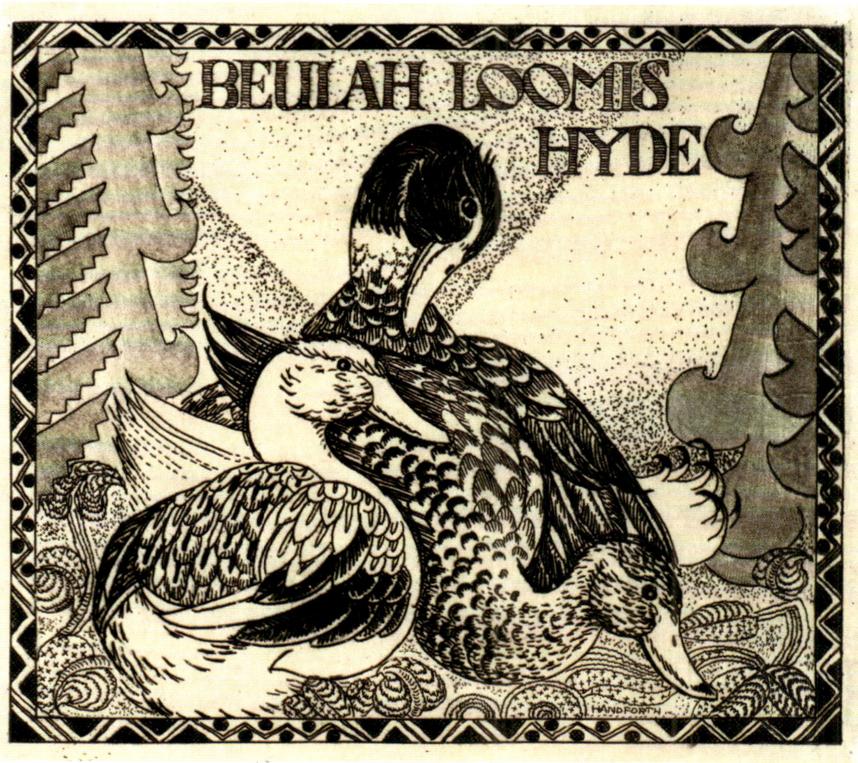
BEULAH LOOMIS
HYDE
HANDFORTH

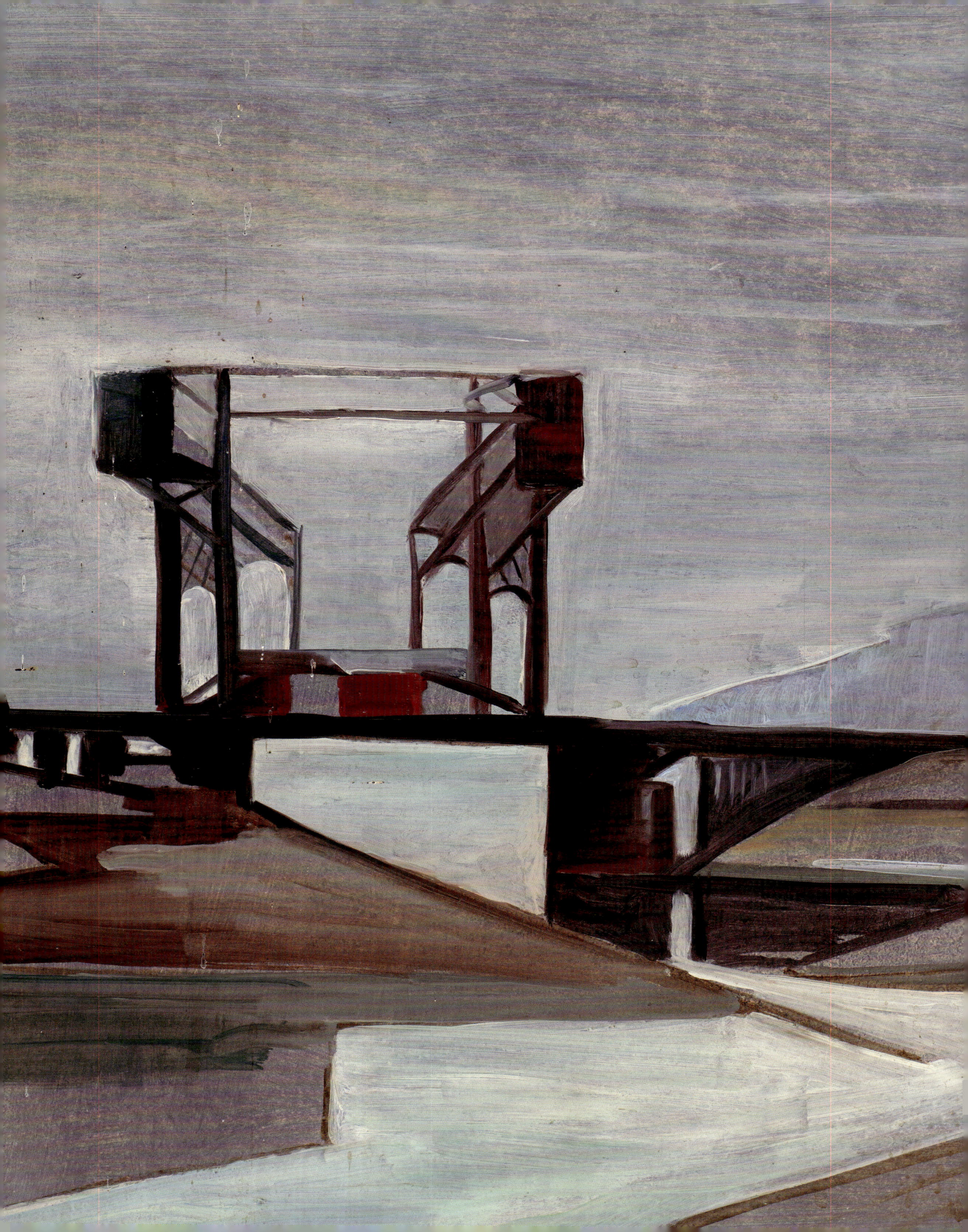

STRUCTURE AND FORM
THE ART OF B. L. HYDE

DAVID F. MARTIN

CASCADIA ART MUSEUM
DISTRIBUTED BY UNIVERSITY OF WASHINGTON PRESS

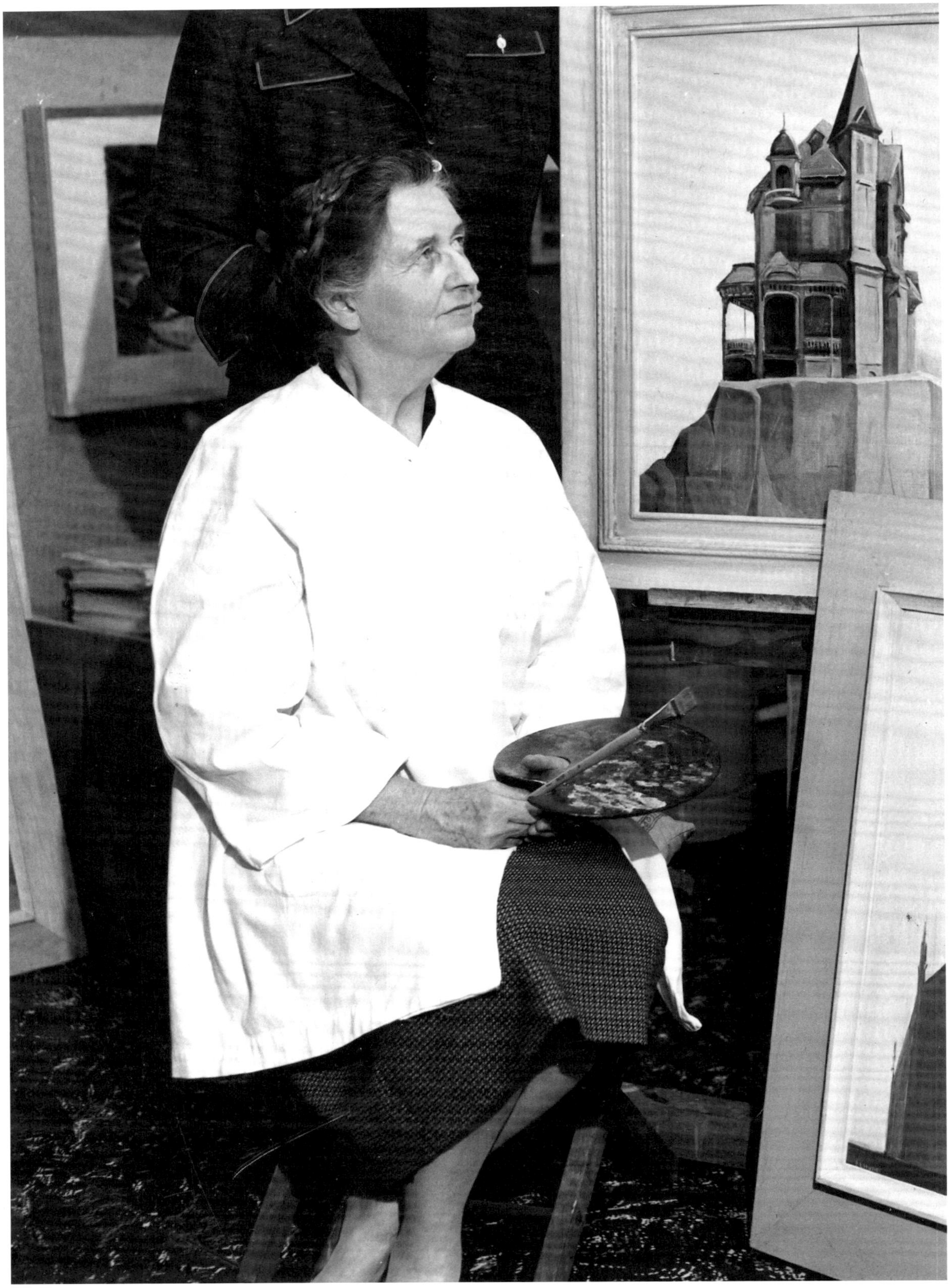

CONTENTS

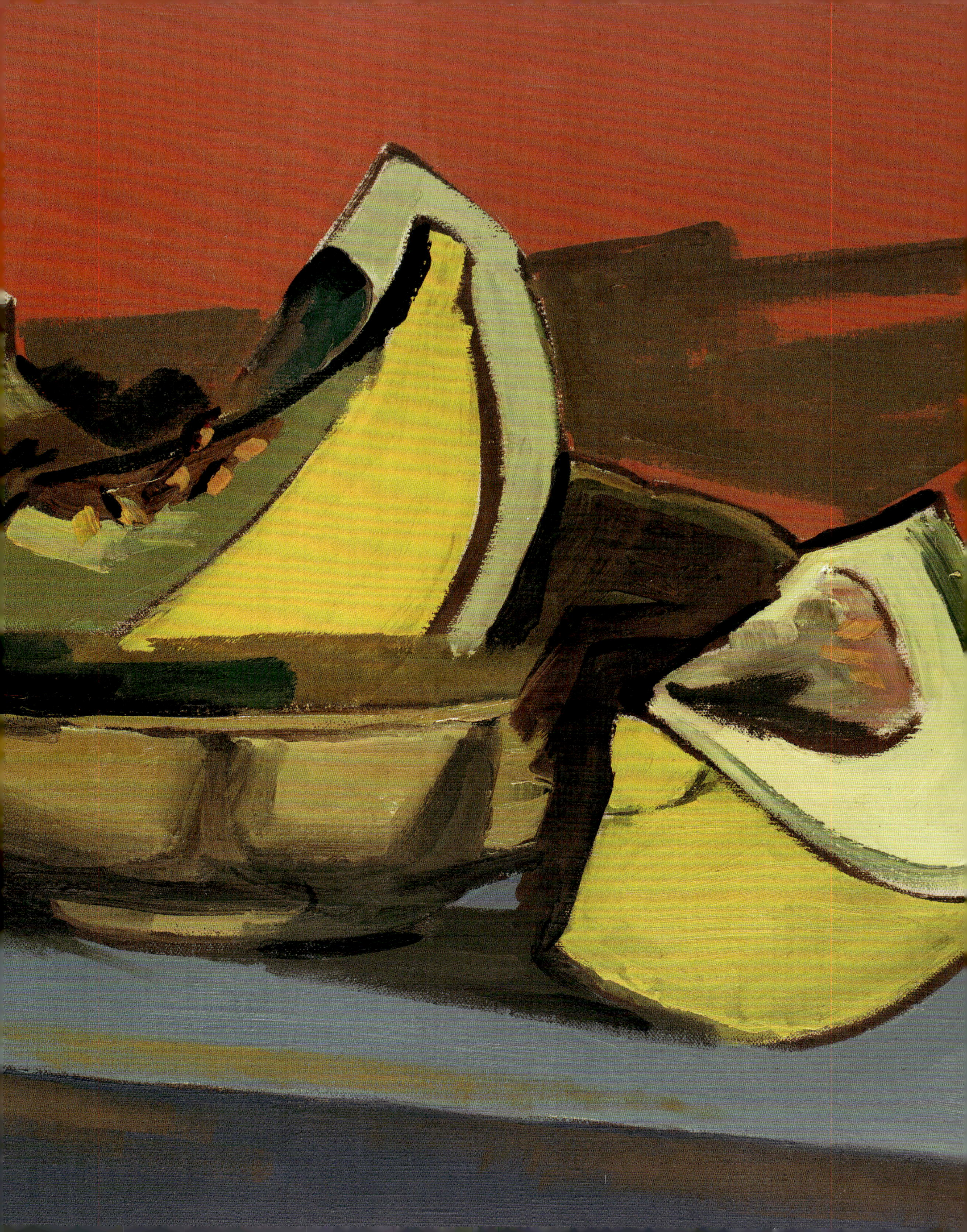

FOREWORD

SALLY RALSTON, EXECUTIVE DIRECTOR
CASCADIA ART MUSEUM

WELCOME TO THE WORLD OF B. L. HYDE, an artist whose legacy we are thrilled to revive and share with you.

Cascadia Art Museum is proud to present this publication and accompanying exhibition featuring the paintings of Beulah Loomis Hyde (1886–1983). Hyde was the principal regional artist to depict Washington State's industrial landscape in the early to mid-twentieth century. This book sheds light on her legacy, an artistic journey that has remained obscured for too long.

B. L. Hyde's decision to use her initials to mask her gender speaks to the challenges she faced as a woman in the early twentieth-century art world. She overcame these obstacles and emerged as one of the region's most innovative painters. Besides her own impressive body of work, Hyde was an early arts activist and important cultural figure in Tacoma. Her contributions to early arts organizations and her role as a collector and student of other Northwest artists, including the renowned Mark Tobey, highlight her deep commitment to regional art.

Despite her significant accomplishments and respected status among her peers, Hyde chose to limit her exhibition opportunities to regional venues and organizations, such as Women Painters of Washington. Emphasizing her own development as an artist and eschewing attention from larger cities, she was content to focus on her art rather than seeking a national reputation.

As part of our own unwavering commitment to historical Northwest art and to the artists who often go unrecognized, we are proud to reintroduce to the public the extraordinary work of B. L. Hyde. This publication and exhibition are more than a collection of her paintings; they are a celebration of a life dedicated to art.

Our deepest appreciation goes to the University of Washington Press for its ongoing partnership and to our loyal donors who allow us to fulfill our mission.

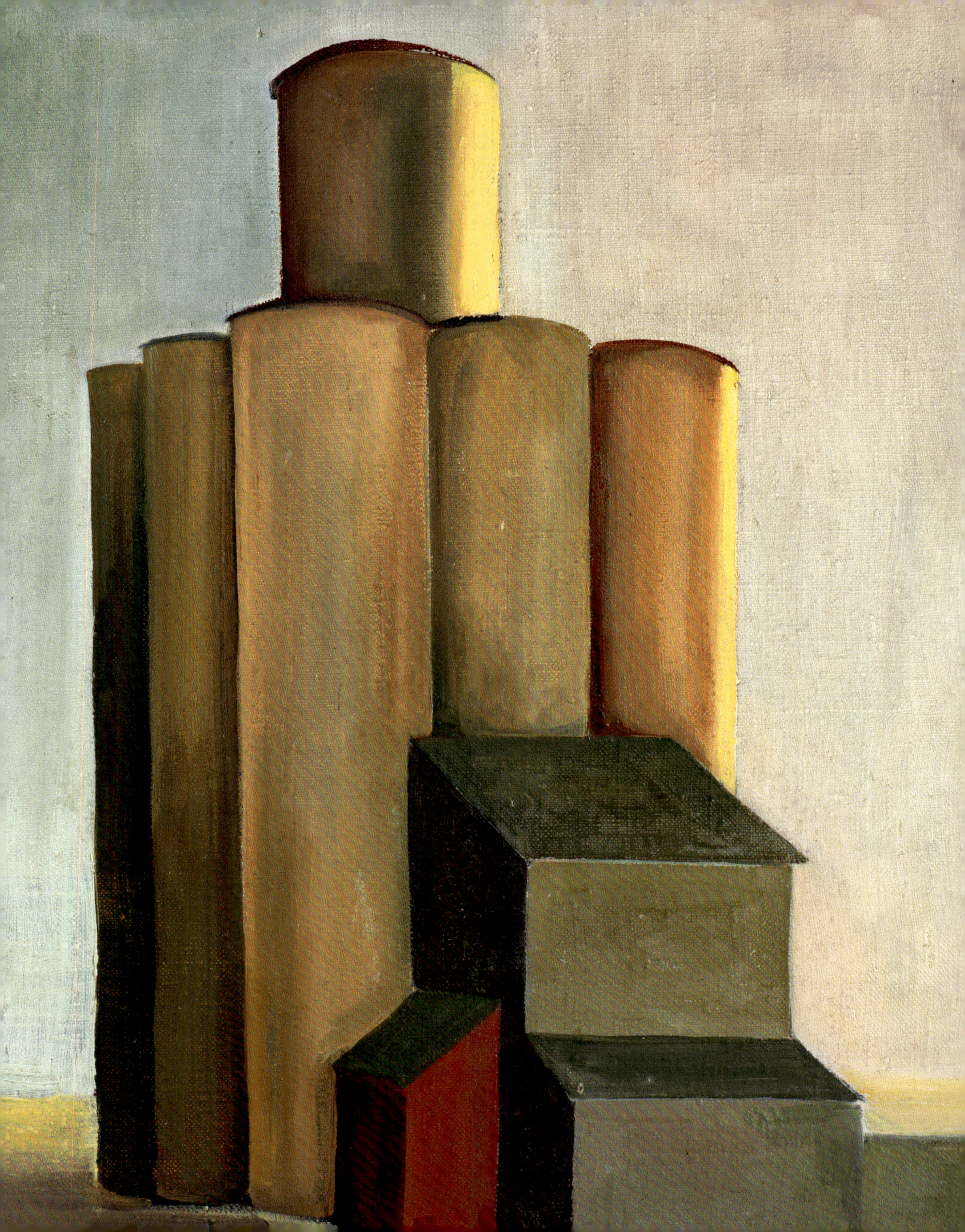

INTRODUCTION

CASCADIA ART MUSEUM performs a wonderful service to art, to the Pacific Northwest, and to our family by drawing long-awaited attention to the work of Beulah Loomis Hyde. Cascadia's exhibition and this catalogue will place her in art history forever, as she deserves.

We in her family revered and loved her, and her influence on us persists today. We're proud of her development as an artist, and seeing so many of her paintings together enhances their impact. Her style and subjects were unique, bold, and beautiful. She had a keen intellect. I remember fierce Scrabble games, brainy conversations about literature, and perspectives more worldly than from anyone I knew. She had a wonderful spirit of adventure. Who else rode a horse around Mount Rainier at seventy-five, skied until she was eighty-five, was among the first visitors to post–World War II Moscow, or caught the theater season in London most autumns? She inspired us.

"Nonnie," as we all called her, could be formidable, but she was also warm, good-humored, infinitely tolerant, and delighted by life's joys. Her large archive of correspondence from her school days on reveals, as our memories do, her devotion to her family and the Pacific Northwest.

We are especially grateful to curator David F. Martin, the expert and engine behind this exhibition. We hope that the spirit of B. L. Hyde comes through to you in her paintings.

PAMELA HYDE SMITH

Her oldest grandchild, speaking for B. L. Hyde's family, her sons, the late Charles H. Hyde II, Robert H. Hyde, and William B. Hyde; her other grandchildren, Douglas Hyde Land, Chris Hyde Lee, and Charles H. Hyde III; and her great-grandchildren, Julia K. H. Lee, Paul Ang Lee, Benjamin B. Land, Catherine S. Ebert, Marian H. Smith, Allison A. T. Hyde, Carrie D. Land-Steves, Charles H. Hyde IV, and Nicola M. Hyde

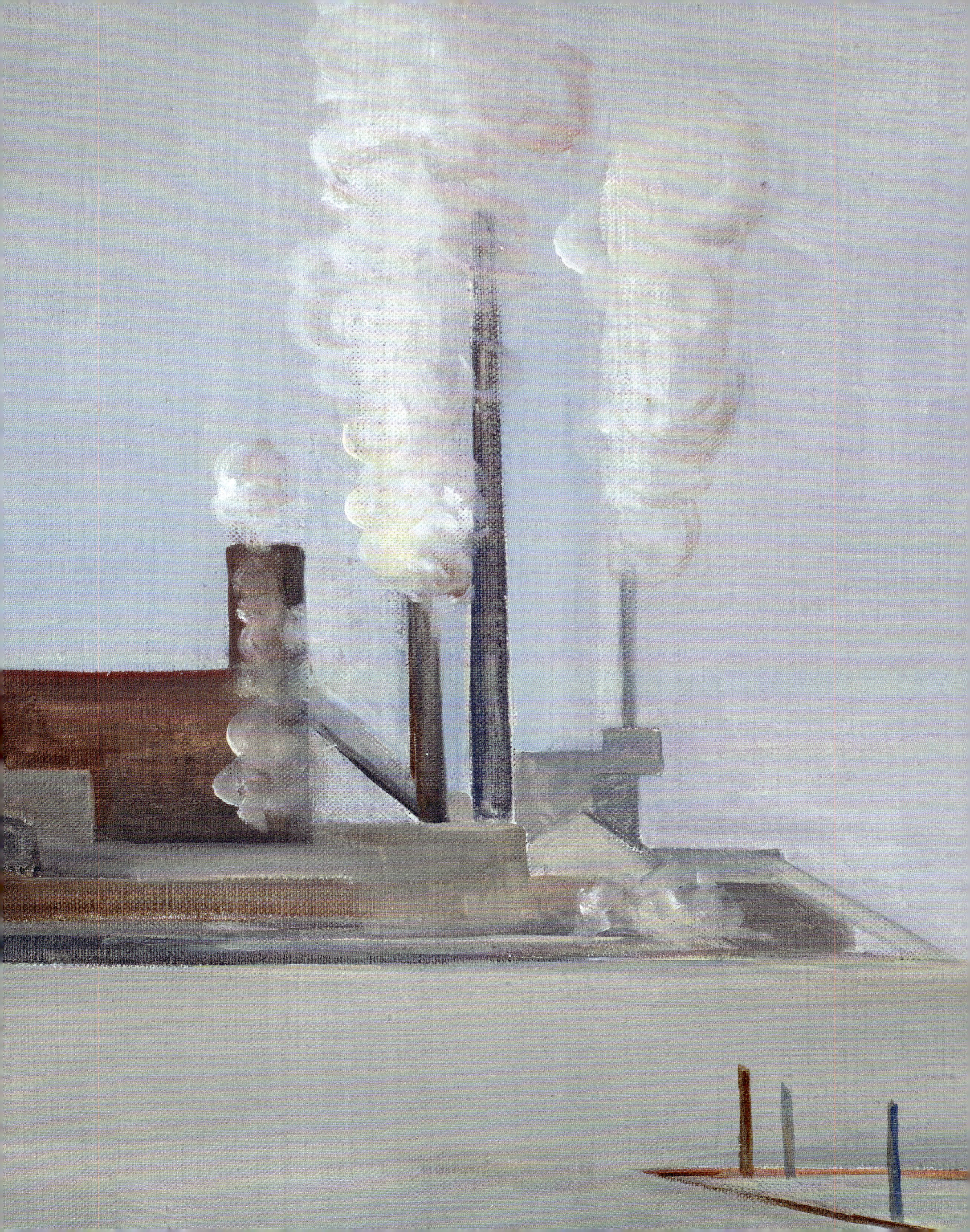

CURATOR'S NOTE

DAVID F. MARTIN
CASCADIA ART MUSEUM

BEULAH LOOMIS HYDE left an incredible body of work along with the challenging dilemma of attempting to title and date her paintings.

With the exception of a few of her early sketchbooks, she never dated any of her works, nor did she assign titles anywhere on the stretcher bars or the canvas verso. If she documented the information on the frames, most have been replaced or re-used. If she documented the art through photographs, they are no longer extant. Consequently, we have no means of definitively placing her work into a chronological order.

I have attempted to estimate the dates by putting a year range next to each work. Luckily, an intact cache of paintings created in her classes with Mark Tobey from 1935 to circa 1940 recently surfaced. These are all oil on paper, so I can safely assume that the works in this medium are from this earlier period. Some titles derived from exhibition catalogues, where the subject is literal (such as *Gas Station*), also allowed the paintings to be identified. Unfortunately, Hyde used very few descriptive titles and opted for brevity.

Hyde's obsession with industrial forms does not reflect an insensitivity to the ecological damage that we have now been able to assess nearly one hundred years later. For instance, one of her finest paintings depicts the Asarco copper smelter in the Tacoma, Washington, suburb of Ruston. At the time, this was the largest smokestack in the world. Back then, the community held a sense of local pride for the plant's employment opportunities and industrial strength. However, we now know that the site was extremely harmful to the environment, taking decades of work to reclaim the land and clear it of the toxins released by the plant. I personally witnessed this same type of ecological problem in my hometown of Niagara Falls, in western New York. Once a mighty industrial force in the early twentieth century, the area became a toxic nightmare by the 1970s and reached international notoriety when the Love Canal became a symbol of shortsighted political and industrial greed. The natural beauty of Niagara Falls together with Mount Rainier and Puget Sound, on the opposite side of the country, leaves a legacy of the ongoing tension between nature and industry.

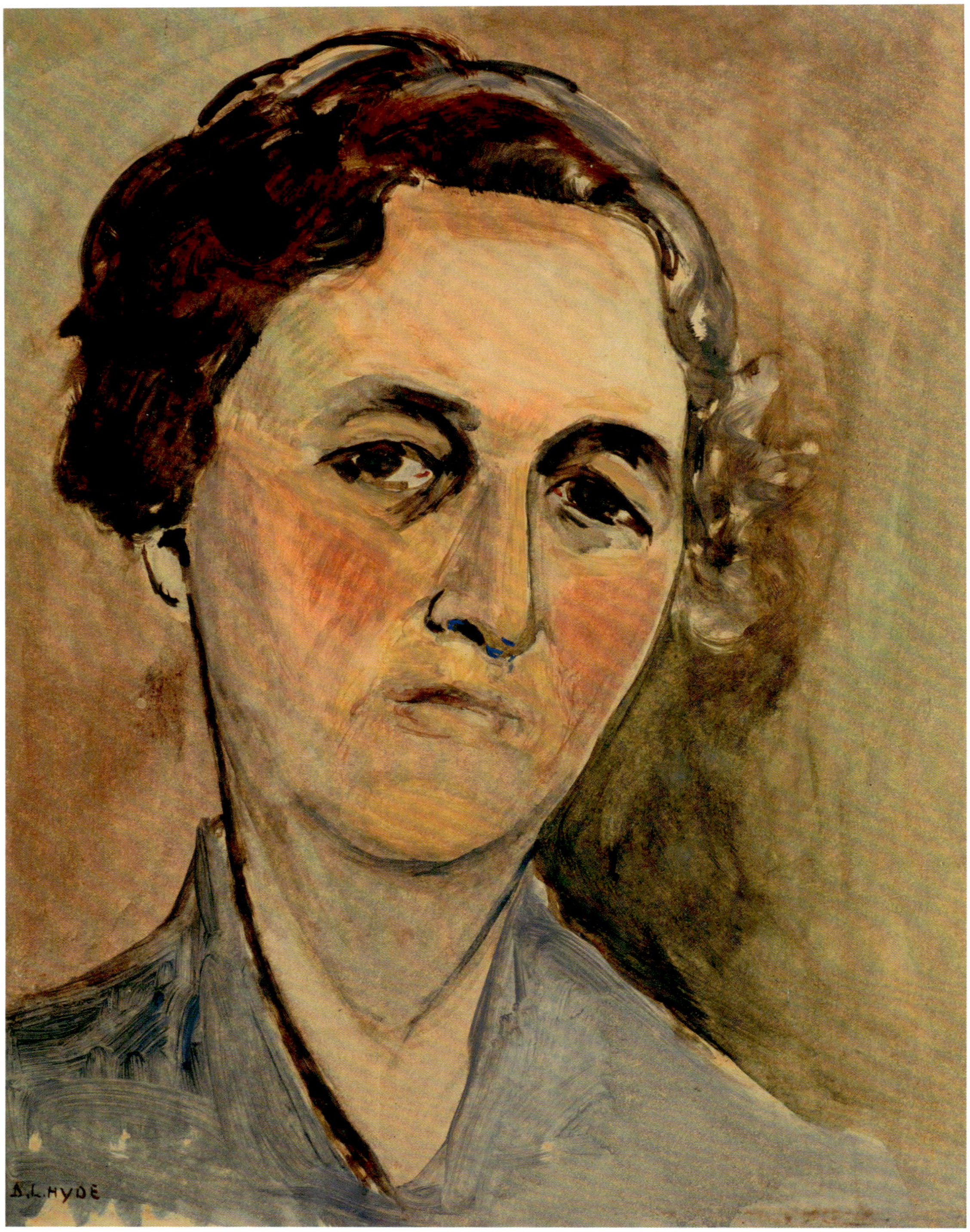
D.L. HYDE

STRUCTURE AND FORM
THE ART OF B. L. HYDE

DAVID F. MARTIN

THE ABILITY TO SIMPLIFY MEANS TO ELIMINATE THE UNNECESSARY SO THAT THE NECESSARY MAY SPEAK.

HANS HOFMANN

Beulah Loomis Hyde held a unique position in the history of art in Washington State. The trajectory of her artistic production encompasses national and international developments in creative visual representation.

She was born on January 24, 1886, in McPherson, Kansas, to Lyman U. Loomis (1857–1934) and Elizabeth "Lizzie" Beaton Loomis (1865–1942), who had married in 1882. She was the younger of their two daughters. Her sister, Winifred Loomis Labbe (1883–1959), was an exemplary older sibling, who also shared her artistic interests.

Beulah's entry into the world was not an easy one. Her frail physical beginnings were recorded in her mother's personal journals.

> "Business gone to thunder. Will you live on a claim?" This telegram came to me from Dodge City, Kansas, in May, 1886, signed by my husband. We had one child two years and eleven months old, and a baby four months old, the baby very delicate, having arrived quite suddenly in a blizzard in January, with neither doctor nor nurse on hand. The baby was blue with cold and wheezing every breath before they came. My sister was with me, but inexperienced and more or less frightened, while the head of the family was on his way three blocks to summon the doctor and his wife, who was the nurse. It took them from five until eight a.m. to put in their appearance!

Beulah Loomis Hyde
(1886–1983)
Self-portrait, ca. 1935–40
Oil on paper
20 × 15 in.
Collection of Pamela Hyde Smith

> The baby suffered the most, as when she was born she had been laid on a bed between a door and a window, with blankets loosely thrown over her. She did not recover from that blizzard until she was nearly grown.[1]

The Loomises and their two young daughters left McPherson with only the bare necessities, riding in a two-wheel horse-drawn cart. They were headed for Dodge City, Kansas, where Lyman had started a small manufacturing business that included making windmills and farm equipment. This was just the latest adventure for the young family, who followed Lyman in his multiple unsuccessful attempts at forming a lucrative business and finding a home in order to care for his family. Lizzie was growing weary of what appeared to be the promise of an unstable, itinerant future and being left the sole responsibility of raising the girls. This new home in Dodge City was basically a twelve-by-sixteen-foot shack, with no access to water and the closest available well seven miles away on a stranger's farm. Lyman negotiated with the farmer to deliver a barrel each week to his wife and daughters. The water, however, was often putrid before the week had ended. Lyman left them alone to fend for themselves while he traveled for work opportunities. Resourceful out of necessity, Lizzie made the best of her dismal surroundings. Surviving on small amounts of basic necessities, she planted a garden as a source for fresh fruits and vegetables, but the harsh climate and poor-quality soil limited the harvest. Her friends from McPherson sent her a bay mare and a buckboard carriage, allowing her and the girls to travel nearby for water and meager food supplies while their well was being dug. Lizzie encountered numerous rattlesnakes and poisonous insects, which she had to kill to protect herself and the children. To keep warm, she papered the walls of the shack with newspapers for insulation. After nearly a year, the young family headed for Wichita. The stability was short-lived, as their home was foreclosed in 1887.

For reasons unknown, the young family arrived in Tacoma, Washington, the following year. Lyman's tenacity finally paid off with the opportunities available in their new home in the Pacific Northwest. He filed articles of incorporation for a business titled Southern Pacific Town Company on February 12, 1889, with two partners, Benjamin J. Boulton and E. E. Bair. Little more than two years later, in May 1891, he was co-owner of the Bair-Loomis Banking and Investment Company.

Having left behind the poverty and bleak future of Kansas, Lizzie and Lyman became a part of Tacoma's burgeoning cultural development as their finances substantially increased. In 1892, Lizzie became a charter member of the Nesika Club in Tacoma. The name of the organization originated from the Chinook word meaning "our place." Lizzie was one of the twelve women founders of the group, formed "for the united study of American Literature, History and Art."[2]

Not content with his success in Tacoma, Lyman relocated to Helena, Montana, abandoning Lizzie and his daughters. By February 1896, he was general manager of the Gold Coin Company and was already well known in the mining field. This success extended to an additional business venture with Gold Reef Mines in Philipsburg, Montana. By 1910, Lyman was living in New York City.

From the start, Lizzie was the head of the family due to her husband's unstable personality and wanderlust. She remained in the Tacoma area with the girls, and with the newfound wealth from Lyman's success and her own farming operation, their future

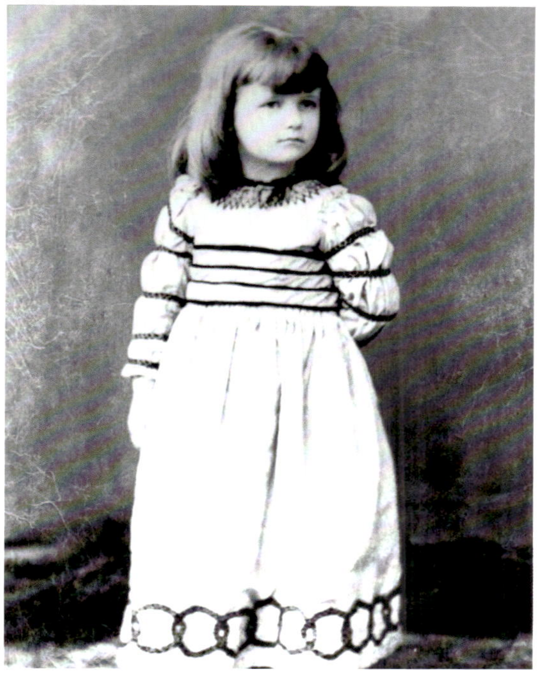

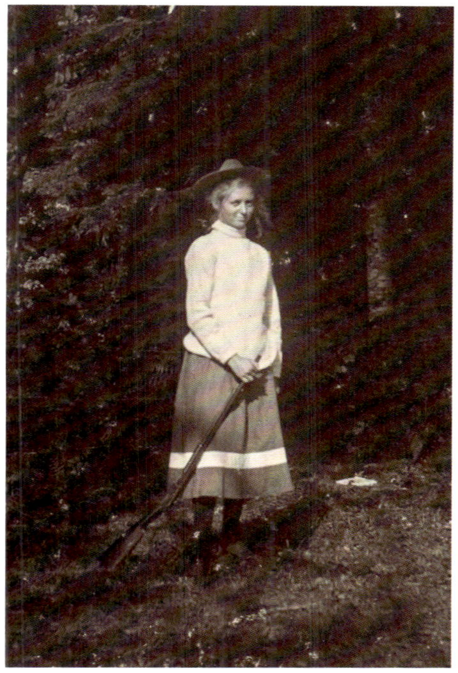

Left: Beulah Loomis at approximately age four.

Right: Beulah Loomis at approximately age twelve.

appeared bright. Lizzie's multi-acre farm, which she referred to as a ranch, was nine miles from Tacoma and yielded significant crops to sell to wholesalers and distributors. This successful operation lasted for fourteen years.[3] Following in the footsteps of her sister, Winifred, Beulah was enrolled in Tacoma's Annie Wright Seminary as a primary school student in 1893. By that time, Lizzie had acquired a home camp in the Park Lodge district near Lake Steilacoom in Lakewood, Washington. In late 1896, seeking the best education for her daughters, Lizzie headed cross-country with Winifred and Beulah for a two-year stay in Andover, Massachusetts, so the girls could attend the Abbot Academy. Abbot was founded in 1829 for the advanced education of women and girls. During this period, Lizzie and her daughters rented rooms at the Stowe Cabin Mansion House in Andover, formerly the home of the writer and abolitionist Harriet Beecher Stowe. In the school's records, Beulah is listed as a non-graduate in the class of 1898, a common designation at that time.[4]

By July 1899, Lizzie and the girls returned to Tacoma, and Beulah was enrolled again at the Annie Wright Seminary. From such an inauspicious beginning, she grew into a young woman of intelligence, talent, tenacity, and athleticism. During these early years, she became very interested in sports and excelled in horseback riding and tennis, for which she became a local celebrity.

> *The greatest enthusiasm of the day was perhaps evoked by the mixed doubles between (Sam) Hardy, with the dainty little club champion, Beulah Loomis, as a partner and P. J. Fransioli, who had Miss Potter to sweep in the fringed ends. Miss Loomis, who is but 15 years old, received an ovation on her coming upon the courts, and, though somewhat nervous, played an excellent game.*[5]

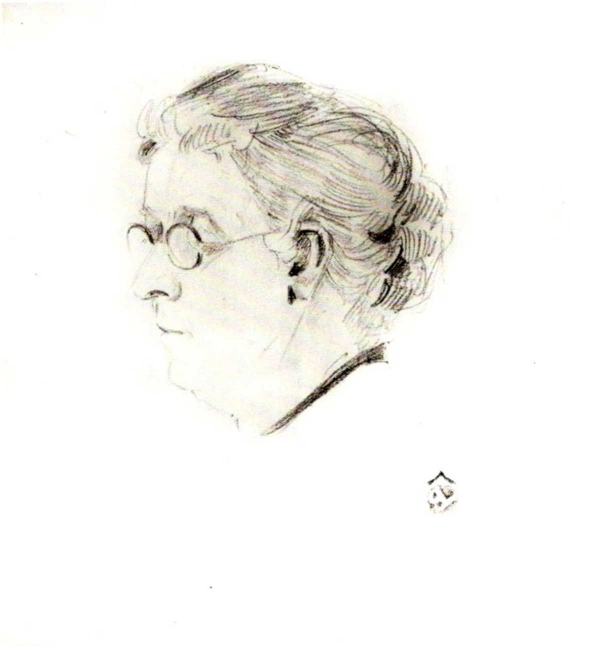

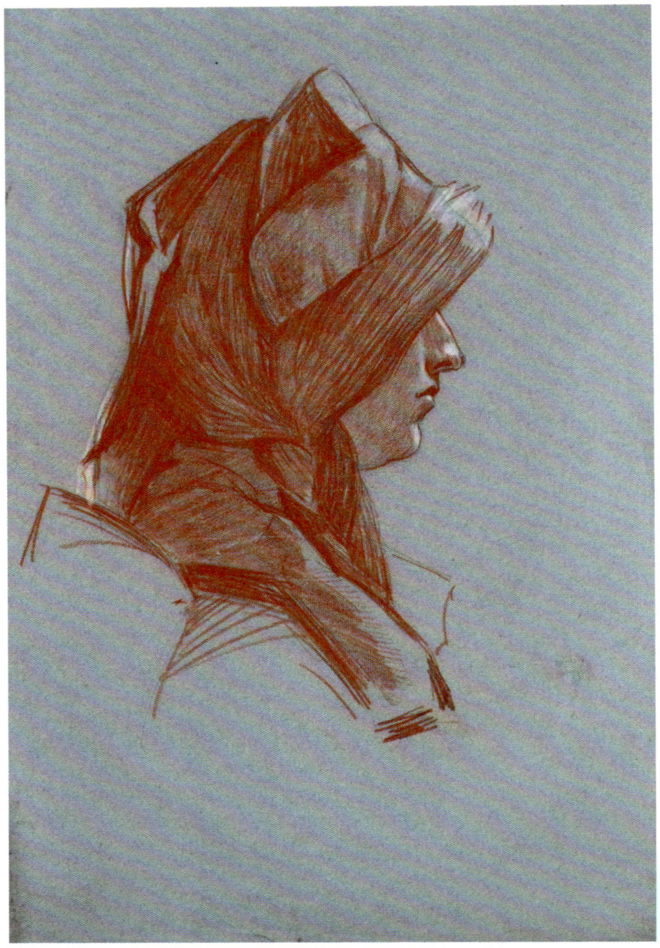

Beulah Loomis (1886–1983)
Sketch of her mother,
Elizabeth Beaton Loomis, ca. 1902
Graphite drawing
9 × 9 in.
Collection of Pamela Hyde Smith

Beulah Loomis (1886–1983)
Untitled, ca. 1902
Sanguine drawing
24 × 19 in.
Collection of Pamela Hyde Smith

Besides her athletic skills, young Beulah was an exemplary student of cultural pursuits. This was evidenced by her translation of Victor Hugo from the original French texts for the school's newspaper, *The Hyak*, in 1902, and playing piano in classical concerts at school recitals.[6] However, it was the visual arts that began to surpass her other interests. Her earliest extant sketchbooks and drawings date from 1902 and display a sensitivity to portraiture and landscapes. An interesting sketchbook from that year includes two drawings created within minutes of each other. One is a sketch of Beulah by an artist named R. de St. Arnaud, and the other is a reciprocal sketch of R. de St. Arnaud by Beulah. The two were riding on "the Flyer" passenger ferry from Seattle to Tacoma and apparently developed a quick rapport based on their mutual artistic interests.

Following the lead of the artist James McNeill Whistler (1834–1903), Beulah created an Asian-inspired graphic seal using a circular design of her initials to sign her work. This was the initial practice that she would use to conceal her gender throughout her professional career.

Her earliest art instructor appears to have been the Dalmatian-born painter Roberto Rascovich (1857–1905), who had a successful career in Chicago before moving to Tacoma. In 1904, Beulah graduated from Annie Wright Seminary as one of only five students in the class. After graduation, and followed by the sudden death of Rascovich, she, Lizzie, and Winifred headed east again for the girls to attend the progressive Ingleside School in New Milford, Connecticut, beginning in 1906. At Ingleside, Beulah enhanced her artistic skills and wrote essays for the school's

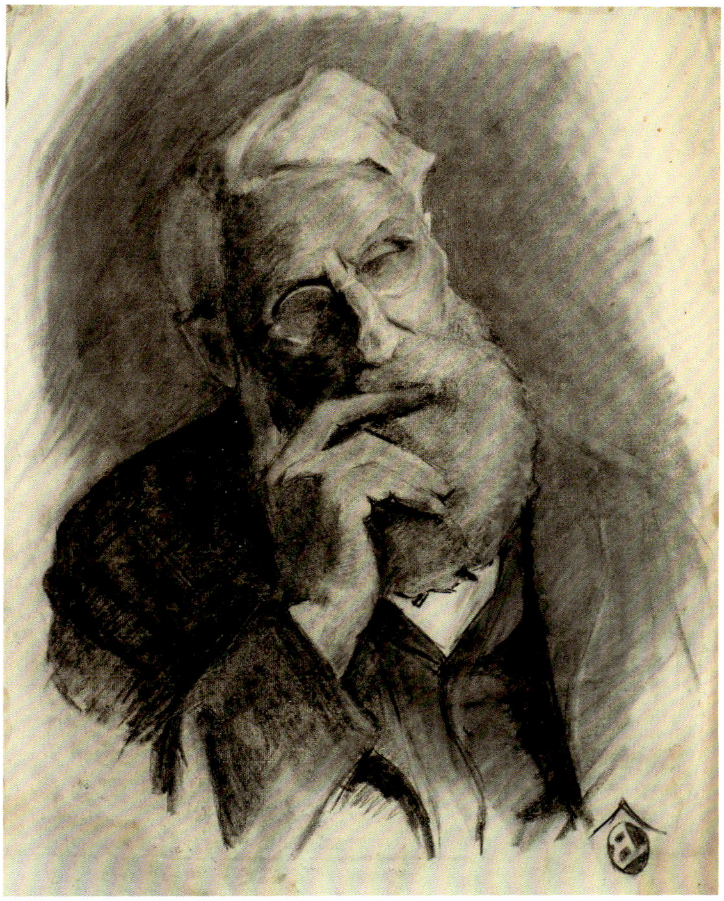

Beulah Loomis (1886–1983)
Untitled, ca. 1902
Charcoal
24 × 18 in.
Collection of Pamela Hyde Smith

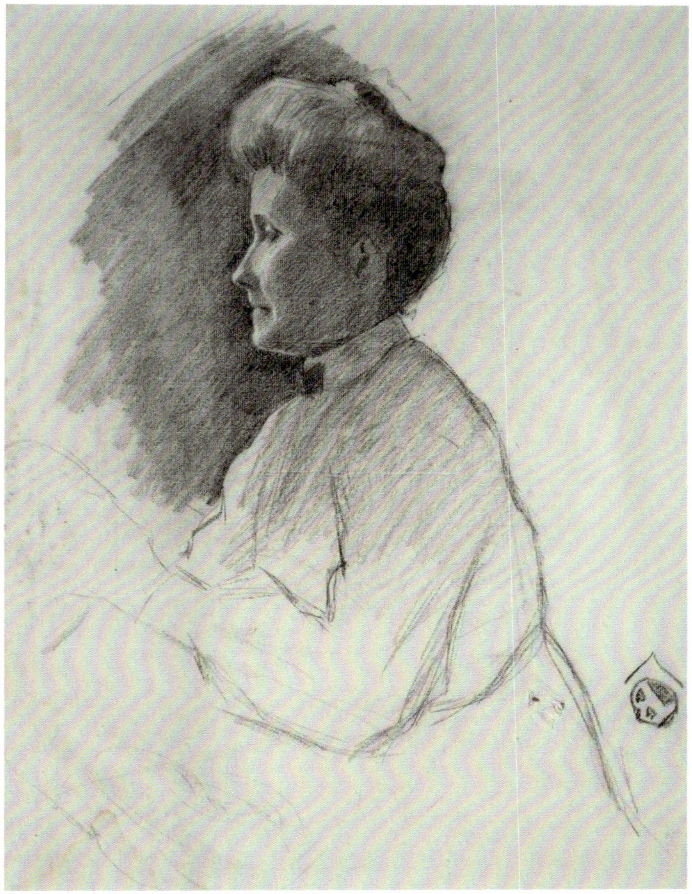

Beulah Loomis (1886–1983)
Untitled, ca. 1902
Graphite
24 × 18 in.
Collection of Pamela Hyde Smith

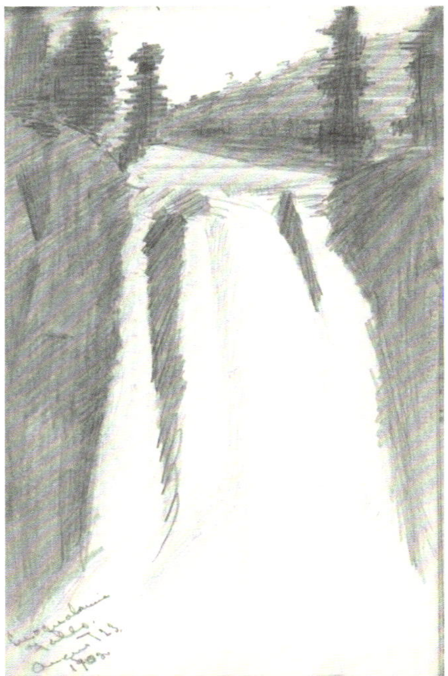

Beulah Loomis (1886–1983)
Sketch of Snoqualmie Falls, 1902
Graphite
7¾ × 5 in.
Collection of Pamela Hyde Smith

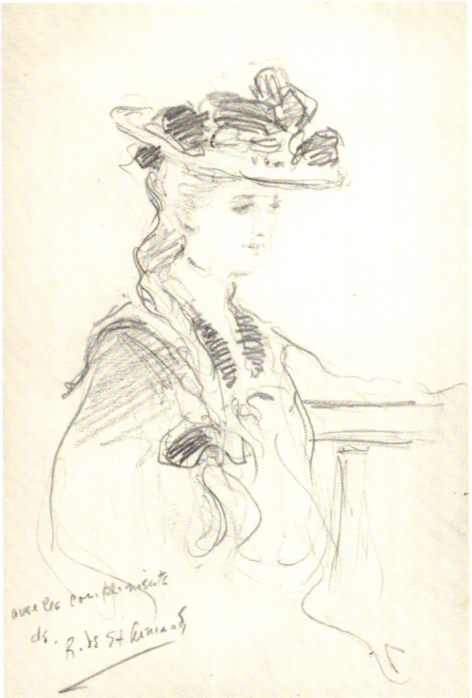

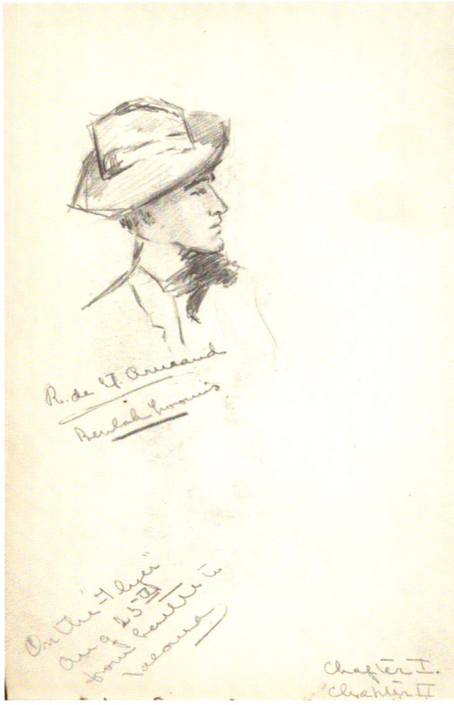

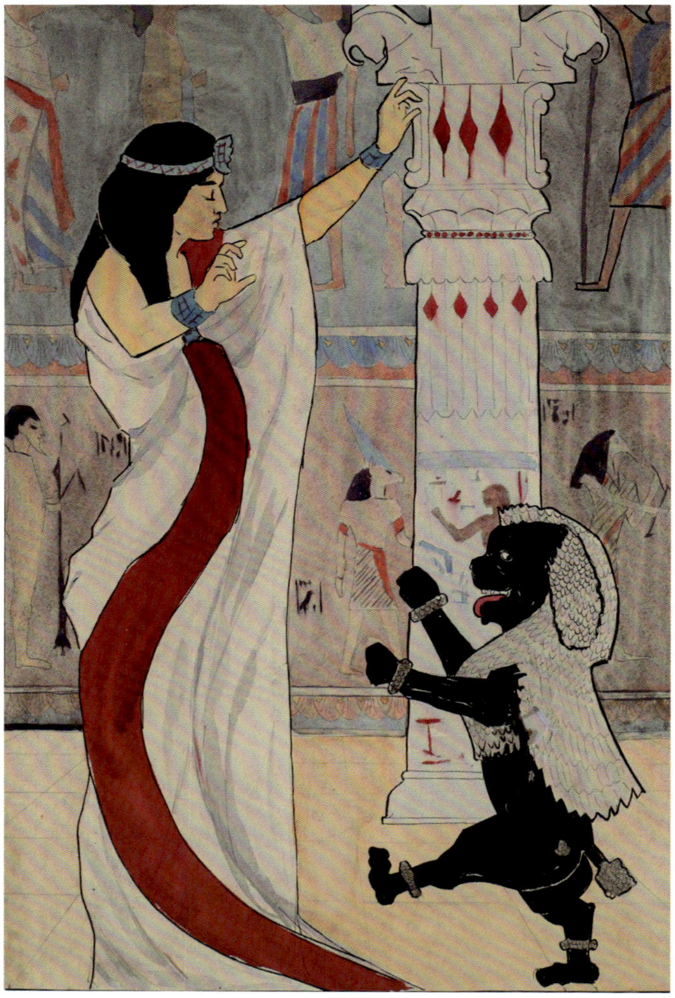

R. de St. Arnaud (dates unknown)
Sketch of Beulah Loomis, 1902
Graphite
7¾ × 5 in.
Collection of Pamela Hyde Smith

Beulah Loomis (1886–1983)
Sketch of R. de St. Arnaud, 1902
Graphite
7¾ × 5 in.
Collection of Pamela Hyde Smith

Beulah Loomis (1886–1983)
Untitled, ca. 1902–4
Ink and watercolor
24 × 16¾ in.
Collection of Pamela Hyde Smith

Beulah Loomis (1886–1983)
Untitled, ca. 1902–4
Ink and gouache
23 × 16¼ in.
Collection of Pamela Hyde Smith

Beulah Loomis, ca. 1903

Annie Wright Seminary graduating class of 1904. Beulah Loomis is in the center.
Courtesy of Annie Wright Schools, Tacoma, WA

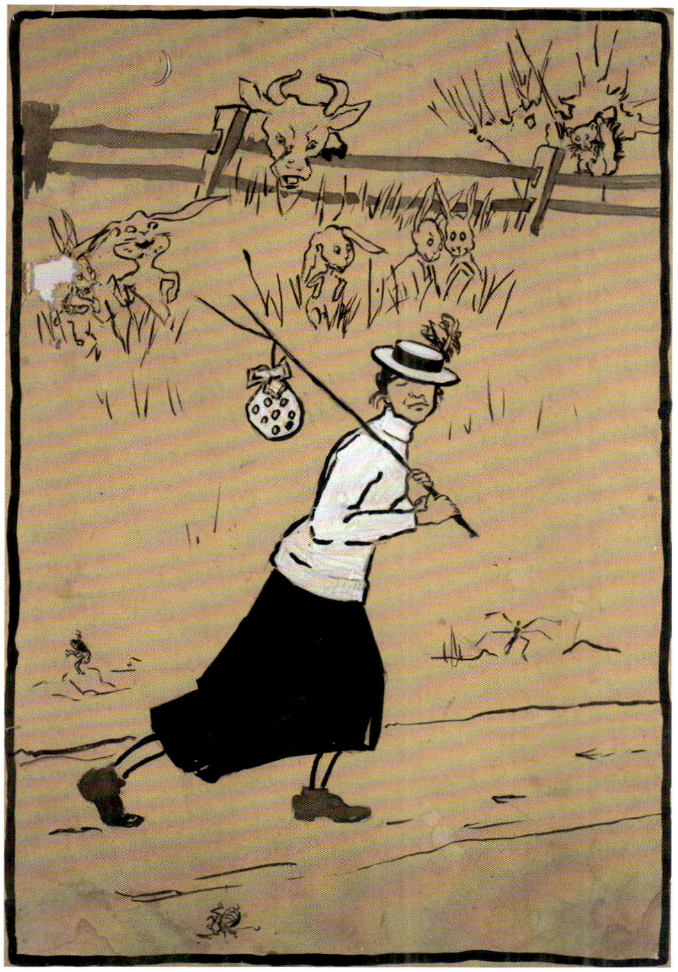

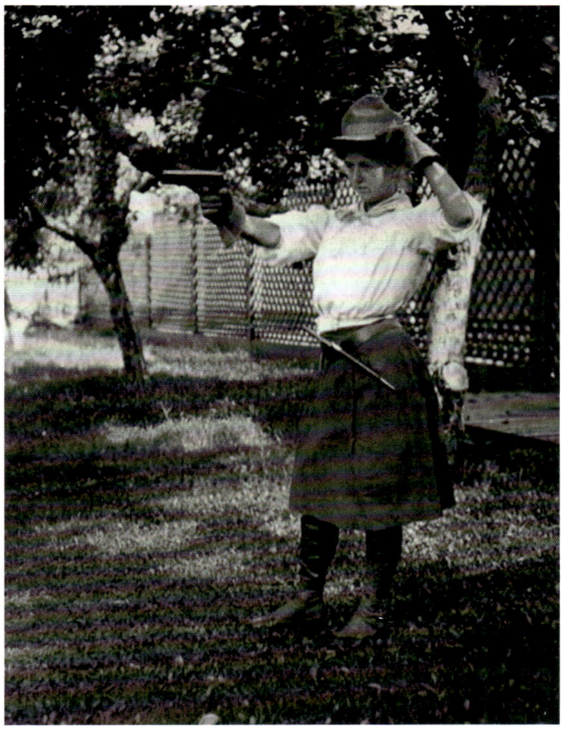

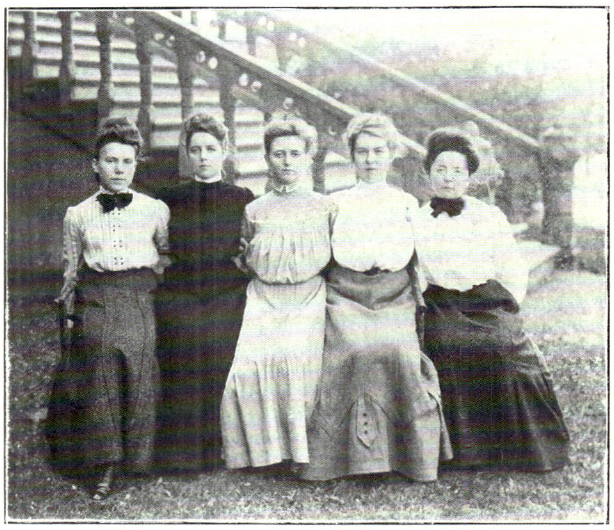

CLASS OF 1904

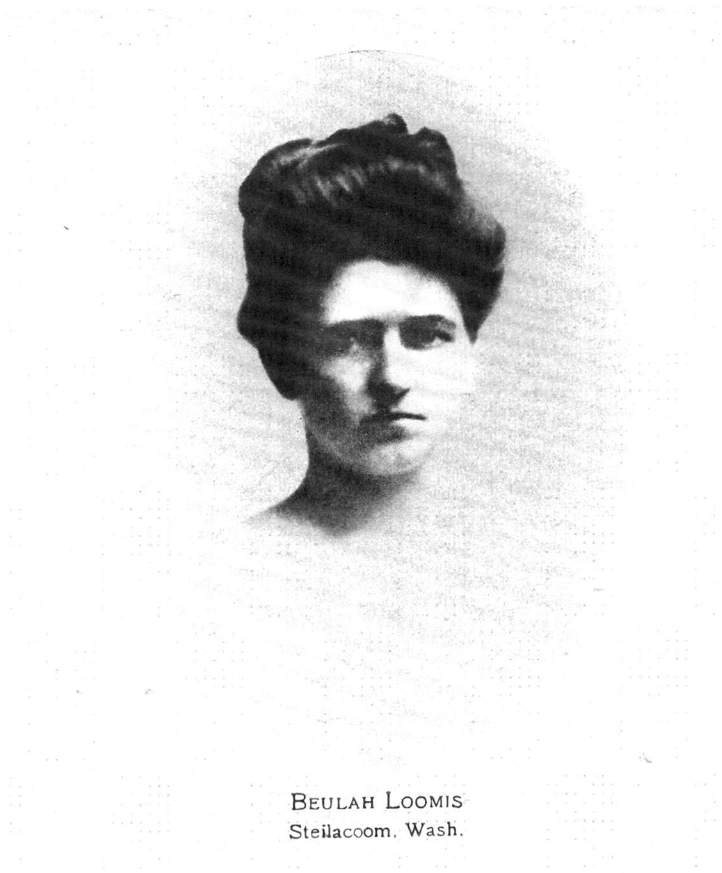

publications. The following year, they returned to Tacoma by July 1907, as well-rounded, educated young women.

During her training at various schools, Beulah undoubtedly learned of the teachings of the artist Arthur Wesley Dow (1857–1922). After training in the United States and Paris, Dow became the assistant curator of the Japanese Collection at the Museum of Fine Arts in Boston in 1893. This position allowed him access to study, in particular, the color woodcuts of masters such as Hokusai and Hiroshige. Adapting Japanese methods to his Western training, Dow developed a new vision of delineating pictorial space and a unique modern expression formed by the synthesis of multiple cultures. His seminal book *Composition: A Series of Exercises in Art Structure for the Use of Students and Teacher* was originally published in 1899 and became the standard guide for most art instructors in the United States. Dow's teachings are evident in several of Beulah's early watercolor studies. These characteristics include the simplification of form, non-Western pictorial placement, and the tonal variations created by observation of the atmospheric effects caused by natural sunlight. Two of Dow's most prominent students, Georgia O'Keeffe and Charles Sheeler, would later have an impact on Beulah's work, beginning in the 1930s.

In 1909, Minnesota artist George Zell Heuston (1855–1939) arrived in Tacoma following studies at the Art Institute of Chicago. He opened a studio and became a highly respected local art instructor. Some of his Tacoma students went on to have distinguished careers in the arts. They include the sculptor Allan Clark (1896–1950) and

Beulah Loomis, from the Ingleside School for Girls publication *Ingleside Log*, 1907. Honor Girls, Post-Graduate Department Courtesy of New Milford Historical Society, New Milford, CT

Opposite, top: Page from the Ingleside School for Girls publication *Ingleside Log*, 1907, depicting Beulah with a camera, one of her original poems, and one of her landscape photographs. Courtesy of New Milford Historical Society, New Milford, CT.

Opposite, bottom left: Beulah Loomis, ca. 1907

Opposite, bottom right: Beulah Loomis, ca. 1912

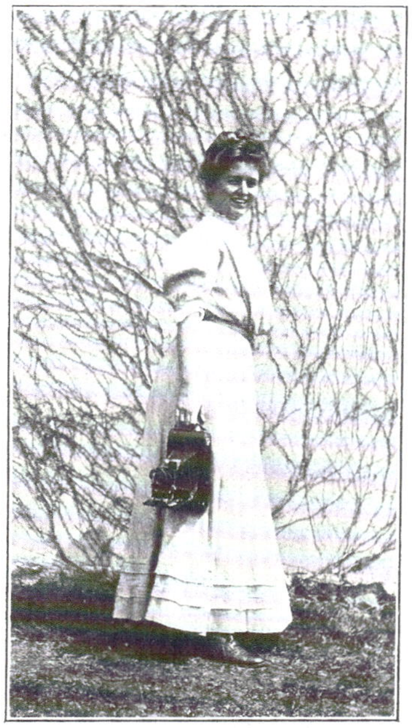

Into a drowsy tone
Transmute the afternoon.

So—Friends with ears and eyes
Which shy divinities
Have opened with their kiss,
We need no balm but this.

A little space for dreams
On care unsullied streams,

Mid task and toil a space,
To dream on nature's face."

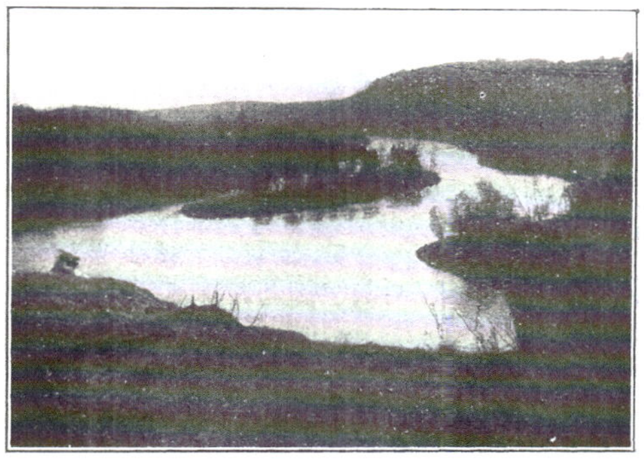

BEULAH LOOMIS

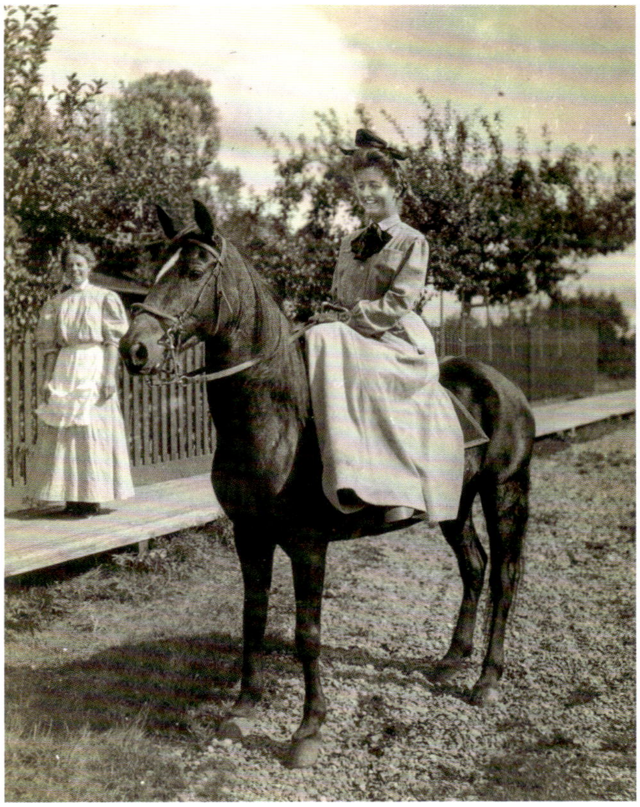

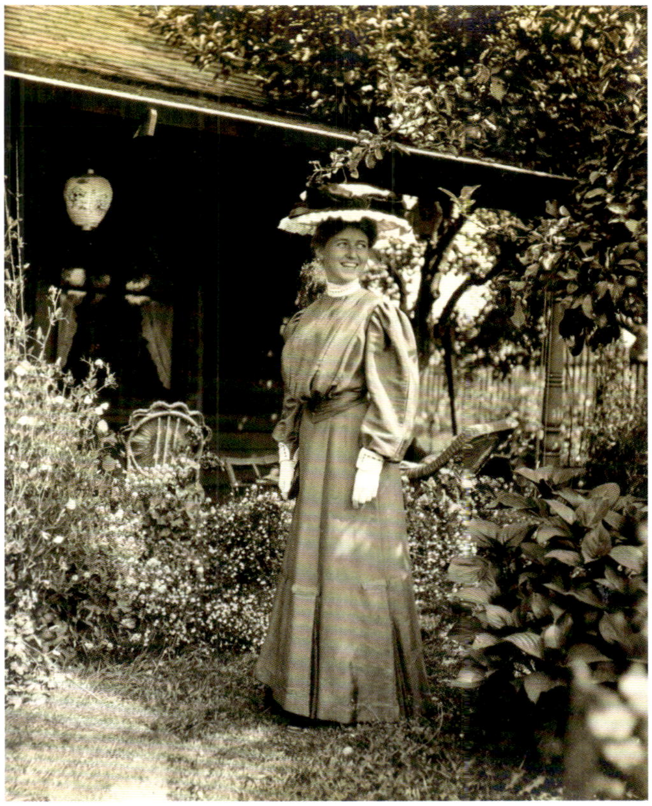

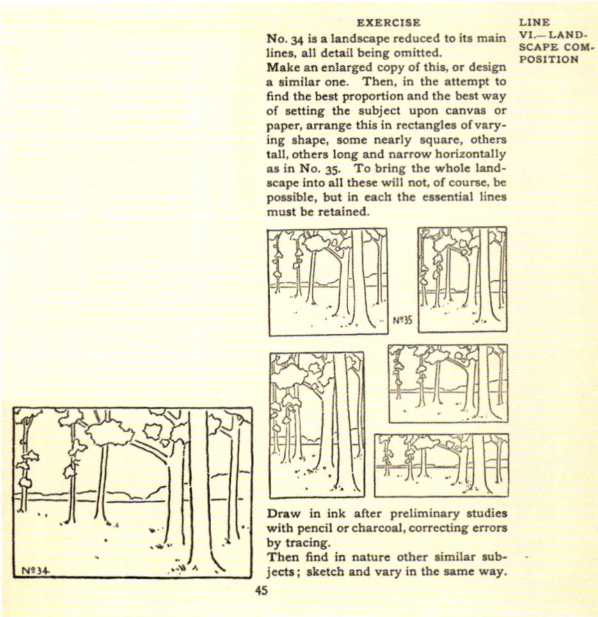

EXERCISE

LINE VI.—LANDSCAPE COMPOSITION

No. 34 is a landscape reduced to its main lines, all detail being omitted.

Make an enlarged copy of this, or design a similar one. Then, in the attempt to find the best proportion and the best way of setting the subject upon canvas or paper, arrange this in rectangles of varying shape, some nearly square, others tall, others long and narrow horizontally as in No. 35. To bring the whole landscape into all these will not, of course, be possible, but in each the essential lines must be retained.

No. 35

No. 34

Draw in ink after preliminary studies with pencil or charcoal, correcting errors by tracing.

Then find in nature other similar subjects; sketch and vary in the same way.

45

Page 45 from *Composition* by Arthur Wesley Dow, 7th edition (Garden City, NY: Doubleday, Page & Company, 1913). Martin-Zambito Archive, Seattle

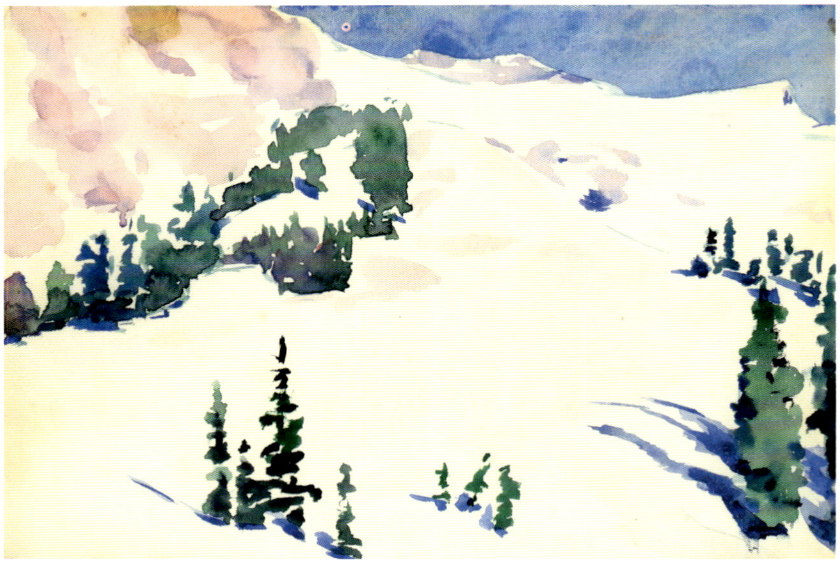

Beulah Loomis (1886–1983)
Exercise sketch in the manner of Arthur Wesley Dow,
ca. 1910–12
Watercolor
7 × 10 in.
Collection of Pamela Hyde Smith

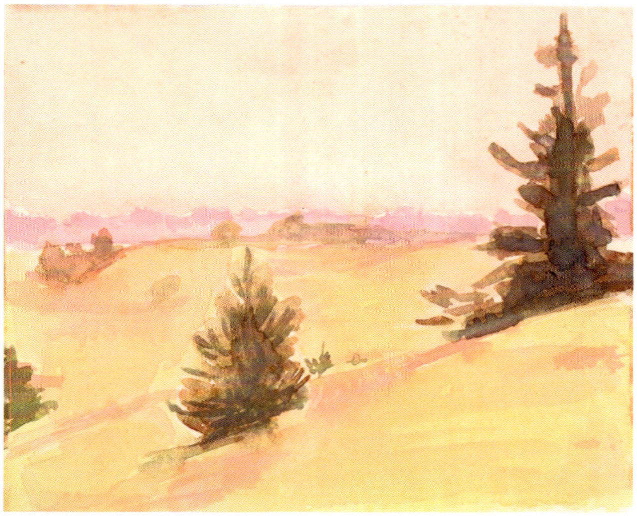

Beulah Loomis (1886–1983)
Exercise sketch in the manner of Arthur Wesley Dow,
ca. 1910–12
Watercolor
4 × 5¼ in.
Collection of Pamela Hyde Smith

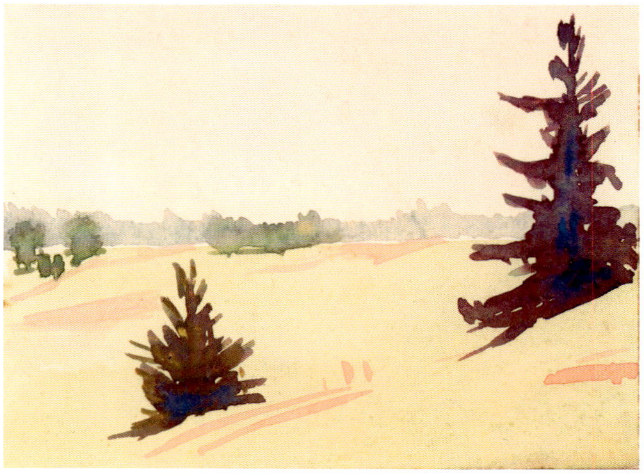

Beulah Loomis (1886–1983)
Exercise sketch in the manner of Arthur Wesley Dow, showing color and atmospheric variation,
ca. 1910–12
Watercolor
4½ × 5⅜ in.
Collection of Pamela Hyde Smith

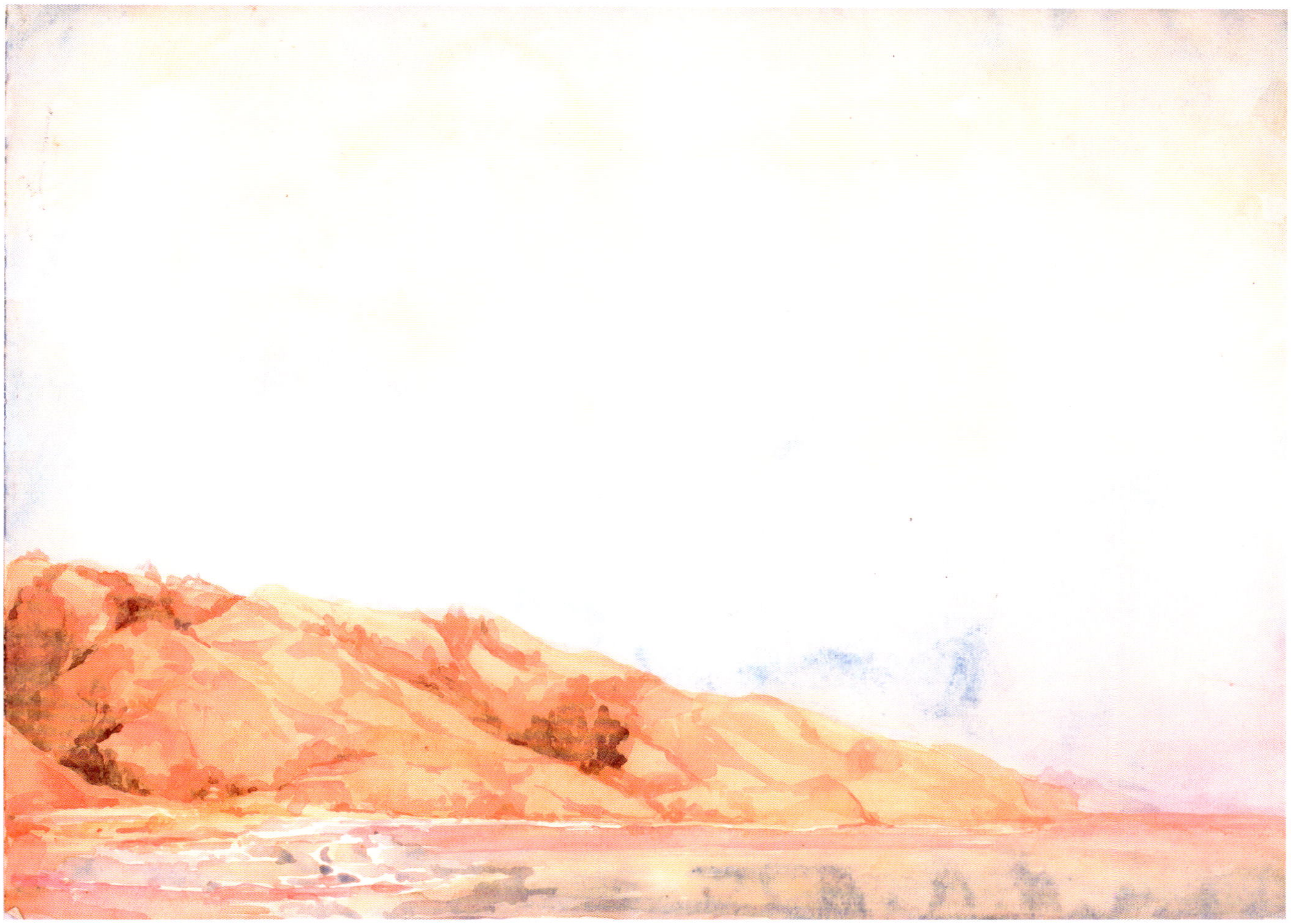

Beulah Loomis Hyde
(1886–1983)
Untitled landscape, ca.
1910–12
Watercolor
9 × 11¾ in.
Collection of Pamela Hyde
Smith

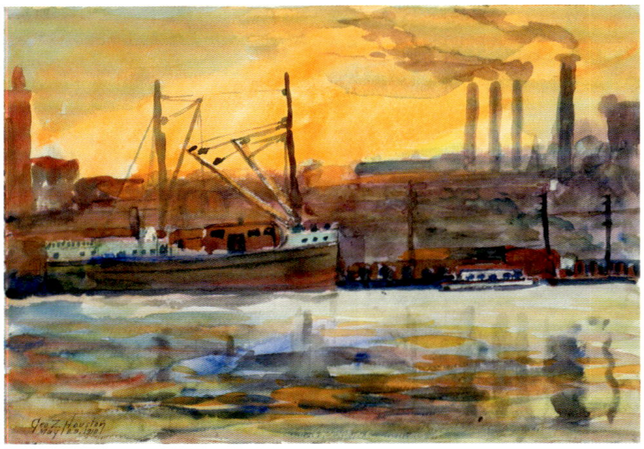

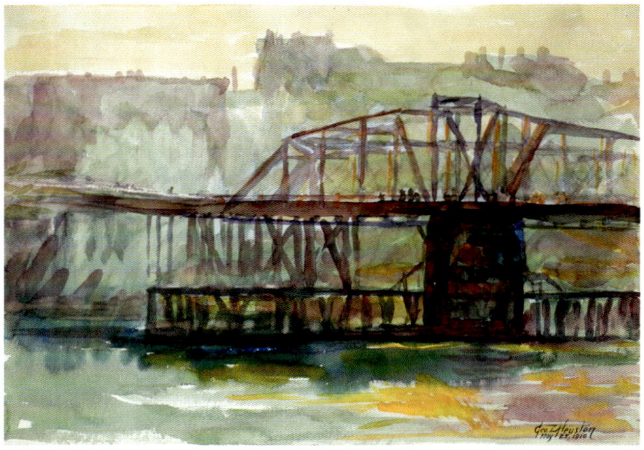

George Zell Heuston (1855–1939)
Untitled, Tacoma waterfront, May 23, 1910
Watercolor
10 × 14 in.
Cascadia Art Museum, Gift of Slava White and Family, CAM 2024.8.1

George Zell Heuston (1855–1939)
Untitled, Tacoma waterfront, May 25, 1910
Watercolor
10 × 14 in.
Cascadia Art Museum, Gift of Slava White and Family, CAM 2024.8.2

Opposite, top: Beulah Loomis Hyde (1886–1983)
Untitled, ca. 1913
Watercolor
6½ × 9½ in.
Collection of Pamela Hyde Smith

Opposite, bottom: Beulah Loomis Hyde (1886–1983)
Untitled landscape with Mount Rainier, ca. 1913
Watercolor
6⅝ × 9¼ in.
Collection of Pamela Hyde Smith

the painter/printmaker Thomas Handforth (1897–1948). Heuston's dual career as both engineer and artist attracted him to Tacoma's burgeoning industrial waterfront to use as subject matter for his paintings. Although it is not known if Hyde formally studied with Heuston, she would certainly have been aware of his high standing in Tacoma's art circles and numerous exhibitions. Besides the teachings of Dow, she was apparently aware of British watercolor techniques of the previous century, and she used both influences in her search for a personal expression. However, many of her extant early watercolors show a compatibility with Heuston's loose, impressionistic paintings and may have provided her the initial inspiration for seeking out Tacoma's industrial areas as subject matter.

Around this time, Beulah met Robert Henry Hyde (1881–1944). Born in Owego, New York, he was the son of Charles H. and Caroline Woodford Hyde. When Robert was six years of age, his parents moved to Tacoma, where Charles founded the West Coast Grocery Company, which developed into one of the largest and most successful grocery concerns on the western coast. The company constructed grocery warehouses from Alaska to Tacoma to Salem, Oregon. The business included the clever company brand name "Amocat," which was Tacoma spelled backwards.

Robert and Beulah married on February 20, 1913, but a few weeks later, in March, Robert was hospitalized in San Francisco for an emergency appendix operation. After his recovery, the couple had an extended three-month honeymoon traveling to the Bermuda Islands, Southern California, Louisiana, New York City, and Washington, DC.

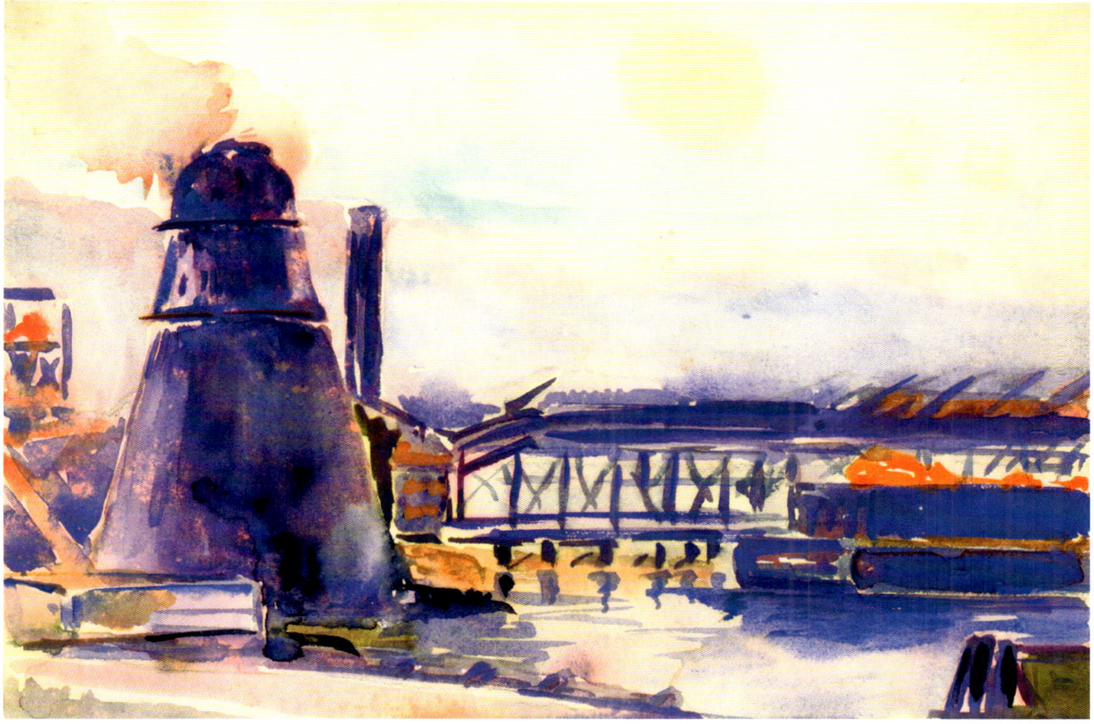

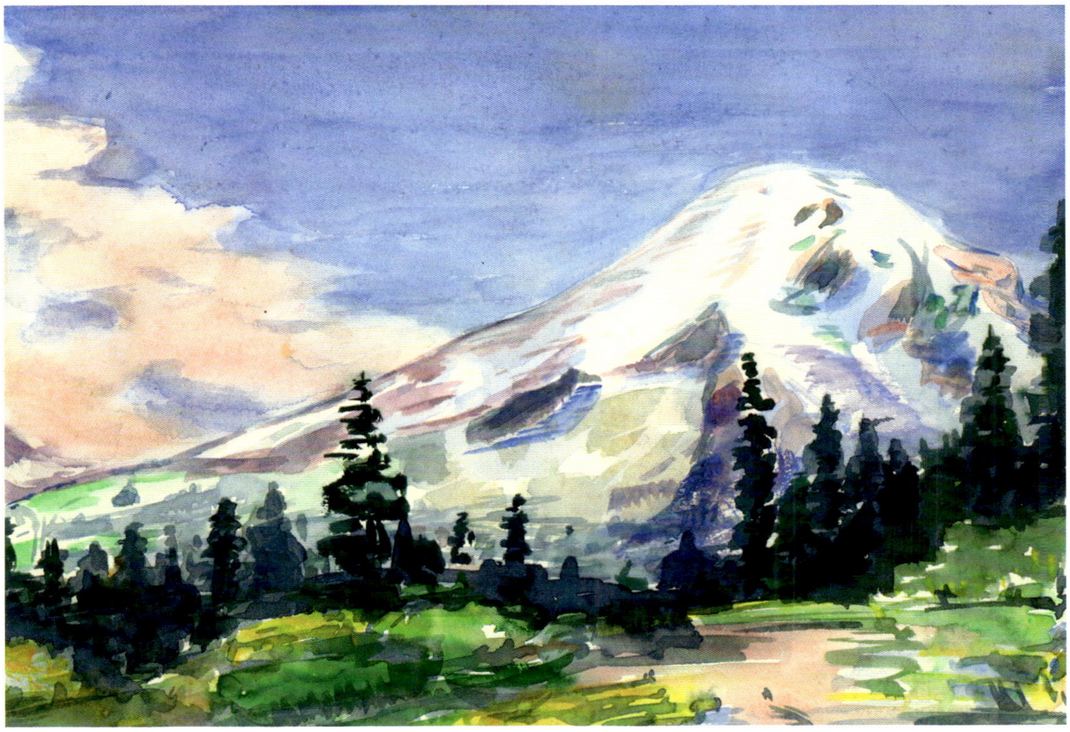

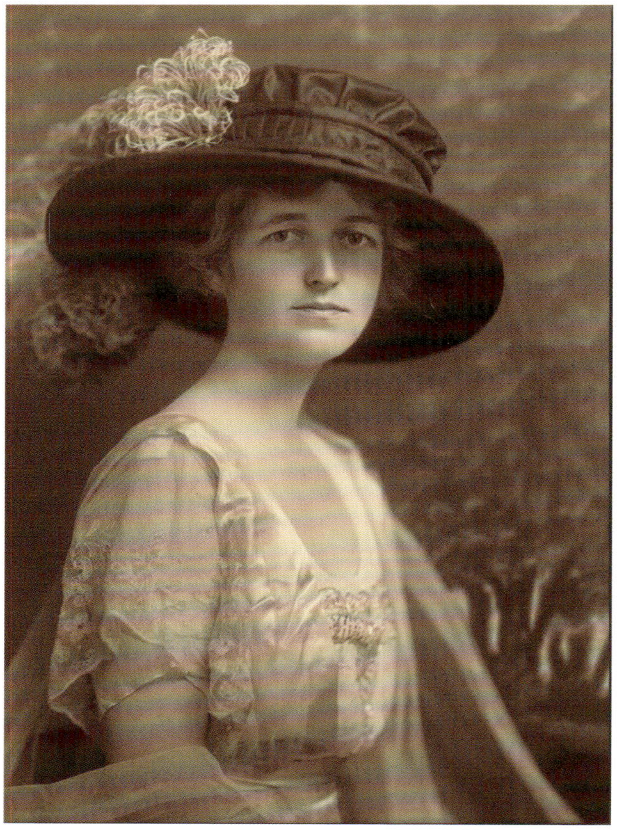

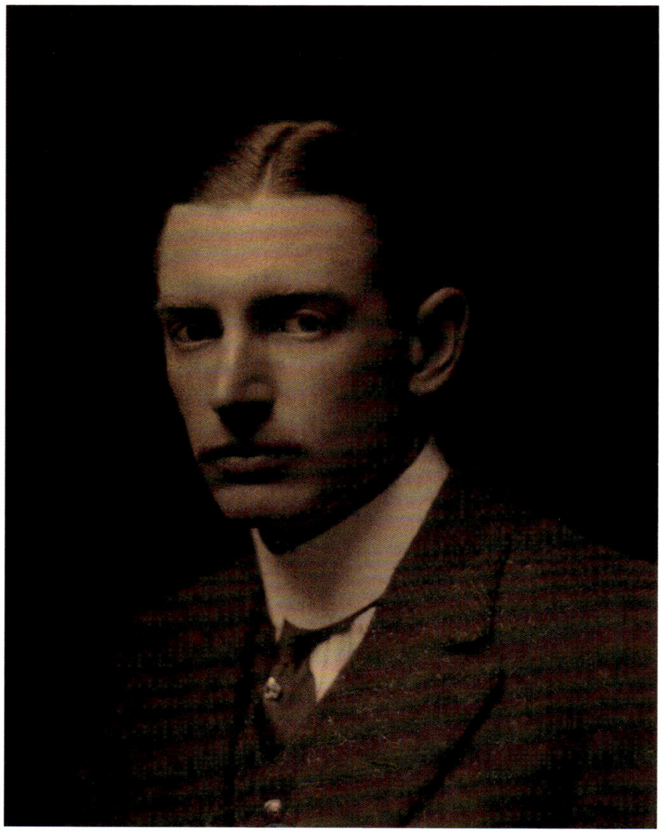

Beulah Loomis Hyde, 1913

William Dassonville
(1879–1957)
Portrait of Robert Henry Hyde, ca. 1913
Platinum print
10 × 8 in.

When they resumed life in Tacoma, they purchased a home in 1914, which they named "Scarlet Oaks," an understated but lovely residence on Gravelly Lake in the Tacoma suburb of Lakewood. The following year, on October 17, 1915, Beulah's estranged father, Lyman, married Gertrude Wilson Deaton in Montana. They intended to settle in New York City but remained in Montana and finally settled in California.[7] Lyman died on April 7, 1934, in Inglewood, California, from tuberculosis.

Beulah and Robert's union produced three sons, Charles Henry Hyde II (1914–1998), Robert H. Hyde (1916–1981), and William B. Hyde (1918–2014). With a loving husband and three sons, each born two years apart, Beulah had an intact, financially secure family, something she had not experienced in her own youth. However, as with many creative women of her generation, her artistic career took second place to raising her sons. By all accounts, Robert and Beulah were exemplary parents, making sure that the boys received a proper education and traveling when time allowed. Beulah used her own athletic inclinations to take her boys camping, skiing, and swimming and participated in other outdoor activities in the beautiful Northwest natural environment.

While parenting kept Beulah busy in the 1920s, her Tacoma colleagues kept the cultural flame alive. Her younger friend Thomas Handforth was establishing himself as an internationally recognized printmaker and portrait artist. He had moved to Paris in 1920 to study at the École Nationale Supérieure des Beaux-Arts, the Académie Colarossi, and the Académie Delécluse. An extraordinarily talented young man, he rented a studio in the Parc Montsouris district, where his fellow Tacoma artist friends,

Wedding portrait of Beulah Loomis and Robert Henry Hyde, 1913

Robert, Beulah, and baby Charles Henry Hyde II, ca. 1914

Beulah with baby Charles Henry Hyde II, ca. 1914

Family photograph, ca. 1916
From left: Robert; Beulah; Robert's father, Charles Henry Hyde, holding baby Robert H. Hyde; Beulah's maternal grandfather, William Beaton, holding the hand of baby Charles Henry Hyde II; and Beulah's mother, Elizabeth Beaton Loomis.

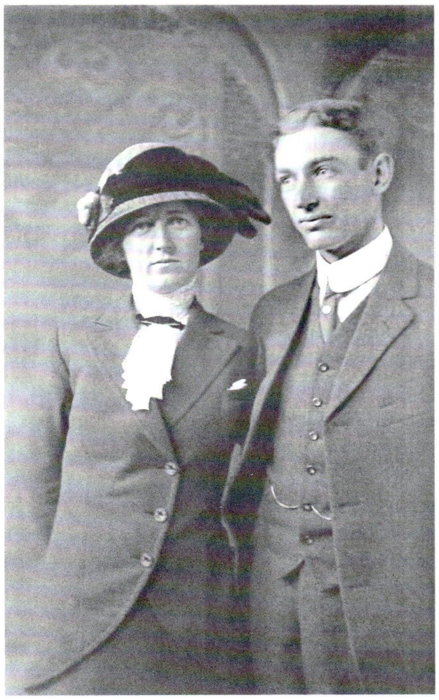

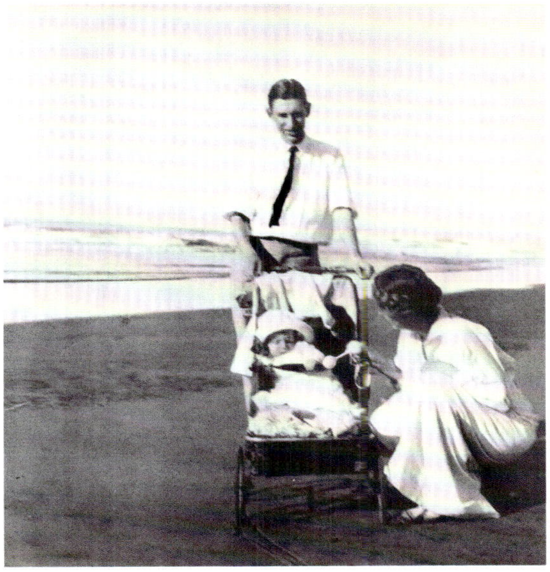

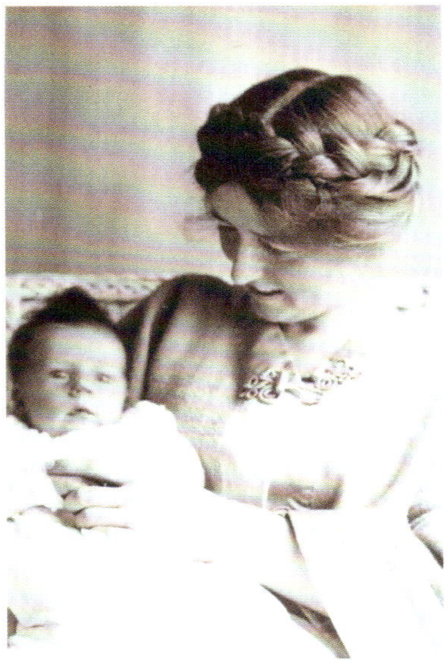

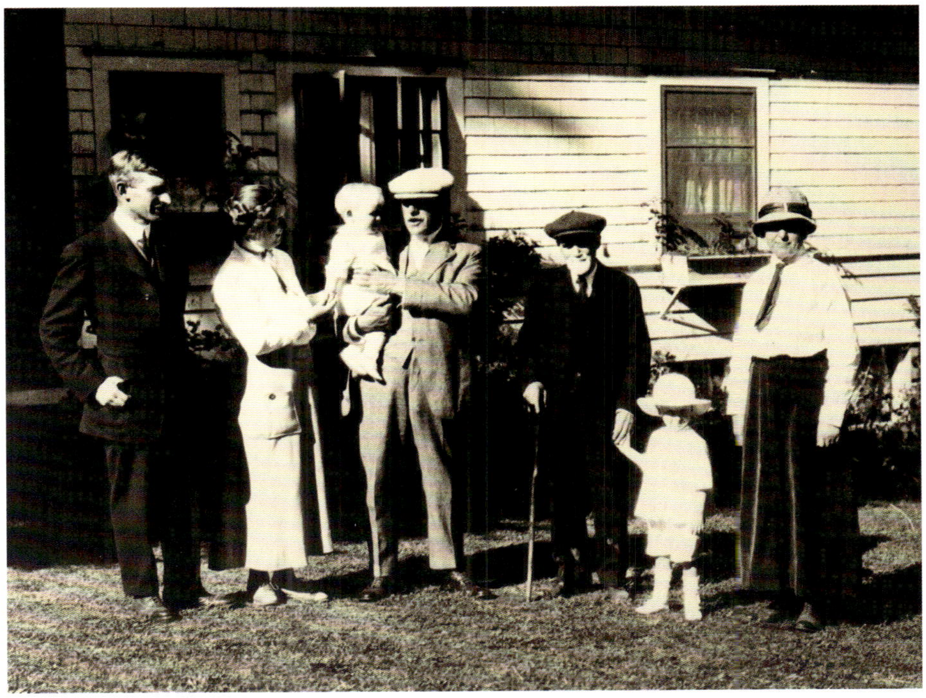

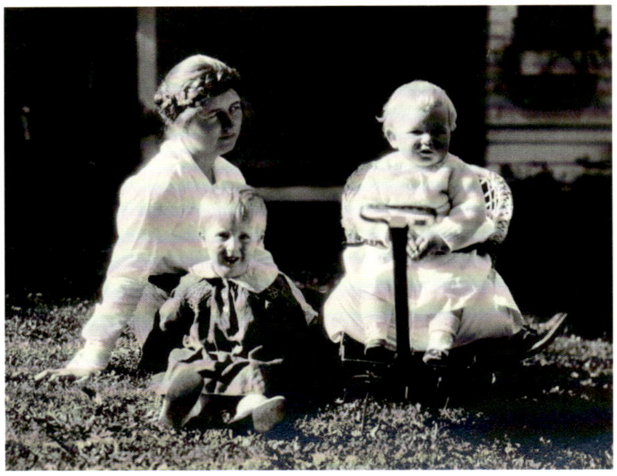

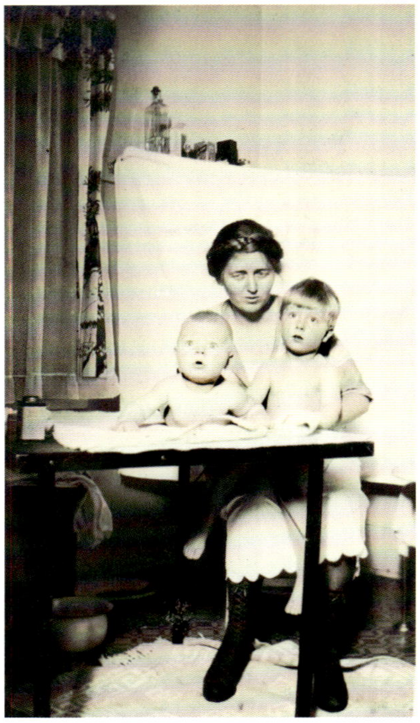

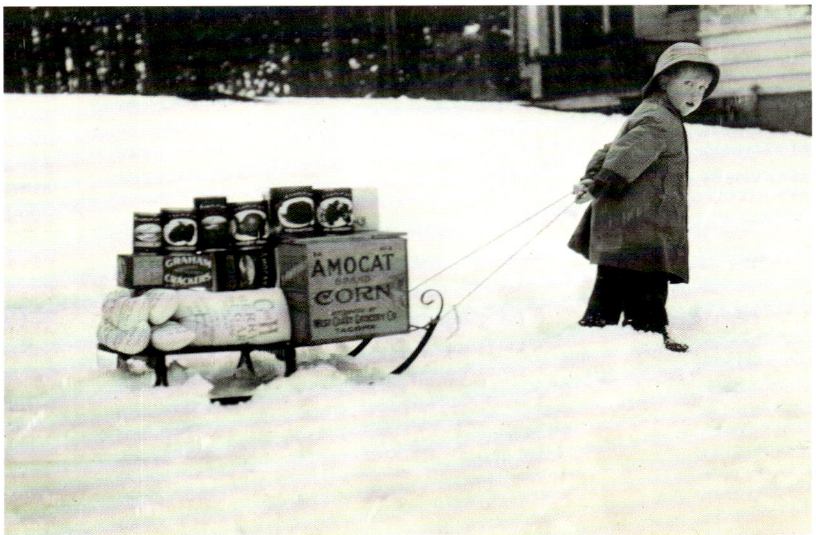

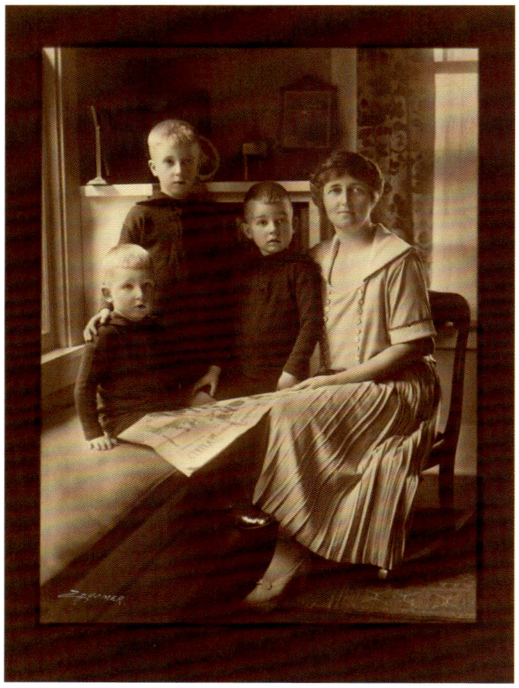

Top: Beulah with children Charles and Robert, ca. 1916

Above, left: Beulah with sons Robert and Charles, ca. 1916

Above: Beulah and Robert's son Charles H. Hyde II pulling a sled full of the family business products "Amocat," ca. 1920

Left: Beulah with her three sons, from oldest to youngest, Charles, Robert, and William, ca. 1922 Marcus Zausmer Studio, Tacoma, WA

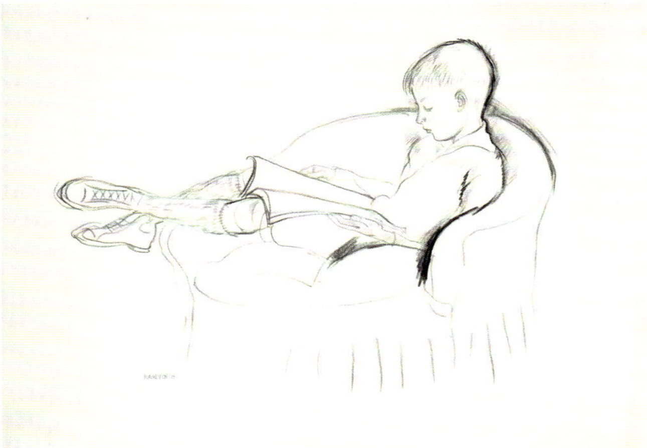

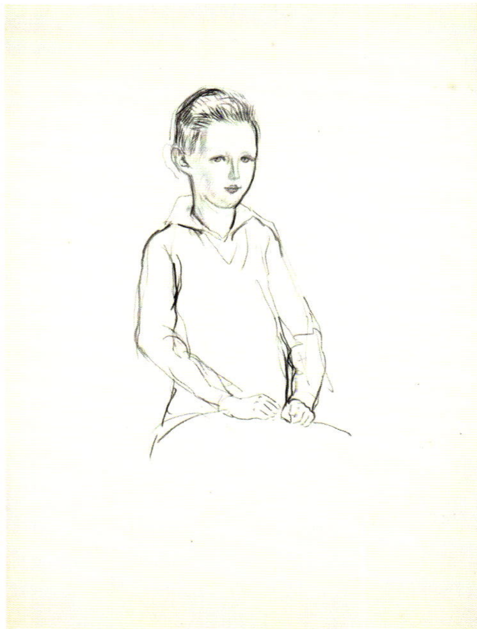

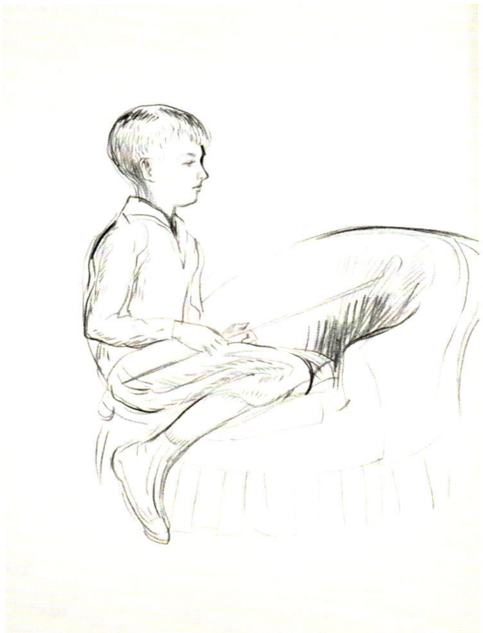

Thomas Handforth (1897–1948)
Portrait drawing of Charles H. Hyde II, ca. 1924
Graphite on paper
$9\frac{3}{4} \times 13\frac{5}{8}$ in.
Collection of Pamela Hyde Smith

Thomas Handforth (1897–1948)
Portrait drawing of William B. Hyde, ca. 1924
Graphite on paper
$13\frac{5}{8} \times 9\frac{3}{4}$ in.
Collection of Pamela Hyde Smith

Thomas Handforth (1897–1948)
Portrait drawing of Robert H. Hyde, ca. 1924
Graphite on paper
$13\frac{5}{8} \times 9\frac{3}{4}$ in.
Collection of Pamela Hyde Smith

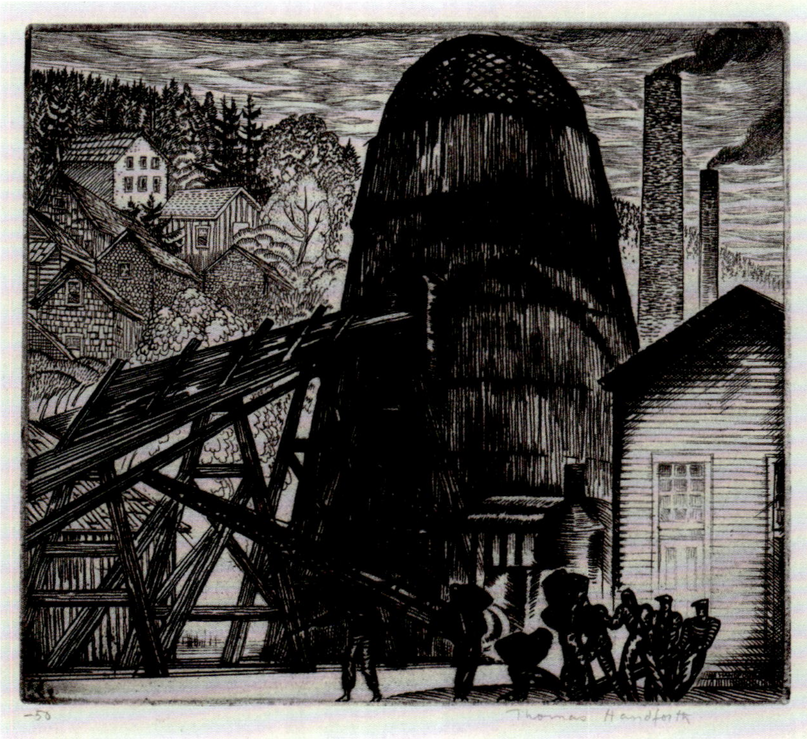

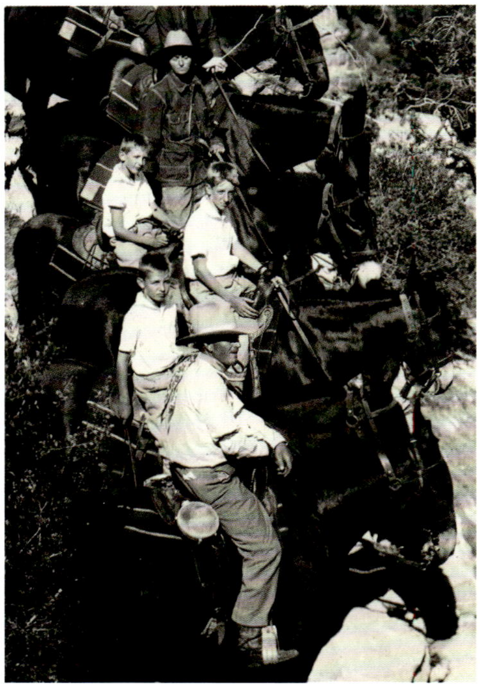

Thomas Handforth (1897–1948)
Sawdust Burner, ca. 1927
Etching and drypoint
5⅞ × 6⅜ in.
Cascadia Art Museum, Margaret Nannie Hartzell Collection, CAM 2021.13.16

Beulah and Robert Hyde with their three sons at Rancho Linda Vista, Oracle, AZ, in 1927

including Allan Clark and the gay couple Mac Harshberger (1901–1975) and Hollande Robinson (1890–1959), also had studios. The Montsouris district was also home to significant French artists, such as Georges Braque (1882–1963), whose studio was next to Handforth's. Harshberger and Robinson became the toast of Paris for their work with Tacoma's outrageous modern dancer Nina Payne (1890–1971), who was attracting attention at the Folies Bergère with compositions and piano accompaniment by Robinson and set and costume designs by both Harshberger and Robinson.

To show her support, Beulah held an exhibition of Handforth's work in her own home to assist the young man in sales and portrait opportunities on one of his many visits home. She commissioned him to create portrait sketches of her young sons and added his work to her own collection. Handforth, like his teacher George Zell Heuston, also turned to Tacoma's industrial sites for inspiration. His circa 1927 etching titled *Sawdust Burner* is one of several industrial subjects that he became known for. Handforth displayed an interest in form but conveyed his subject in a highly scrutinized symphony of line, patterning, and texture.[8]

In 1927, Beulah and Robert brought their sons to Rancho Linda Vista, in Oracle, Arizona. Their oldest son, Charles, had survived tuberculosis, and the warm, dry climate offered an opportunity for a more thorough healing.[9] Beulah used her horse-riding skills to explore the rugged desert terrain with her husband and sons. The desert was the

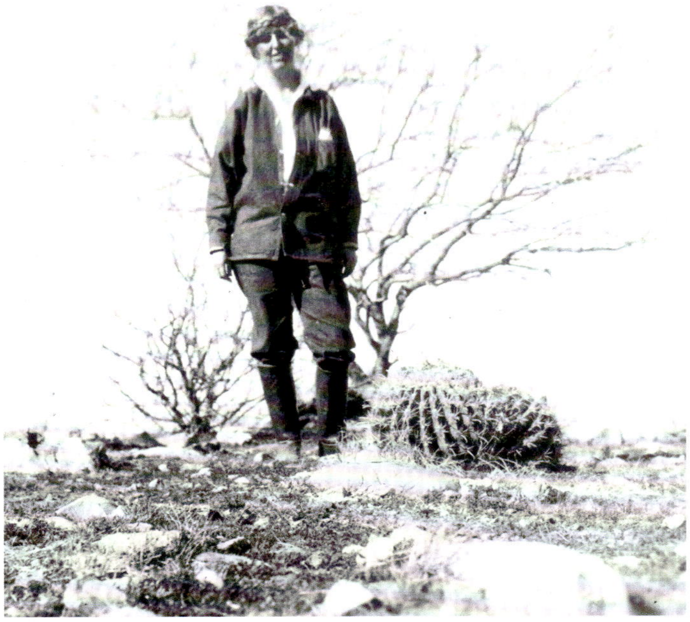

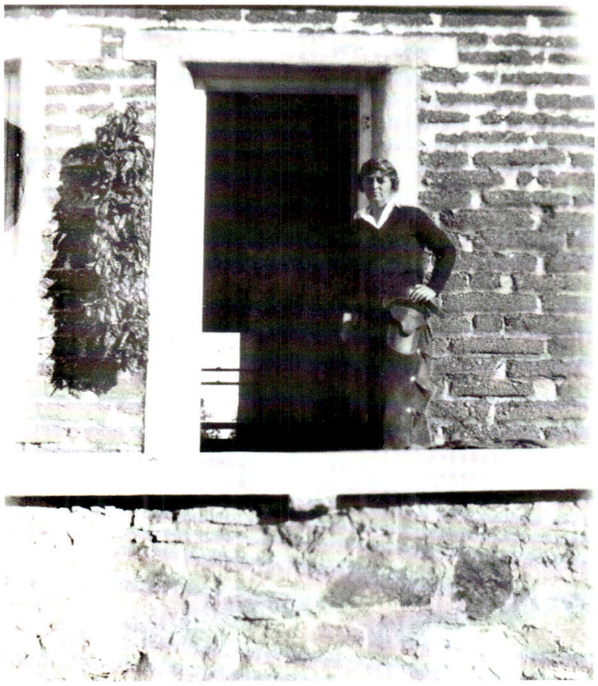

Beulah Hyde at Rancho Linda Vista, Oracle, AZ, ca. 1930s

Beulah Hyde at Rancho Linda Vista, Oracle, AZ, ca. 1930s

Beulah Loomis Hyde, ca. 1930

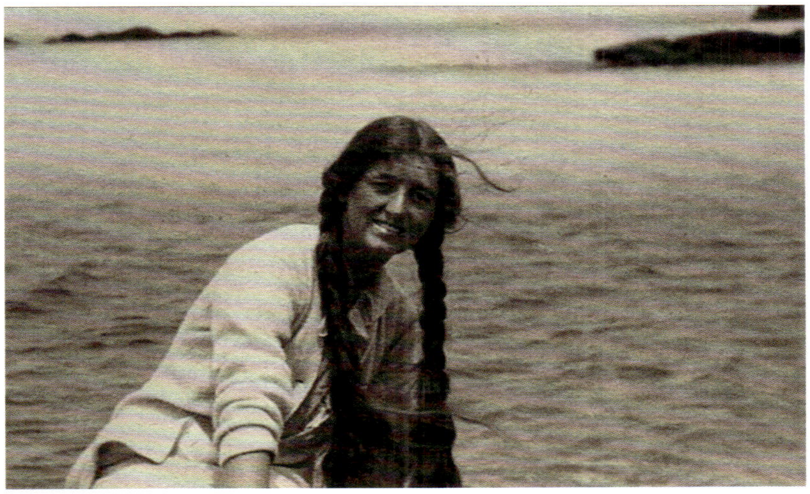

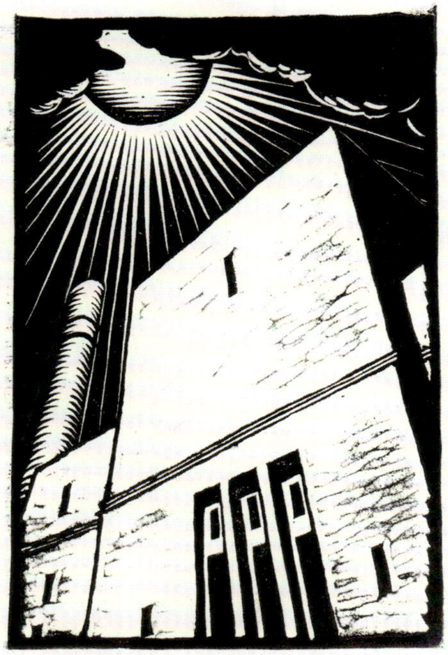

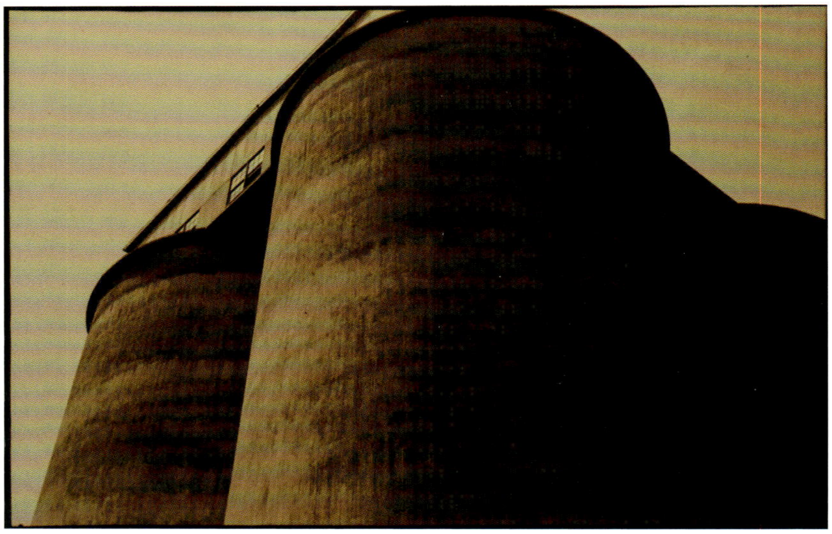

Virna Haffer (1899–1974)
The Big House, ca. 1929
Block print
6¾ × 4½ in.
Private collection

Virna Haffer (1899–1974)
Lime Kiln, ca. 1930
Bromide photograph
6½ × 9¾ in.
Private collection

antithesis of the lush Northwest environment, and the family would often return over the following decades.

During this time, a young Tacoma artist emerged whose impact on regional culture would last for nearly six decades. Virna Haffer (1899–1974) grew up in the nearby Home Colony, a communally inspired progressive encampment on Puget Sound that promoted independent, critical thinking as well as creative pursuits in the arts. Having supported herself since moving to Tacoma at the age of fifteen, Haffer, like Beulah's mother, Lizzie, was hardworking and resourceful and defied the societal expectations of women at that time. In the 1920s, Haffer came into her own as a fine art photographer and printmaker, gaining national and, later, international recognition. Several of her works in both mediums display an interest in industrial subject matter. Block prints like *The Big House* and photographs such as *Lime Kiln* utilize a modernist perspective of depicting the subject from a lower vantage point, emphasizing form and the upward thrust of the massive industrial architecture.[10] Haffer was gaining recognition through her association with the extremely successful Seattle Camera Club (SCC; active 1924–1930), a group of mostly Issei male photographers. She and the only other woman associated with the SCC, Ella McBride (1862–1965), participated in the international renown of the club, which during this time boasted some of the most exhibited pictorialist photographers in the world.[11]

The beginning of the decade of the 1930s saw the impact of the 1929 stock market crash and ensuing economic depression, including the end of organizations such as the SCC, whose membership consisted mostly of working-class men. Luckily, it did not have quite the same devastating effect on artists like Haffer and McBride, who were able to maintain an income through their photography studios in Tacoma and Seattle. The late 1920s and early 1930s also brought continued success for Tacoma artists such as Allan Clark, who had left Paris and traveled to China, Japan, and Korea from 1924 to 1927. Clark's highly stylized Art Deco sculptures were influenced

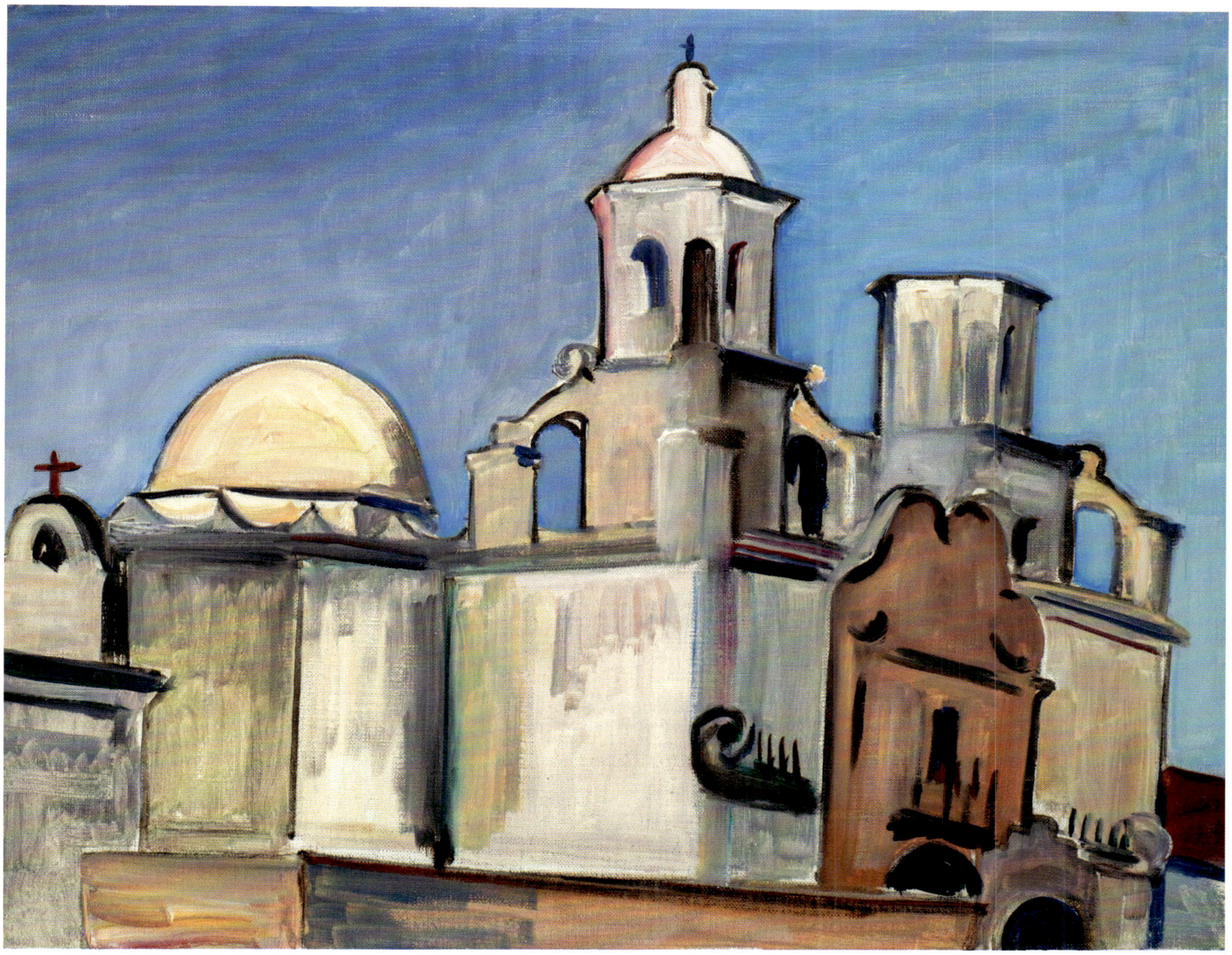

Beulah Loomis Hyde
(1886–1983)
Untitled, Mission San Xavier del Bac, Tucson, AZ,
ca. 1938
Oil on canvas
16 × 20 in.
Collection of Pamela Hyde Smith

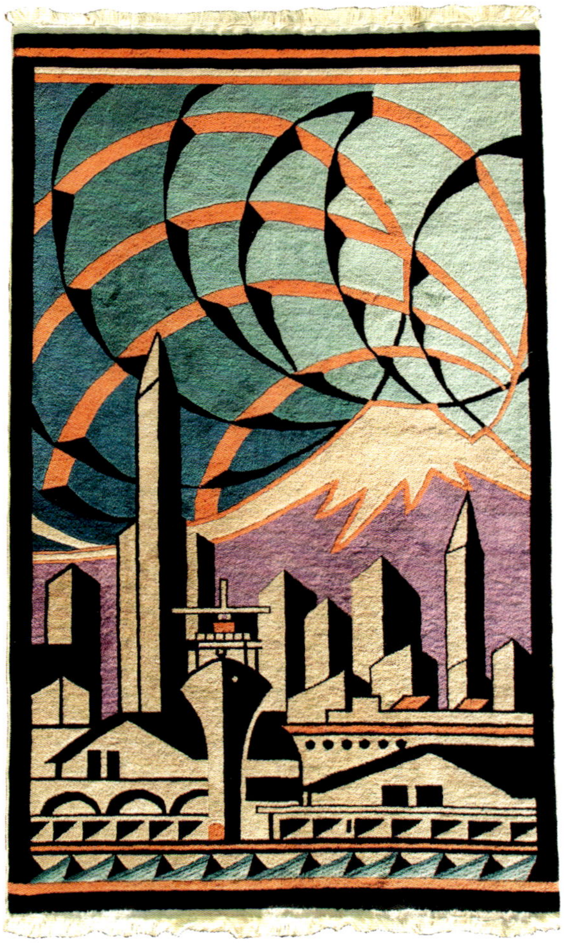

Orre Nelson Nobles
(1894–1967)
Rug designed for the Fette-Li Company, Peking, ca. 1930
Seattle waterfront motif
83 × 49 in.
Courtesy of the Healy Family Collection

by Asian art and were coveted throughout the world. Thomas Handforth and his friend Orre Nelson Nobles (1894–1967), a Tacoma-area artist and designer, were also traveling the world at this time. As early as 1917, Nobles traveled to various ports, including some in China, while working on a tramp steamer. He returned to China in 1927 and again in 1929 when he was hired by the Fette-Li Company in Peking as master designer for its international rug manufacturing business. By the summer of 1931, Handforth arrived in China, sponsored by a Guggenheim Fellowship. He met up with Nobles in Peking, and they traveled and worked together. At this time, Handforth met and developed a relationship with Laurence Sickman (1907–1988), who was traveling through China on a Harvard scholarship. Guided by Handforth and Nobles, Sickman collected important examples of Chinese paintings, sculpture, and objects that would later become the basis of the Nelson-Atkins Museum of Art's Asian art collection in Kansas City, Missouri. Nobles led tours of Asia for interested Northwesterners and imported Chinese and Japanese antiques and objects, to be sold through his sister, who acted as his agent in Seattle.

In the early 1930s, as her sons were maturing, Beulah Hyde appears to have taken an undocumented painting class with a new emphasis on form and altered perspective. Two extant studies from this period depict a still life of geometric blocks and another of ceramic vessels, painted *en grisaille* to emphasize form. In both works, the objects are placed closely together in a confined space with the support and background flattened and using a tilted spatial perspective. These studies foreshadow her mature works

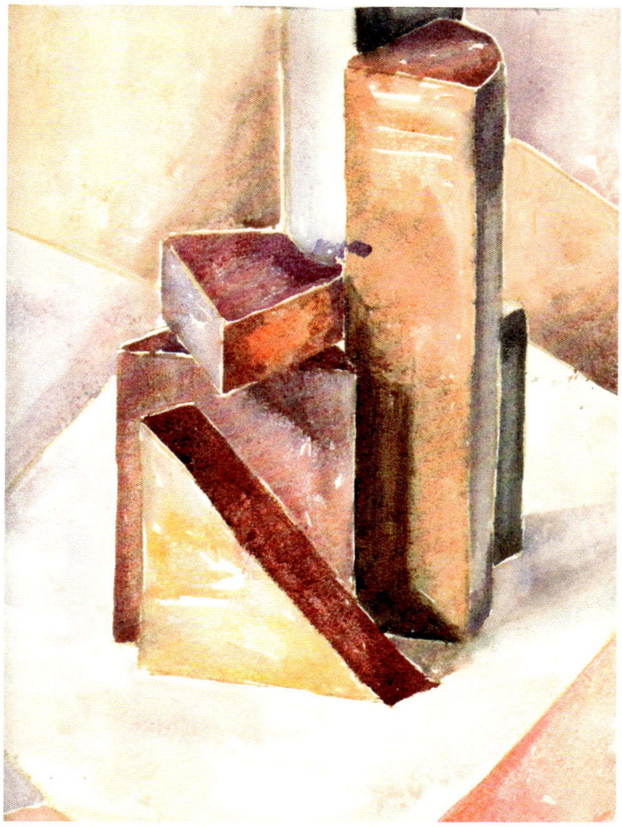

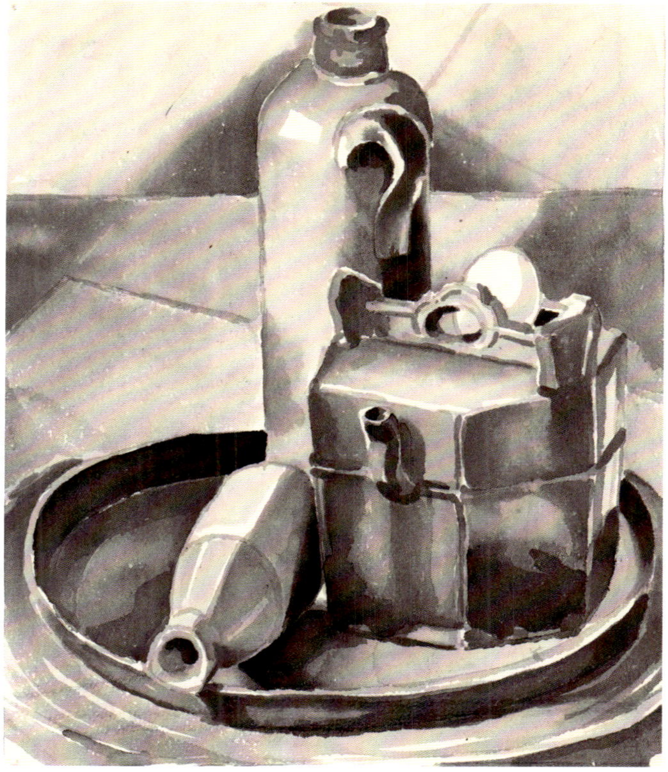

Beulah Loomis Hyde
(1886–1983)
Study, ca. 1930–35
Watercolor
12 × 9 in.
Collection of Pamela Hyde Smith

Beulah Loomis Hyde
(1886–1983)
Still life study, *en grisaille*, ca. 1930–35
Watercolor
9½ × 8 in.
Collection of Pamela Hyde Smith

depicting clustered industrial subjects. Another still life from this period shows a similar type of arrangement with more solid forms, a closer scrutiny of reflective light and texture, and emphasis on pattern (see page 36, top). Using still life as a subject allowed her to stay indoors to make her own arrangements and employ selective lighting, both natural and artificial. However, she would soon venture outdoors to search out the large-scale industrial forms that she could convey with her developing modernist approach.

Hyde's circle of artist friends was soon expanding to other gay men who, like Handforth and Nobles, traveled extensively and promoted a more modernist artistic approach in the Northwest. They included Mark Tobey (1890–1976) and Morris Graves (1910–2001), who would go on to define a unique style of painting in the region by including Asian and Native American influences in their work. Using a limited, low-key palette to reflect the quality of light in the Pacific Northwest, these men would soon go on to international acclaim. After dropping out of high school, Graves traveled as an employee of the American Mail Line with his brother Russell during the period 1928–31. The brothers traveled to numerous Asian ports, giving Graves a foundation for his own artistic creations in the early stages of his career. Tobey, who had arrived in Seattle from New York in 1921, was becoming a leading figure in Seattle's art community by 1930 and was also an inveterate traveler. He befriended the Chinese artist Teng Baiye (1900–1980) in the late 1920s when Teng was attending the University of Washington in Seattle. Teng's unusual finger paintings and mastery of Chinese ink brushwork undoubtedly contributed to Tobey's "white writing" abstractions developed in the later part of the decade. In 1931,

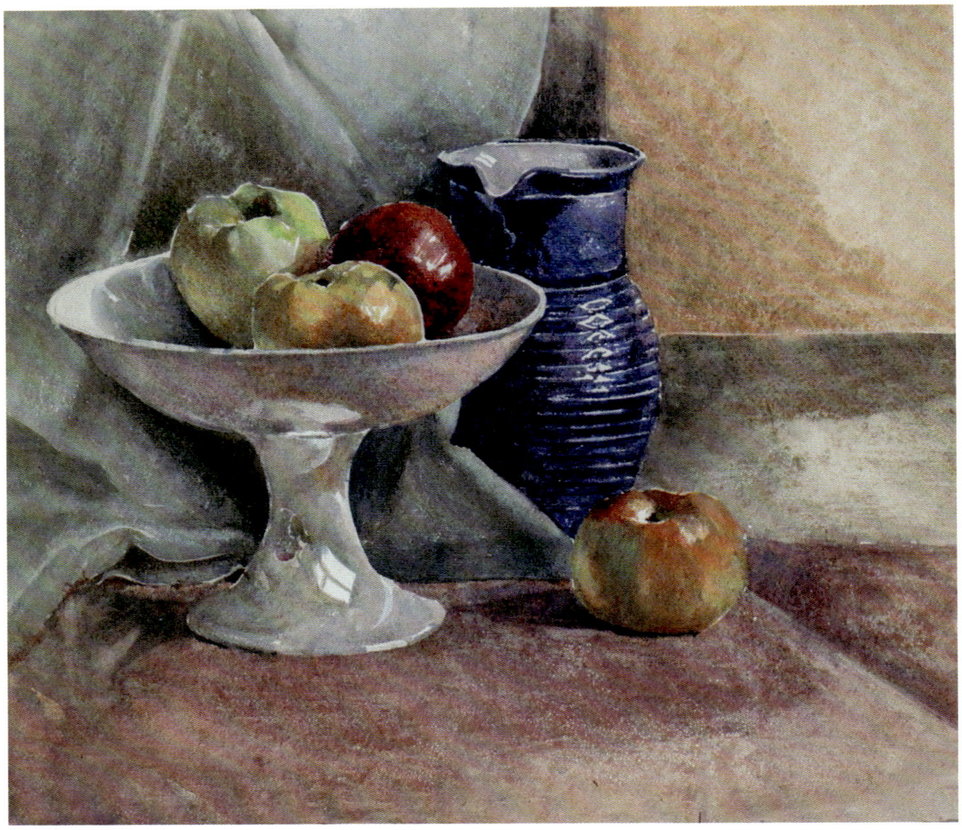

Beulah Loomis Hyde
(1886–1983)
Untitled still life, ca. 1930–35
Watercolor
16 × 18¼ in.
Collection of Pamela Hyde Smith

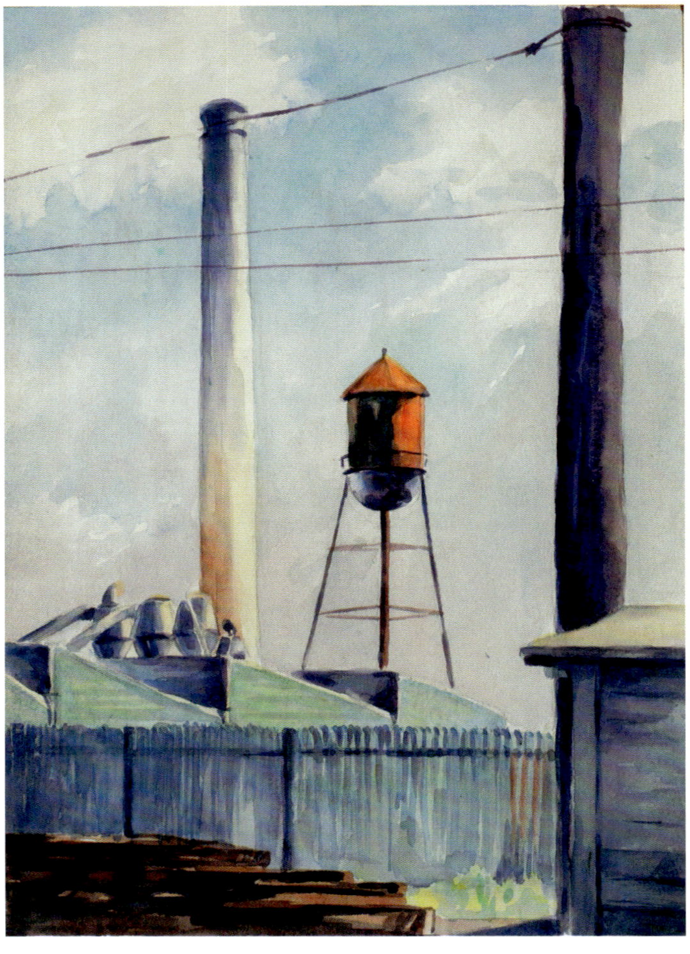

Beulah Loomis Hyde
(1886–1983)
Early industrial scene, ca. 1930–35
Watercolor
15 × 11 in.
Collection of Pamela Hyde Smith

Beulah Loomis Hyde
(1886–1983)
Early industrial scene, ca. 1930–35
Watercolor
15 × 11 in.
Collection of Pamela Hyde Smith

Beulah Loomis Hyde
(1886–1983)
Untitled, abstracted Northwest landscape, ca. 1930–35
Watercolor
10¼ × 10 in.
Collection of Pamela Hyde Smith

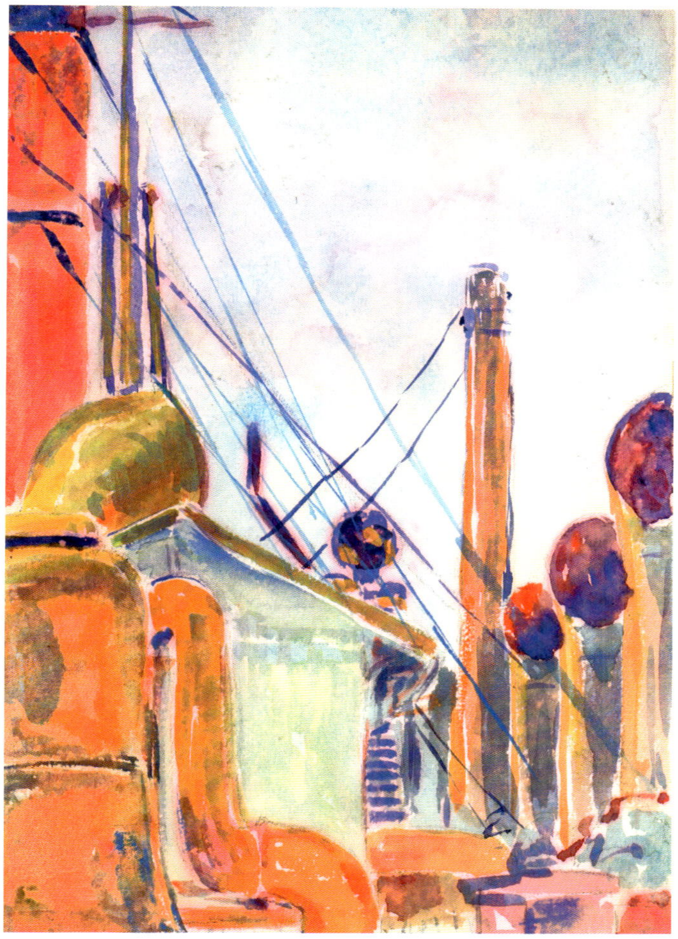

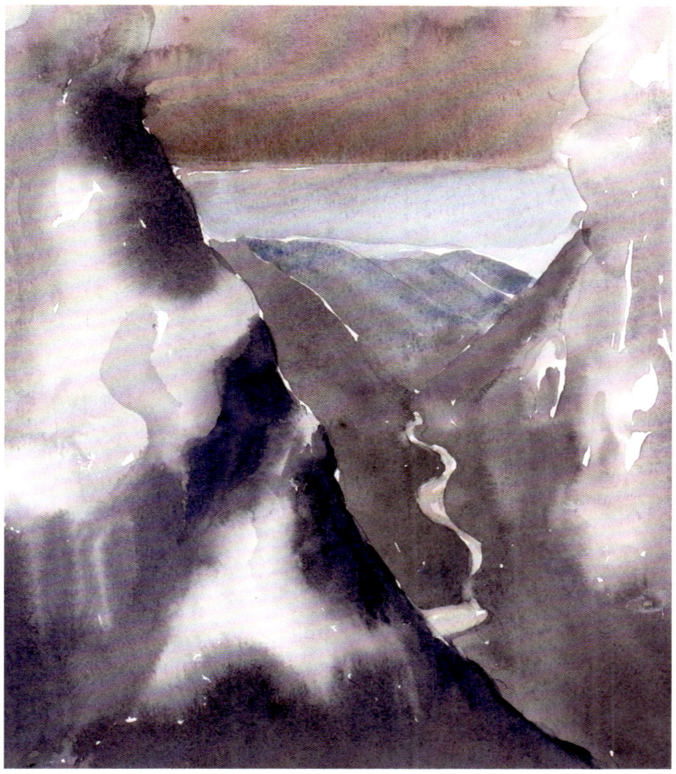

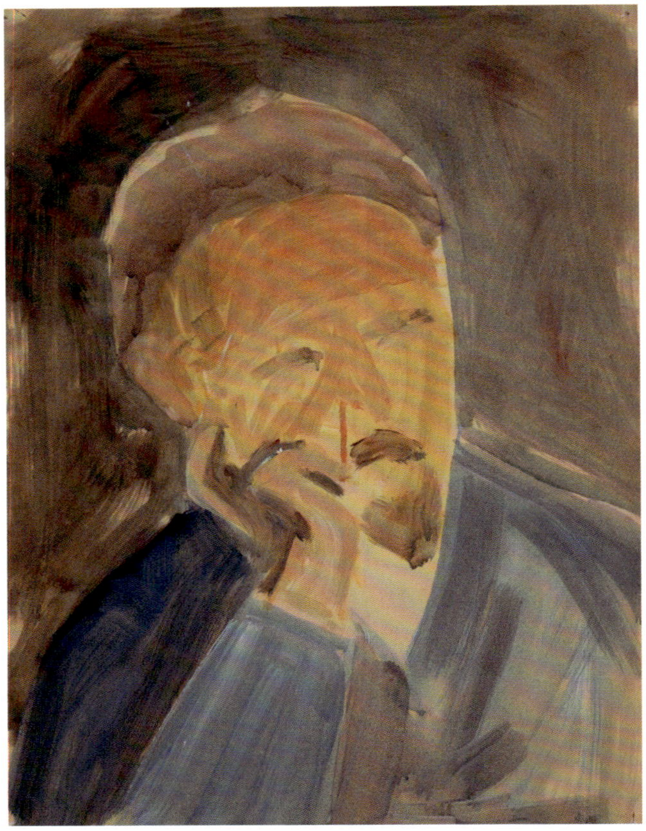

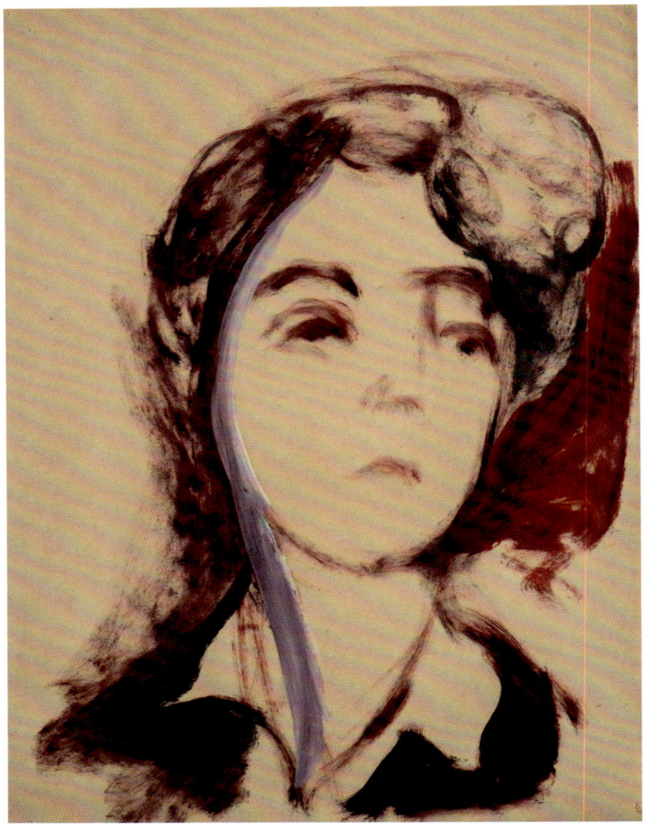

Beulah Loomis Hyde (1886–1983)
Portrait sketch of Mark Tobey, ca. 1935
Oil on paper
20 × 15 in.
Collection of Pamela Hyde Smith

Beulah Loomis Hyde (1886–1983)
Portrait sketch of Ellen Jones Hooker, ca. 1935
Oil on paper
20 × 15 in.
Collection of Pamela Hyde Smith

Tobey was living in England, where he became a resident artist at the Elmhirst Progressive School while teaching at Dartington Hall in Devon. He spent the next few years traveling through Europe and Japan and visited Teng in Shanghai. Returning to Seattle, Tobey had his first solo exhibition at the Seattle Art Museum (SAM) in late 1934. That same year, the Tacoma Art Association (TAA) was formed to provide exhibition opportunities and to emphasize the city's equal standing in the creative arts.

In the summer of 1935, Hyde and fellow Tacoma artists Ellen Jones Hooker (1902–1974) and Helen Keen (1894–1992) formed a private study class in Hooker's studio with Tobey as the instructor.[12] The extant works by Hyde produced in these classes are primarily oil on paper, including portraits that she made of Tobey himself and Hooker. They display the developing modernist approach to her work. Although Tobey had built a substantial reputation for himself by this time, there were other modernist painters in the Seattle region who were far more advanced than he was but lacked his social contacts and tendency for self-promotion. Peter Camfferman (1890–1957) produced a series of abstracted heads in the mid-1920s, all of which were oil on paper and are likely what influenced Tobey in that direction. Camfferman along with his wife, Margaret Gove Camfferman (1881–1964), were two of the most progressive regional artists in Washington State, beginning in 1915 when they relocated to Whidbey Island from Minnesota. Camfferman's abstracted head of his wife from 1926 used Fauvist techniques and shows the influence of Henri Matisse. Hyde would also begin a series of self-portraits during this time that reflect similar influences.

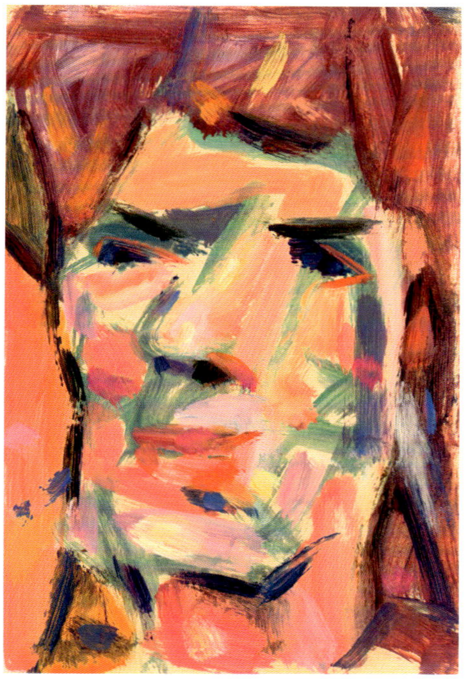

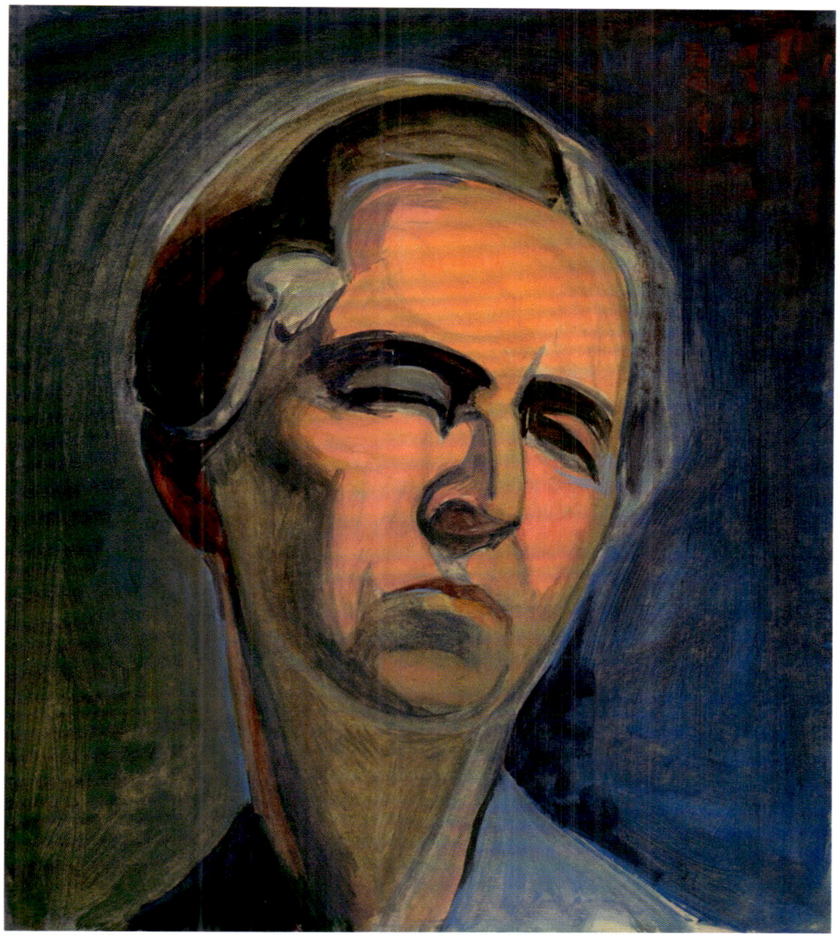

Peter Marienus Camfferman
(1890–1957)
Untitled portrait of his wife, Margaret Gove Camfferman, 1926
Oil on paper
9 × 5¾ in
Private collection

Beulah Loomis Hyde
(1886–1983)
Self-portrait, ca. 1935–38
Oil on paper
23 × 18 in.
Collection of Pamela Hyde Smith

While working under Tobey's guidance, Hyde was still interested in the architecture of industry and attempting to create a method of expressing herself. However, Tobey's style was not fully aligned with the American Precisionist movement in art, which began in the 1920s with artists such as Charles Demuth (1883–1935) and Charles Sheeler (1883–1965). Although most American art was heavily influenced by Europe at that time, Precisionism's hard-edged renderings and fractured planes reflected America's growing industrial power. Some American women artists participated in this movement, including Elsie Driggs (1898–1992) of New York. Her painting *Blast Furnaces*, from 1927, typifies her work of that period, although her emphasis on Precisionist industrial compositions was brief and constituted only a very small part of her oeuvre.

Although Precisionism was not widely practiced by artists in the Northwest in the early 1930s, a few made works that were compatible. This is evident in the work of Seattle's Kenjiro Nomura (1896–1956). His painting *Bridge*, circa 1930–35, uses an emphasized foreshortening with loose brushwork but confined in hard-edged outlines of black or dark blue, similar to the practices of European Post-Impressionists. Nomura's work of the 1930s also reflected his interest in architectural and industrial subjects. Hyde was likely aware of Nomura's work and would begin using this type of outlined structuring in the late 1930s as well. It also ushered in her habit of signing her work with initials to conceal her gender. SAM had opened in September 1933, and its co-founder, Dr. Richard Fuller, was extremely supportive of regional artists. The first solo exhibition at the museum was given to Nomura in June–July 1933.[13]

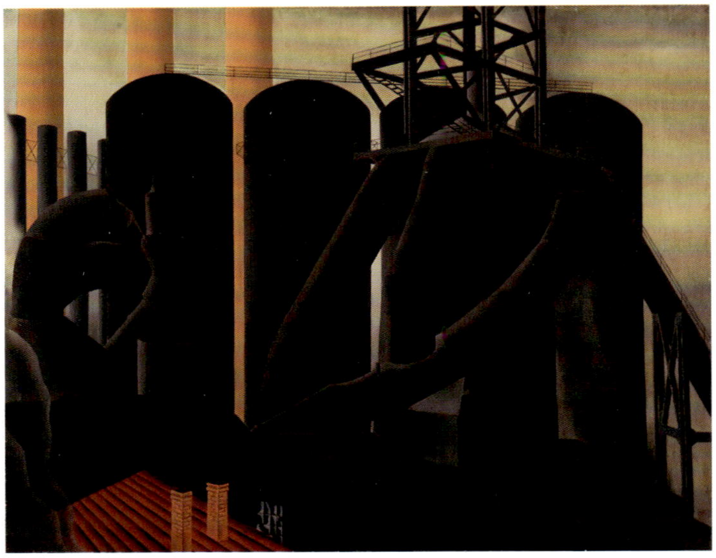

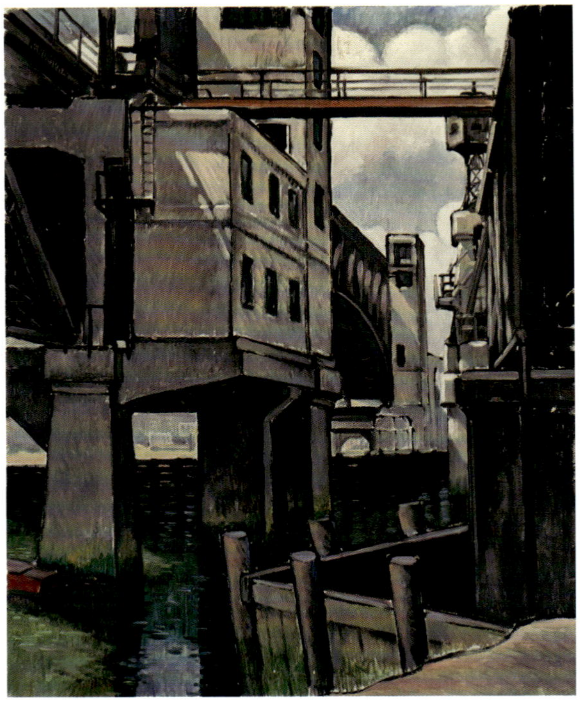

Surrealism was also being integrated into American art during the 1930s and 1940s. An artist whose work wielded an important influence was the Italian painter Giorgio de Chirico (1888–1978). One of his most famous early Surrealist works is *The Anguish of Departure*, 1913–14. This work could be seen as a progenitor of American Precisionism and Surrealism, although de Chirico's painting was likely influenced by Piero della Francesca's fresco *Discovery and Proof of the True Cross*, circa 1460, in the Piazza San Francesco, Arezzo, Italy. Hyde may have seen the de Chirico painting either in person or in color reproduction. Her undated painting *Grain Elevators* displays an influence from the de Chirico work, with similar formal qualities and an almost identical color palette.

Tobey also flirted with a type of Precisionist-inspired Surrealism in the late 1920s. One of his first important achievements was being included in the Museum of Modern Art's (MoMA) exhibition *Painting and Sculpture by Living Americans*, which ran from December 3, 1930, through January 20, 1931, in New York City. His *American Landscape*, painted in 1928 according to the exhibition catalogue, displays such influences and was one of three works by Tobey included in the show. That same MoMA exhibition also included five works by Charles Sheeler, including his iconic *American Landscape*, 1930. Even though their paintings shared the same title, the two approaches had little if anything in common. These works were made during the time when American artists were attempting to break away from the dominant European influences and establish a new American aesthetic. Tobey's painting used the same concept of European modernism, while Sheeler

Elsie Driggs (1898–1992)
Blast Furnaces, 1927
Oil on canvas
33 × 39 in.
Crystal Bridges Museum of American Art, Bentonville, AR, 2017.1
Photo: Edward C. Robinson III

Kenjiro Nomura (1896–1956)
Bridge, ca. 1930–35
Oil on canvas
30 × 24 in.
Wing Luke Museum, Gift of Sean Callahan, 1991.073.003

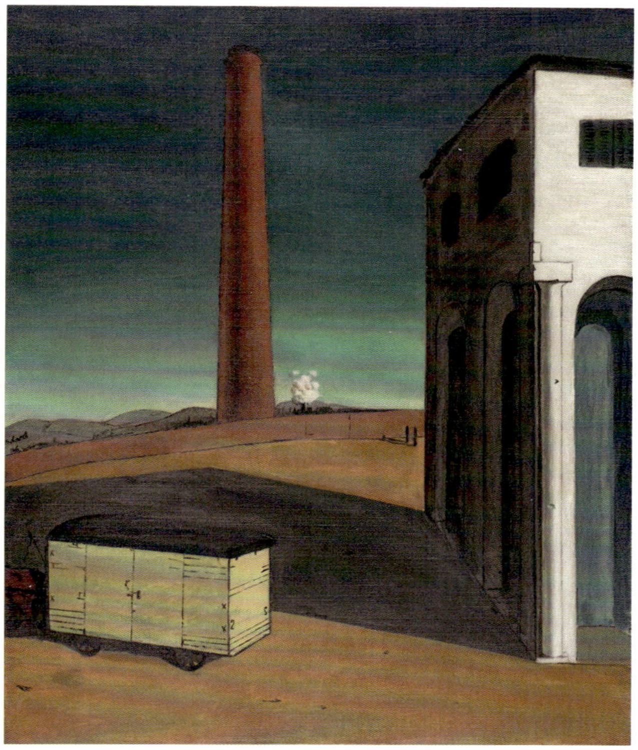

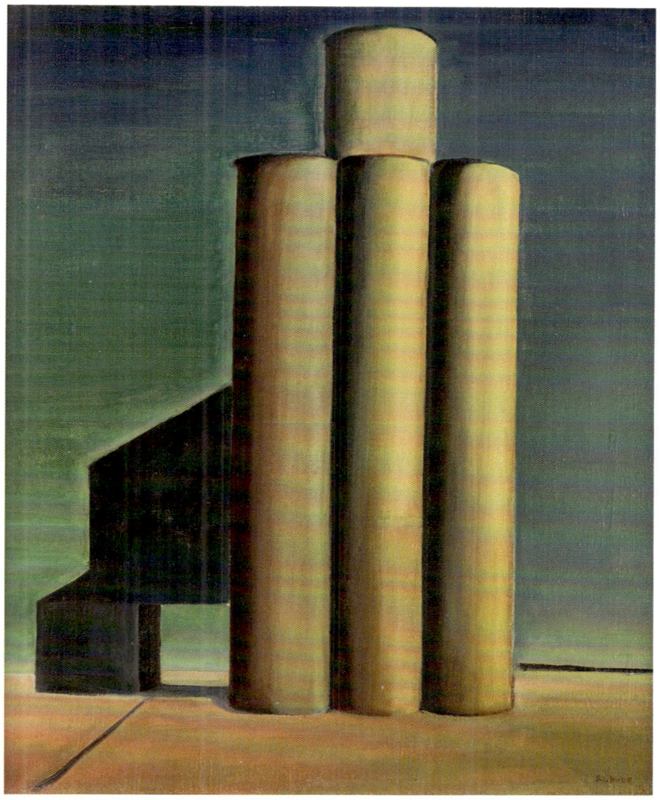

Giorgio de Chirico (Italian, 1888–1978)
The Anguish of Departure, 1913–14
Oil on canvas
33⅞ × 27⅝ × 1¼ in. (86.04 × 70.17 × 3.18 cm)
Collection Buffalo AKG Art Museum; Room of Contemporary Art Fund, 1939 (RCA1939:14.3)

Photo: Brenda Bieger, Buffalo AKG Art Museum

Beulah Loomis Hyde (1886–1983)
Grain Elevators, ca. 1940–47
Oil on canvas
24 × 20 in.
Private collection

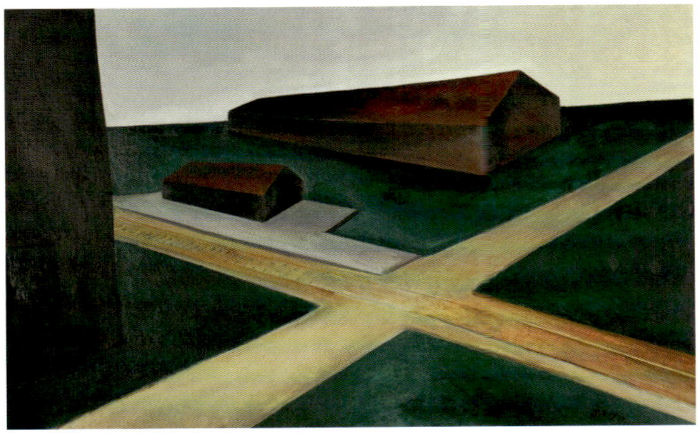

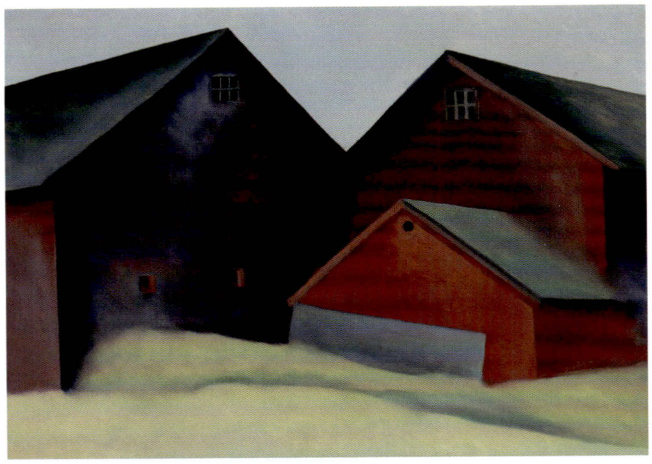

was breaking new ground in his paintings and photography. Whether intentional or not, Tobey's *American Landscape* has almost a primitive feeling to it due to its highly unusual perspective and confusing scale. The painting's tilted picture plane suggests an incongruous uphill motion that conflicts with the totality of the image. Hyde would certainly have been aware of the Tobey painting and created an undated abstraction of a lumber mill in a similar type of composition. Hyde's successful use of converging perspective lines common with dynamic symmetry, convincing spatial placement and scale, and a subdued, unified color palette gives evidence to her unique and growing skill.

Another artist whose work Hyde was likely aware of at that time was Georgia O'Keeffe (1887–1986), whose early works created on the East Coast are compatible with Precisionism. O'Keeffe's 1922 painting titled *Ends of Barns* takes a typical American subject and utilizes a hard-edged composition to convey the architecture and an almost dreamlike foreground of loosely blended edges. Hyde's graceful depiction of a Northwest English gambrel–style barn eliminates details such as windows and doors to give prominence to the form. This painting, one of several barn paintings that Hyde would produce, also displays a distinctive characteristic that she would use with success in several of her architectural/industrial subjects. By using chromatically contrasting colors in the sky, she vertically divides the picture plane with a cool color (blue) and a warm color (pink) to cause a visual sensation that makes the painting appear less flat. Cool colors cause the visual reaction to recede, while warmer colors cause the image to come forward. Employing this technique, she was able to add visual interest by turning the axis of the barn with the use of background color and forgoing traditional modeling using light and shadow. This vertical delineation is normally a device used in portraiture, and Hyde's use of it in landscape and industrial subjects was unique to her. She would successfully utilize this technique in many of her paintings.

Although O'Keeffe has become one of America's most recognized artists today, back in the 1930s she was barely known in the Northwest. However, local regional women artists were supportive of the work of other women in the arts and were often open to new ideas. On February 8, 1938, the artist Elizabeth Warhanik (1880–1968), who co-founded Women Painters of Washington (WPW) in 1930, gave a lecture for the Study Guild at SAM that substantiates this support.

Mark Tobey (American, 1890–1976)
Middle West; also *American Landscape*, 1929
Oil on canvas
37 × 59⅛ in. (94 × 150.2 cm)
Collection of Seattle Art Museum
Gift of Mrs. Thomas D. Stimson, 42.20
Photo: Elizabeth Mann

Georgia O'Keeffe (American, 1887–1986)
Ends of Barns, 1922
Oil on canvas
16 × 22 in. (40.64 × 55.88 cm)
Museum of Fine Arts, Boston
Gift of William H. and Saundra B. Lane, Juliana Cheney Edwards Collection—Robert Jacob Edwards Fund, Emily L. Ainsley Fund, and Grant Walker Fund, 1990.380

Beulah Loomis Hyde
(1886–1983)
Untitled, ca. 1935–40
Oil on canvas
16 × 20 in.
Collection of Pamela Hyde Smith

Beulah Loomis Hyde
(1886–1983)
Untitled, ca. 1935–40
Oil on paper
16 × 20 in.
Collection of Douglas Hyde Land

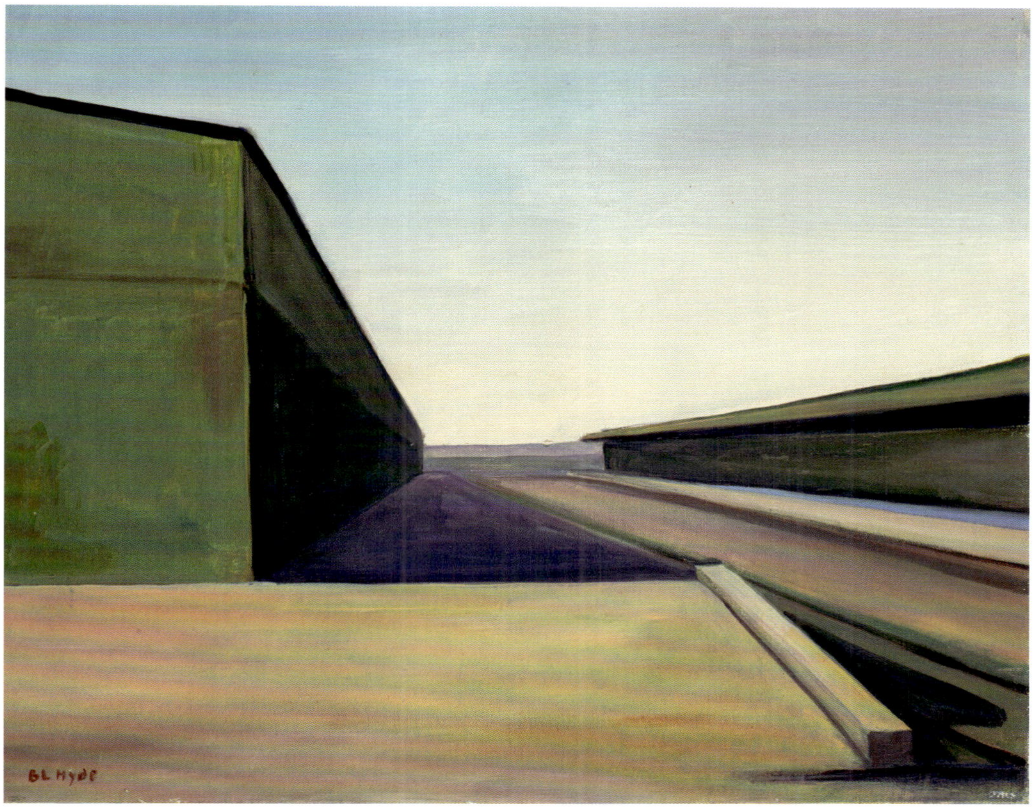

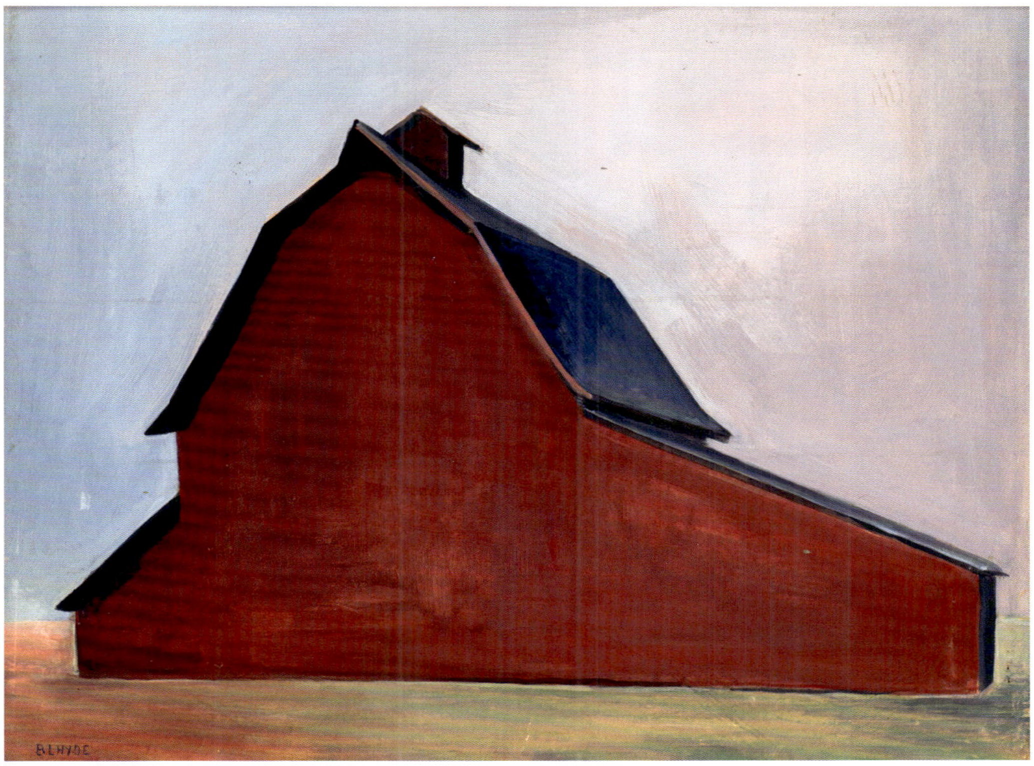

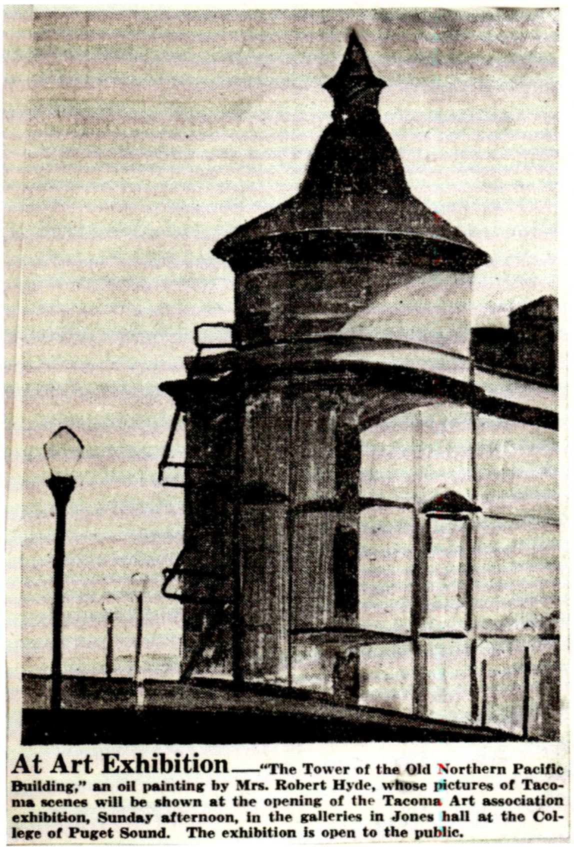
At Art Exhibition—"The Tower of the Old Northern Pacific Building," an oil painting by Mrs. Robert Hyde, whose pictures of Tacoma scenes will be shown at the opening of the Tacoma Art association exhibition, Sunday afternoon, in the galleries in Jones hall at the College of Puget Sound. The exhibition is open to the public.

Clipping from the *Tacoma Daily Ledger*, October 13, 1940
Northwest Room, Tacoma Public Library

> *"All-American," as applied to a modernist painter, is a term that startled some in the Study Guild audience at the SAM yesterday afternoon. Mrs. C. A. Warhanik (Elizabeth Warhanik, the artist) speaking of abstractions and other works of Georgia O'Keefe [sic] also called this artist "an individualist in spite of her training and of her experience as a commercial artist," and a "sincere symbolist." She characterized her as a painter who, with any subject, gives a sincere expression "barn-ness" if the subject is a barn, and similarly "chair-ness," "church-ness," and to continue the idea in one noted canvas, "skunk cabbage–ness."*[14]

The 1938 date of Warhanik's lecture coincides with the likely time that Hyde painted her barns, and she would return to the subject matter for several additional paintings over the next decade. Hyde would eventually become an associate member of the WPW and attained full membership in 1952.

In the summer of 1939, Hyde and her family traveled to San Francisco to attend the Golden Gate International Exposition. Inspired by the cultural infusion, she returned to Tacoma anxious to make advances in her art production. Although founded in 1934, the TAA held its first juried exhibition in April 1940, at Jones Hall at the College of Puget Sound in Tacoma. Hyde had two paintings accepted, *Mill* and *Highway Flower Stand*, which won an honorable mention. Six months later, in October, she was given a solo exhibition at the same venue.

That same month marked Hyde's first work to be accepted in SAM's prestigious Northwest Annual Exhibition, with her two oil paintings *Factory* and *The Yellow*

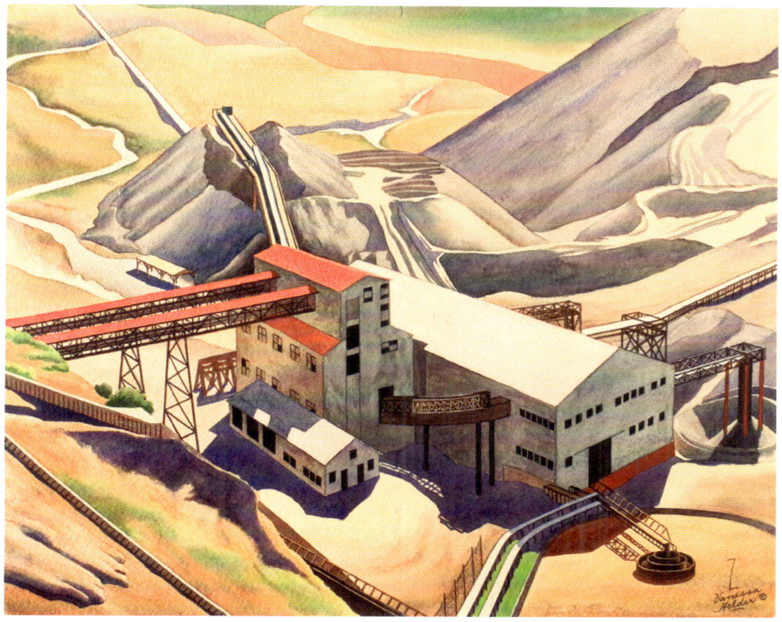

Z. Vanessa Helder (1904–1968)
Sand and Gravel Works, 1939–41
Watercolor on paper
17⅞ × 22 in.
Northwest Museum of Arts and Culture / Eastern Washington State Historical Society, Spokane, WA, 2585.19

House included. The SAM annual also featured two Precisionist-style watercolors by Z. Vanessa Helder (1904–1968). A prominent member of the WPW, Helder was one of the only other regional artists, besides Hyde, to work in a Precisionist manner with a focus on urban and industrial subject matter. Helder had relocated to Spokane the previous year to teach at the Spokane Art Center, an organization federally funded by the Works Progress Administration (WPA) under Franklin D. Roosevelt's New Deal program. SAM gave Helder a solo exhibition in May 1939. While teaching in Spokane, Helder began working on a series of Precisionist watercolors depicting the Grand Coulee Dam and its environs. When she returned to Seattle in 1941, she had completed this series consisting of twenty-three watercolors. Twelve of her Precisionist paintings were shown in a prominent 1943 exhibition at MoMA, *American Realists and Magic Realists*, including four from the Coulee Dam series.[15]

Besides Hyde, Helder, and Blanche Morgan Losey (1912–1981), whom Hyde had known through her activities in Tacoma's art circles, these women were the only Precisionists working in western Washington at that time. That changed with the arrival of the artist Yvonne Twining Humber (1907–2004) in 1943. A highly talented and successful WPA artist active in New York and Boston before moving to Seattle, she was one of very few painters, male or female, using a hard-edged, formalist realism style that was derived from elements of Precisionism and early pre-Renaissance art. Humber was also a member of the WPW and served as its president in 1947–48.[16]

Another talented member of the WPW was Peggy Strong (1912–1956), also a Tacoma native, whose family lived close to the Hydes in Lakewood. Strong and Hyde were arguably two of Tacoma's most successful artists of the period. They were often

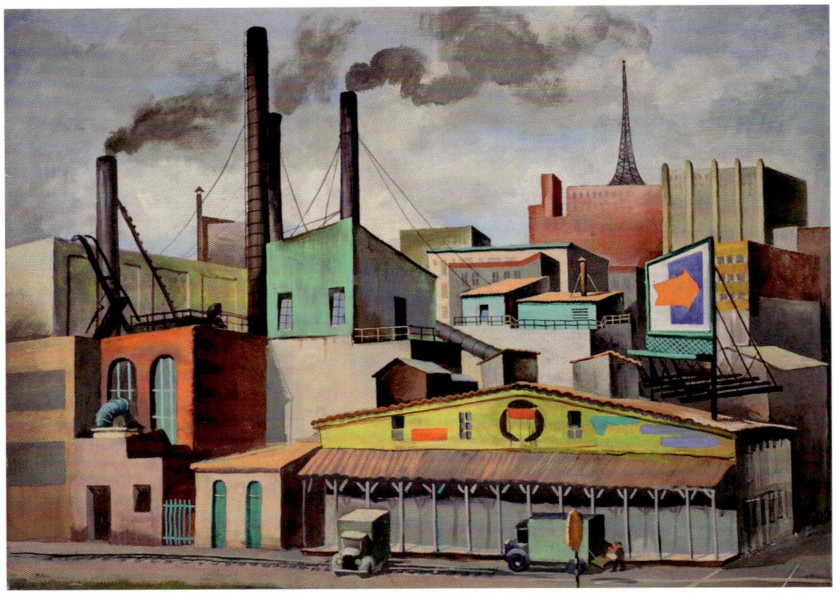

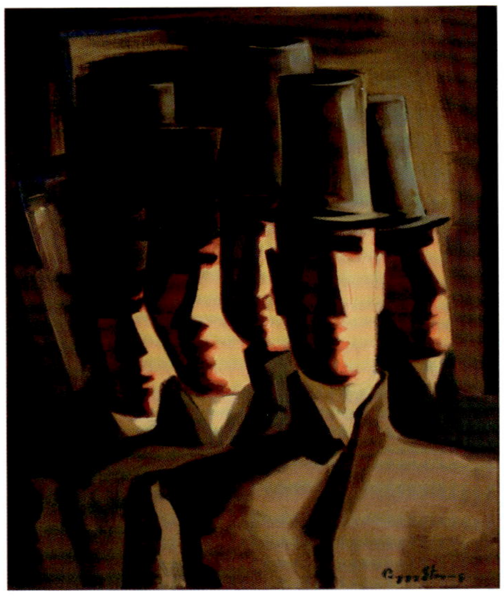

Yvonne Twining Humber (1907–2004)
City View, ca. 1946
Oil on panel
20 × 26 in.
Private collection

Peggy Strong (1912–1956)
Men in Tall Hats, ca. 1939
Oil on canvas
24 × 21 in.
Collection of John Strong

included in the same exhibitions and usually cited as among the better painters singled out by reviews in the local press. Strong began her career as a promising young artist of note whose life was dramatically altered in August 1933, when a car accident resulted in a severe spinal injury that left her paralyzed from the chest down. Luckily, she maintained the use of her arms, allowing her to continue painting, but was confined to a wheelchair for the remainder of her life. Not one for self-pity, the resourceful Strong continued her career as a painter, even producing several large murals during the Depression by using a platform that she could manually operate to reach the entirety of the mural's surface. The platform was designed by Strong's father, an engineer, who also created a system that allowed her to drive her car independently by steering, accelerating, and braking using her hands and arms. Unlike Hyde, Strong never produced any industrial subjects or urban scenes. Perhaps she felt that the senior Hyde had established success with the subject. Instead, Strong concentrated on portraiture and figure painting, which brought her tremendous national success. Before her accident, Strong, like Hyde, was an expert horsewoman and also athletically inclined. Her painting *Men in Tall Hats*, circa 1939, is a modernist depiction of a group of men in riding gear with elongated faces and tall, tubular hats that mimic the shapes of smokestacks.[17]

After Hyde's extremely successful entry into the new decade of 1940, she resumed exhibiting, primarily in Tacoma. She participated in the community-minded National Art Week in November of that year, following her solo exhibition with the TAA. National Art Week, a highly publicized event across the country, began in 1940 and continued for several years during the Depression. Its motto, "American art for every American home," encouraged the public to purchase the work of American artists during this difficult economic time.

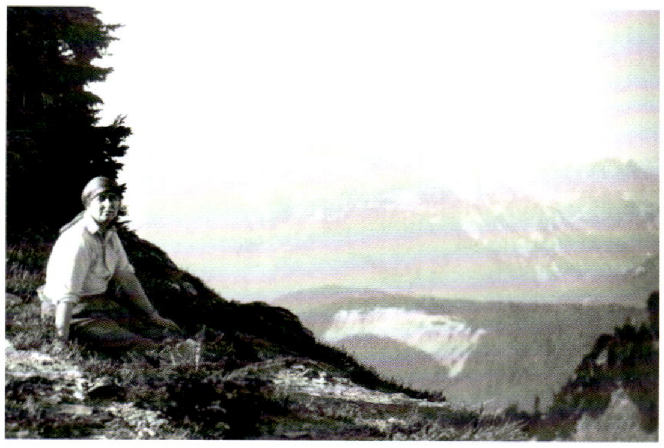

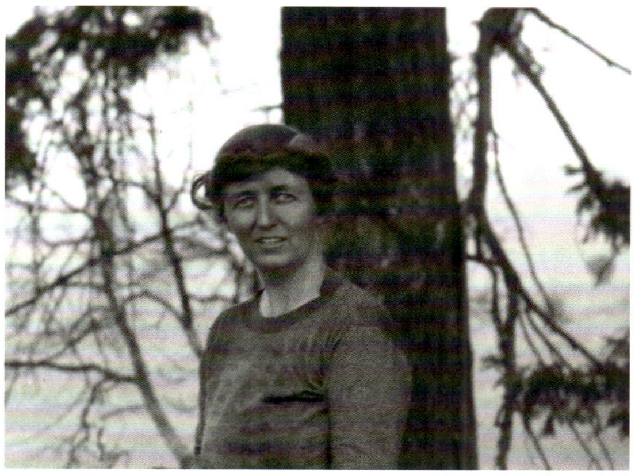

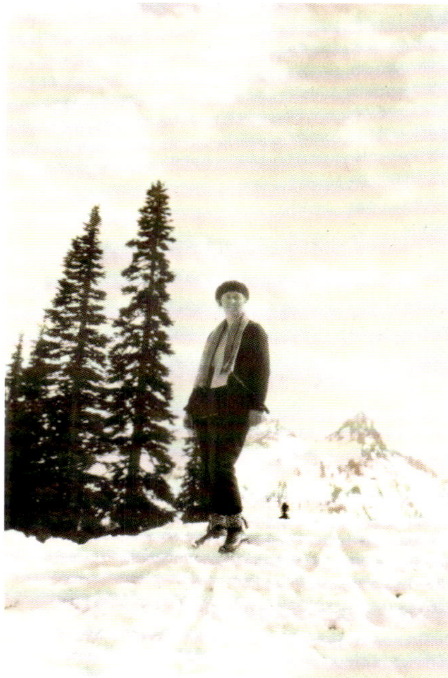

Beulah Hyde, ca. 1935

The year 1941 brought a continuation of advancement for the TAA and Hyde herself. Under the brilliant leadership of director Melvin Kohler (1911–1984), the quality of the TAA exhibitions at the College of Puget Sound, where Kohler was an instructor, increased and prominent speakers gave lectures, such as "Why Modern Art?" by Mark Tobey.

Kohler was also involved with the art exhibitions for the Western Washington Fair Art Galleries in nearby Puyallup. At the time, even though they were part of the Washington State Fair, the Puyallup exhibitions produced some of the finest shows in the state, held yearly in late August and September. The 1941 exhibition titled *Contemporary American Art* included Hyde's oil painting *Gas Station*, which won second prize. Other artists in this exhibition included prominent American painters such as Thomas Hart Benton, Paul Cadmus, Edward Hopper, and Raphael Soyer. To provide regional context, the show also included, besides Hyde, Seattle's Nomura and Tobey as well as Tacoma's Strong and Handforth. Kohler knew the value of including regional artists with well-known figures from the East Coast, as it demonstrated how lesser-known regional artists could hold their own with the big names whose access to large galleries and museums was mostly unavailable in the Northwest, with few exceptions. Immediately following the successful show at Puyallup, Kohler miraculously arranged for an exhibition of fourteen original Van Gogh paintings at the TAA galleries at the College of Puget Sound. Lasting for ten days, the show directly followed their exhibition at the San Francisco exposition that Hyde had attended. These exhibitions were quite an achievement for such a humble college gallery. Kohler, an art history professor at the college and director of the TAA, produced another extraordinary show in April for the Third Annual TAA exhibition. Hyde won honorable mention for

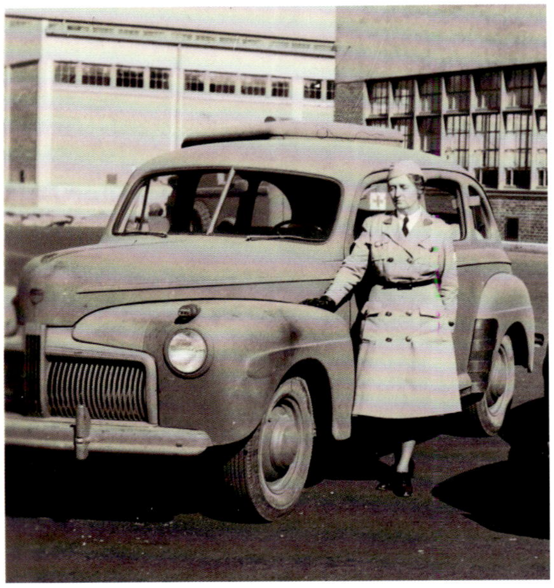

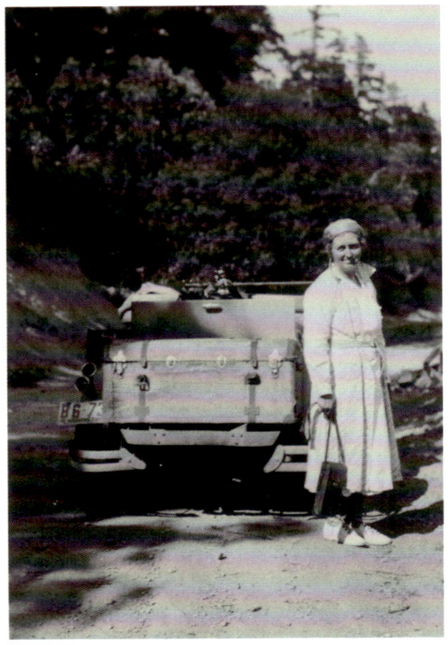

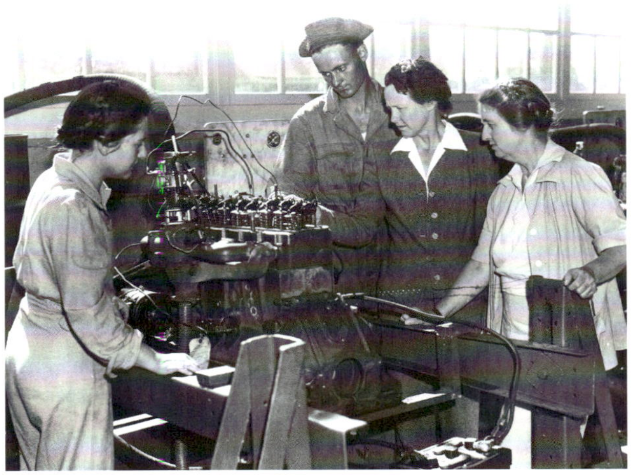

Beulah Hyde, ca. 1942

Beulah Hyde, ca. 1942

Tacoma Times, August 22, 1942, p. 5
Richards Photography Studio
Northwest Room, Tacoma Public Library
"Supporting the war effort by learning auto mechanics are, left to right, Mrs. Thomas (Otis) Henderson, an unidentified instructor, Mrs. Everett (Mary) Griggs II and Mrs. Robert (Beulah) Hyde. In August of 1942, about 40 members of the Red Cross Motor Corps took classes in automobile mechanics at Fort Lewis. Presently they transported medical supplies, blood and members of armed servicemen's families, but in the case of an emergency they would replace all drivers called up by the military."

Church, one of her three oil paintings in the show. For this exhibition, she was again in extraordinary company, as it included works by the internationally known sculptors Alexander Archipenko, Ernst Barlach, Auguste Rodin, and Tacoma's own Allan Clark. The year ended with an alarming disaster when Japan bombed Pearl Harbor, ushering the United States into World War II.

Kohler enlisted in the army in June 1942, to join the war effort. Hyde herself was determined to do her share as well. In August of that year, she and her future daughter-in-law Otis Henderson, as members of the Red Cross Motor Corps, attended classes at Fort Lewis to learn automobile mechanics. They delivered medical supplies, transported military families, and even drove tanks between military bases as replacements for drivers called into service. Along with her community service, Hyde continued to exhibit and win awards. Unfortunately, the year came to a sad ending when her mother, Lizzie, died on November 25.

The war slowed down arts activities the following year, with many artists and teachers throughout the state serving in the military. Although Hyde exhibited with the TAA's Fourth Juried Annual, she continued with her civilian war efforts as well as participated in National Art Week, held in November of that year at the Fort Lewis Inn. Hyde's son

Beulah Loomis Hyde
(1886–1983)
Untitled, ca. 1942–44
Oil on canvas
16 × 20 in.
Collection of Pamela Hyde Smith

Hyde placed the word "Dead" inconspicuously on the front of the tank as a grim reminder of the function of the armored combat vehicle.

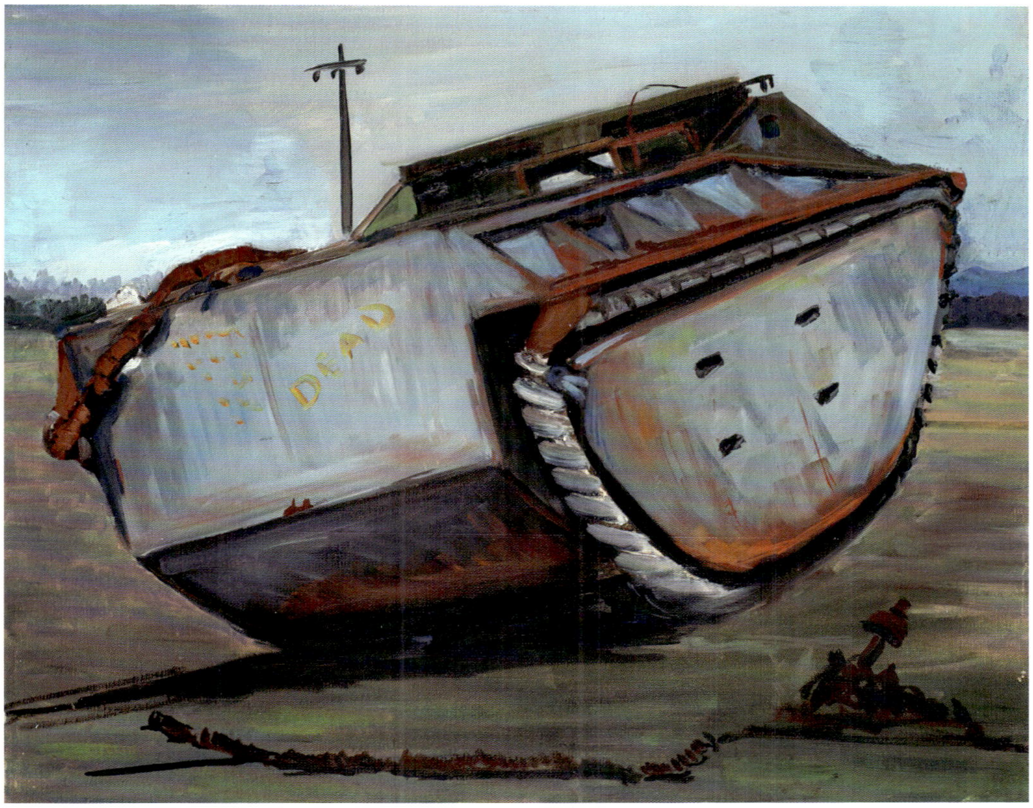

Robert entered the air force in 1944 and attended officer's candidate school, eventually reaching the position of captain. On June 24, 1944, Beulah's beloved husband, Robert, died. Her sons took over the family businesses, which carried on with great success while continuing to patronize social and cultural institutions in the Northwest.

One of Hyde's most important champions, Kohler, was severely injured in 1945 when a Japanese plane carrying large explosives made a suicide dive into the ammunition ship he was aboard. He and his troops were headed for the invasion of Mindoro in the Philippines. Among other awards, he was presented with the Purple Heart for meritorious service and for the injuries he sustained.[18] Kohler returned to Tacoma in late 1945, after the war ended on September 2, determined to continue his teaching position and his promotion of regional art despite the continuing debilitating effects from his injuries. Dealing with the grief of losing her husband, Hyde resumed painting and exhibiting. In the Sixth Annual Exhibition of the TAA in 1945, she won honorable mention for her painting *Ordnance Depot Warehouse*, one of her three oils that were accepted. She also participated in SAM's Thirty-First Annual Exhibition of Northwest Artists, which included her oil painting titled *Warehouse B*.

In May 1946, the TAA merged with the Art Guild of Tacoma (organized during World War II) to form the Tacoma Art League. It held an exhibition that year at the State Historical Museum on Stadium Way in Tacoma. Hyde was represented by three oils. In September, the exhibitions at the Puyallup Fair resumed, with Hyde's oil painting *Composition* included. A month later, Hyde's work was again accepted at SAM's Thirty-Second Annual Exhibition of Northwest Artists, represented by her oil *Lumber Shed*. The fair had ceased in 1942 to house "Camp Harmony" on the site of the Western Washington Fairgrounds. The camp, also known as the Puyallup Assembly Center, was a

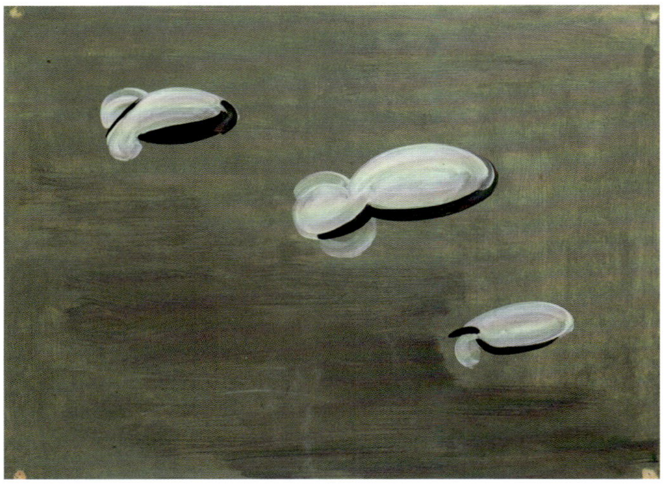

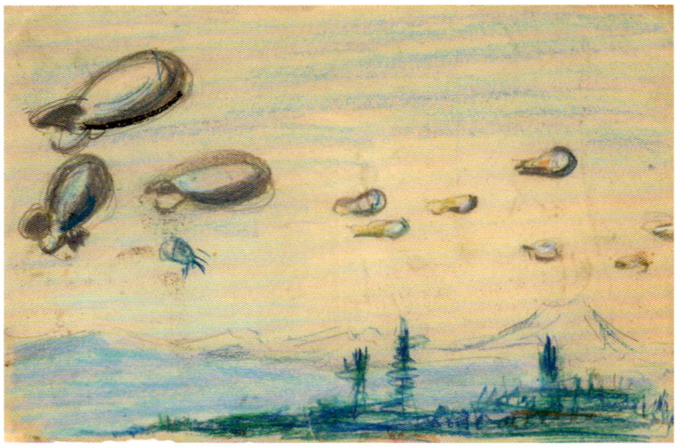

temporary facility that unjustly housed Japanese Americans who were forcibly removed from their homes and awaited transport to incarceration centers in other states against their will. Among them were the artists Kenjiro Nomura, Kamekichi Tokita, and Takuichi Fujii, all of whom were included in many exhibitions that Hyde participated in.

In December 1947, Hyde received her second solo exhibition, this time sponsored by the Tacoma Art League and held at the State Historical Museum in Tacoma. The exhibition featured over twenty of her paintings. Hyde's old friend Kohler favorably reviewed her exhibition, describing her paintings as possessing "a quiet mysterious quality of emptiness," perhaps referencing that Hyde refrained from using human figures in her works.[19] In the same venue, a selection of works was on loan from the Perls Gallery in New York and included pieces by well-known artists such as Marie Laurencin, Georges Rouault, Pablo Picasso, and Amedeo Modigliani. Hyde was now a firmly established artist in the region, and the local press used a photo of her in her studio to announce the exhibition. The photographer, Frank Herbert (1920–1986), would go on to international acclaim decades later as the science fiction author of the Dune series, which he based on the ruins of Tacoma's industrial sites that Hyde had painted decades earlier.

As the decade of the 1940s was getting closer to the end, Hyde remained actively exhibiting in regional venues while refining her technique. She continued to reduce the formal structure of her subjects and used a nuanced blending of warm and cool colors that produced a subtle, almost dreamlike opalescent quality. Hyde had developed into a master of composition and values. As she continued to stress form and structure, contemporaries like Tobey and Graves delved even further into Asian influences. Unlike so many Northwest artists of that era, Hyde never followed their lead in her own work, no matter how successful the two were becoming. She did, however, begin patronizing them by actively collecting the work of both artists. In the winter of 1948, Hyde traveled to New York City to visit her artist friends and fellow Annie Wright Seminary alumnae Vera Fraser and Helen Keen, both of whom had studios there.

Beulah Loomis Hyde
(1886–1983)
Untitled, sketch of barrage balloons, ca. 1942
Gouache on paper
15 × 20 in.
Collection of Pamela Hyde Smith

Beulah Loomis Hyde
(1886–1983)
Untitled, sketch of barrage balloons, ca. 1942
Pastel on paper
6 × 9 in.
Collection of Pamela Hyde Smith

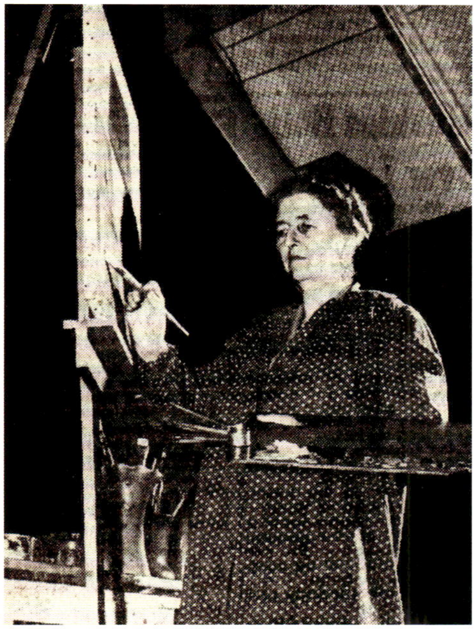

Beulah Loomis Hyde in her studio, December 6, 1947
Photograph by Frank Herbert for the *Tacoma News Tribune*
Northwest Room, Tacoma Public Library

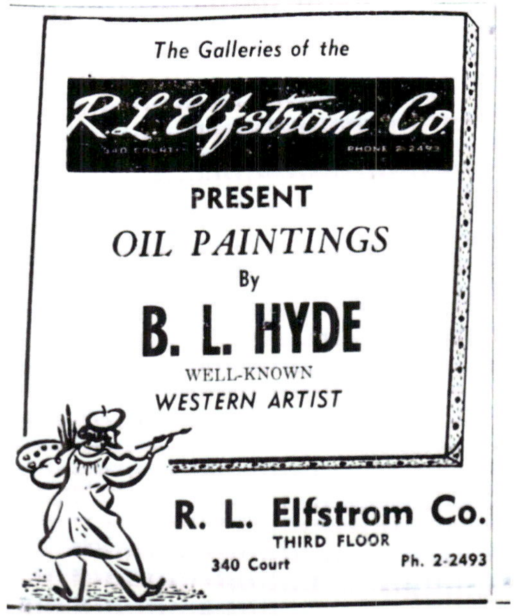

Advertising for Hyde's solo exhibition at the R. L. Elfstrom Company
Capitol Journal (Salem, OR), April 13, 1949, p. 21

In April 1949, Hyde had a solo exhibition of over twenty-five paintings at the R. L. Elfstrom Galleries in Salem, Oregon. This furniture and appliance company modeled itself after department stores like Macy's in New York City, Gump's in San Francisco, and Frederick & Nelson in Seattle, adding galleries for the purchase of high-quality original art for the home. Salem, the capital of Oregon, was trying to develop its own identity as an art center through the Salem Art Association. The gallery had opened in 1946 and featured primarily artists from Oregon, Washington, and California with a leaning toward realism.

In March 1950, the Tacoma Art League added an interesting and impressive feature to its exhibition at Jones Hall, College of Puget Sound. This time, works by Winslow Homer and Eastman Johnson were displayed, on loan from Wildenstein & Company, in New York City. This show afforded the public a rare opportunity to see the work of the nineteenth-century American masters while also exposing them to artists from their own state. As an interesting juxtaposition, contemporary regional modernist artists, including Hyde and the printmaker/sculptor Glen Alps, were represented, along with an entire room of paintings by the legendary Canadian modernist Emily Carr, who had died five years earlier.[20]

This new decade would prove to be a very busy time for Hyde. She was included in three additional exhibitions through the Tacoma Art League shows at Jones Hall. She was also included in SAM's Thirty-Sixth Annual Exhibition of Northwest Artists and became an associate member of the WPW. The following year, she once again exhibited in SAM's Northwest Annual, but 1951 also marked her first showing at the University of Washington's Henry Art Gallery. The Henry exhibition indicates the prominence that Hyde attained, as it was not a juried show but an invitational that featured only the finest artists of the region. She would continue in this invitational exhibition until 1955, where the year before she also served as a juror for the prizes. During the 1950s, she continued exhibiting at the SAM annuals and various WPW shows, winning an honorable mention for her painting *Church at Port Gamble* in 1953.

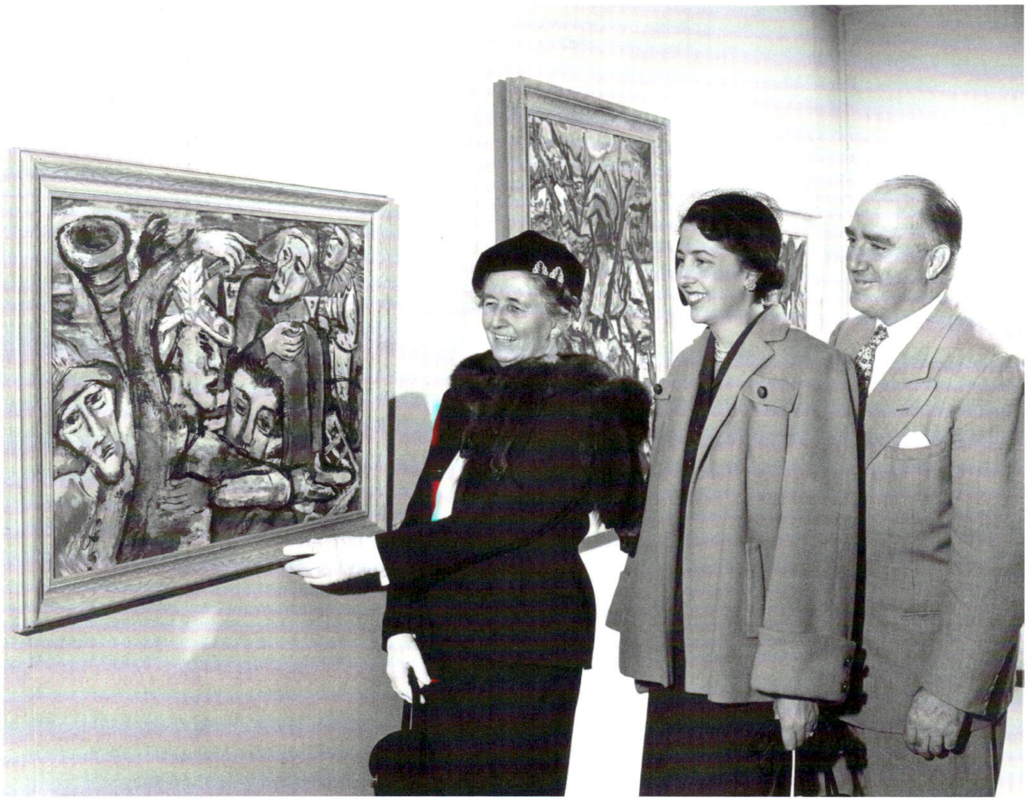

Tacoma News Tribune, October 8, 1950, p. D-4
Richards Photography Studio
Northwest Room, Tacoma Public Library

Original caption: "Mrs. Robert Hyde directs the attention of Mrs. Lucille and Dr. R. Franklin Thompson to the painting entitled 'Carnival,' on loan to the exhibition at the College of Puget Sound. Dr. Thompson was the president of C.P.S. He and his wife were on hand to attend the Tacoma Art League's preview on October 3, 1950, of an exhibit featuring the work of two local artists, Mrs. Vera Fraser and Nelson Sears. Dr. Thompson became President of C.P.S. in 1942 and served as president for 30 years."

In 1952, Hyde had entered a competition for Kansas artists. She was born there and, although she moved away at an early age, was still eligible to participate. Her oil painting *Bridge* was accepted. The show, sponsored by the Kansas State Teachers College's Fourth Annual Kansas Painters Exhibition, began in June 1952 and then traveled to other venues, including the Kansas State Teachers College in Emporia, the Wichita Art Museum, the Topeka Art Guild, and, finally, to the Nelson-Atkins Museum of Art, Kansas City, Missouri. This traveling show represents the only known national exhibition in which Hyde participated.

Back in her hometown, the Tacoma Public Library's Handforth Gallery sponsored the Pacific Gallery Artists Annual Open Exhibition, which ran from February 7 through March 5, 1954. The competition, judged by the prominent Seattle artist Fay Chong, included Hyde's *Self-Portrait*, which won first prize. The self-portrait (see page 154) is highly unusual with its blunt, unflattering self-depiction and emotionless, confrontational gaze. The award must have been particularly poignant, as the venue was, and continues to be, named after her old friend Thomas Handforth, who died unexpectedly in 1948 at the age of fifty-one.

In March, Hyde's same award-winning self-portrait was included in Artists of Washington: An Annual Invitational, presented by the Music and Art Foundation of Seattle and the Henry Art Gallery, University of Washington. For this, an even more prominent exhibition, she also served as a juror with well-established local artists Walter Isaacs, James Peck, and Wirth McCoy and University of Washington professor Millard B. Rogers. As the year was coming to an end, Hyde was included in SAM's Fortieth Annual Exhibition of Northwest Artists, followed by yet another solo exhibition sponsored by the Tacoma Art League and held at Jones Hall, College of Puget

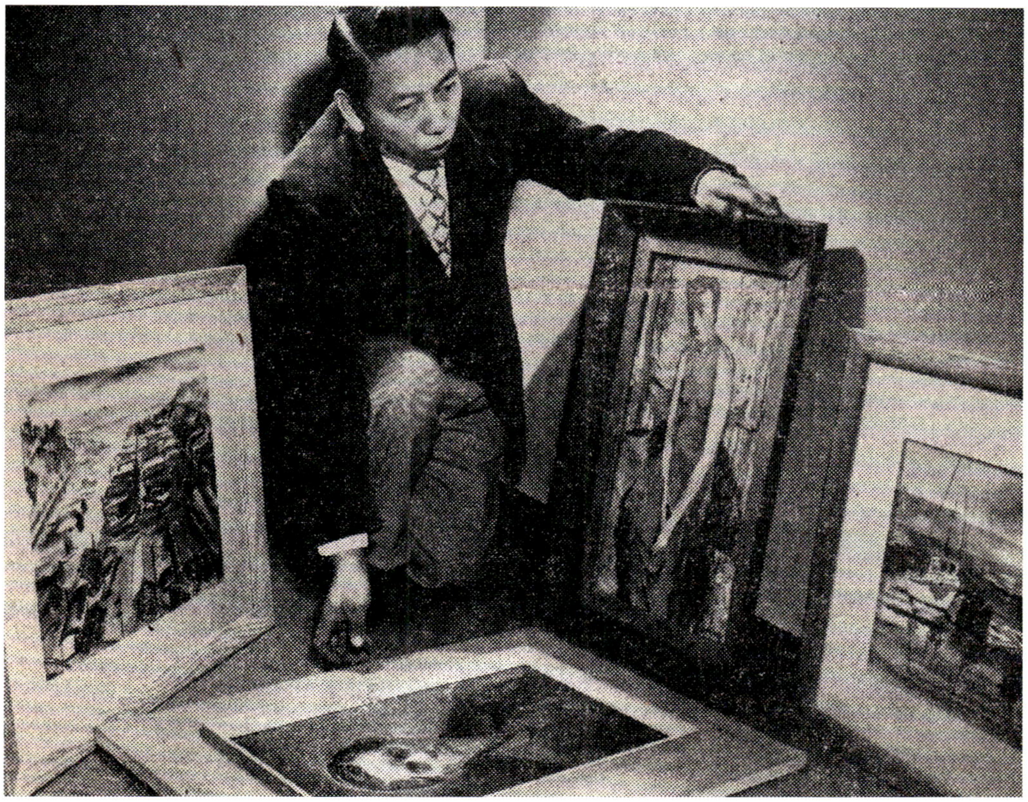

Tacoma News Tribune, February 7, 1954, p. 58

Artist Fay Chong acting as judge for the annual open show of the Pacific Gallery Artists at the Handforth Gallery of the Tacoma Public Library. Hyde's self-portrait, which won first prize, can be seen on the floor.

Sound. The exhibition ran from November to December 1954 as part of the "Meet the Artist" series and featured twenty-three of Hyde's paintings. This series had begun the previous year, with the artist Kenneth Callahan (1906–1986) as the first recipient. The series was intended to celebrate the more prominent artists of the region and included George Tsutakawa (1910–1997) and Ebba Rapp (1909–1985) before Hyde.

In May 1955, Hyde was honored with a two-person exhibition at Seattle's prominent Zoe Dusanne Gallery. Her co-exhibitor, Vera Fraser (1924–1963), was a highly regarded Tacoma painter in the beginning stages of a promising career. Dusanne, a black woman raised in Seattle, had lived in New York City for several years until returning to Seattle, where she opened a gallery in 1950. Using connections she made in New York, Dusanne opened the first Northwest commercial gallery to feature important nationally and internationally acclaimed artists. Like Kohler, she showcased works by talented regional artists along with "big names" in the same exhibitions. Not only did this practice allow the public to view and purchase works by famous, familiar artists that they would normally see only in art books or museums, but it also elevated the reputation of regional artists who deserved the patronage. Dusanne was particularly supportive of Seattle's Japanese modernists like Paul Horiuchi (1906–1999), John Matsudaira (1922–2007), Nomura, and Tsutakawa. A positive review of the Hyde-Fraser exhibition in the *Seattle Post-Intelligencer* created a comical imaginary discussion between two people attending the show and holding different opinions on the work of the two artists.

> *"Ha!" cried Mr. Traditional. "Ho!" cried Mr. Abstraction. (We overheard the conversation at Zoe Dusanne's Gallery, where paintings by two Tacoma artists, Mrs. B. L. Hyde and Vera Fraser, are on display).* What

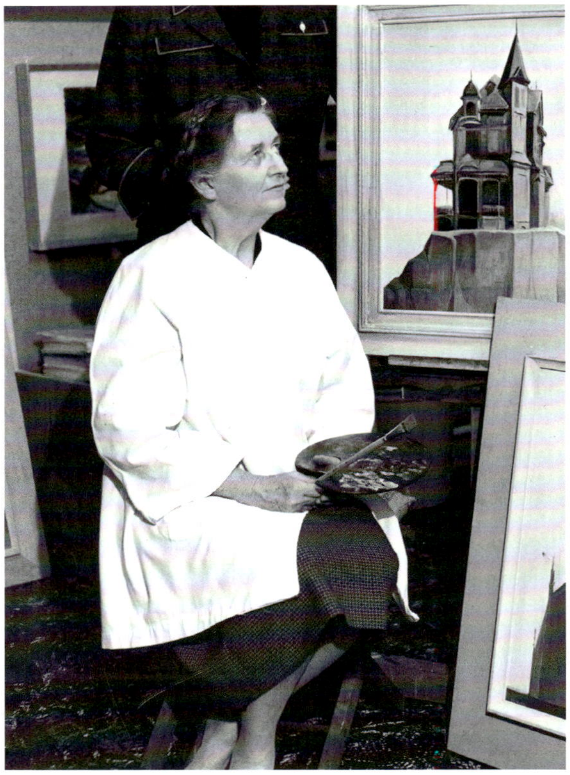

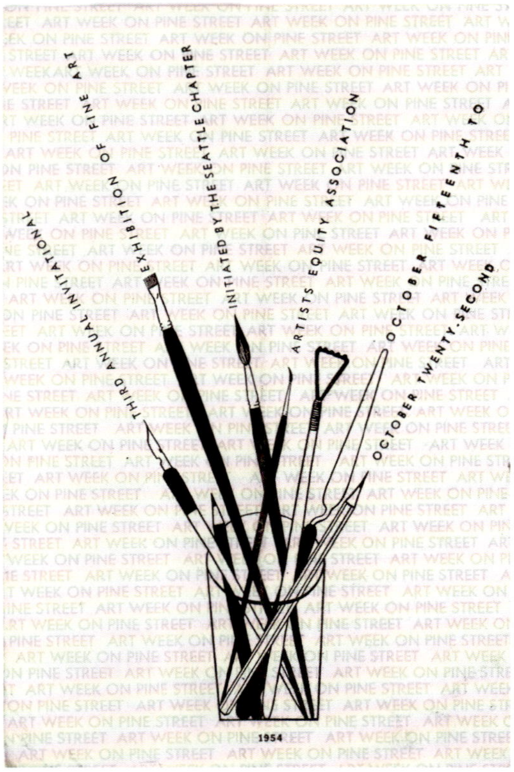

Beulah Loomis Hyde in her studio, 1954
Photography by Chapin Bowen (1900–1956)
Northwest Room, Tacoma Public Library

Cover of the booklet for the Third Annual Invitational Exhibition of Fine Art, initiated by the Seattle Chapter of Artists Equity Association. Hyde's oil painting *Bridge* was displayed in the Jean Hall department store, October 15–22, 1954. Beulah Loomis Hyde Estate.

> do you mean "Ho" said Mr. Traditional. Instead of crying "Ho" you should be enjoying these excellent paintings by Mrs. Hyde. She doesn't go in for throwing paint all over a canvas and calling it some foolish title like "Midsummer Madness." (Mr. Abstraction sputtered at that.)

The issues are finally resolved by Dusanne, who stated,

> I like Mrs Hyde's paintings for their simplicity, their subtle colors and their interestingly handled forms.[21]

A more concise assessment was given by the artist Callahan: "Mrs. Hyde's paintings are as flat and simple in form as Miss Fraser's are complicated and jagged; as calm and considered in method as Miss Fraser's are violent and unrestrained; as petite and refined in color as Miss Fraser's are rich and daring."[22] The success of this exhibition led Dusanne to feature Hyde in her popular Summer Exhibition in August 1955. Besides Hyde's paintings, the exhibition featured works by a few other regional painters as well as pieces by Wassily Kandinsky, Paul Klee, and Marcel Duchamp that Dusanne had purchased in Europe the year before.[23]

Immediately following the opening of this show, Hyde traveled to Europe on an extended painting study trip. She was also fascinated by other lands and cultures, stating, "Since reading Rebecca West's Black Lamb and Grey Falcon several years ago, I have wanted to see the coast and mountain country she describes," referring to the former Yugoslavia.[24] Fraser died eight years later in New York at the age of thirty-nine, ending a promising career and relegating her reputation to obscurity.

Dusanne was quite successful in her practice of pairing talented regional and

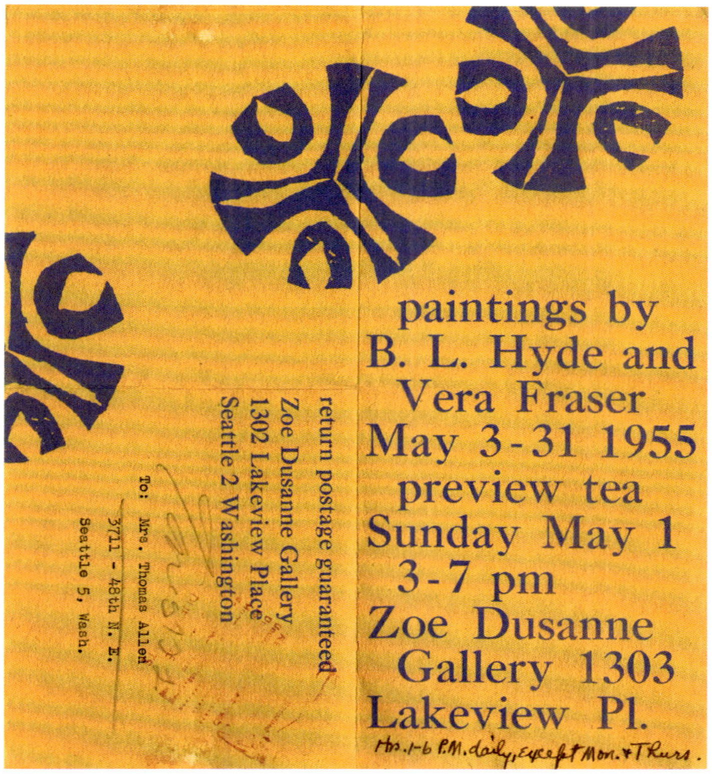

Advertising brochure for Hyde's two-person exhibition with Vera Fraser at the Zoe Dusanne Gallery. University of Washington, Special Collections, Zoe Dusanne Papers, accession no. 2430-4, box 1/42, negative no. UW 42164.

international artists as well as recognizing promising newcomers. Hers was the first gallery to offer Sam Francis a solo exhibition (Hyde purchased one of his early works), and it gave the Japanese artist Yayoi Kusama her first American exhibition, which began on December 10, 1957, with twenty-five paintings.[25]

Hyde would continue to paint throughout the 1950s, but by the 1960s, her production waned as she approached the age of eighty. She found time to enjoy the excellent Tacoma Art League shows displaying regional and international art. These shows included a rare exhibition of the Blue Four group of German Expressionists in May 1962, featuring works by Klee, Kandinsky, Alexei Jawlensky, and Lyonel Feininger. Two years later, the Tacoma Art League formed what today is known as the Tacoma Art Museum, where Hyde and her family became long-term benefactors.

The final recorded exhibition to include Hyde's work in her lifetime was at the Annie Wright Seminary, on the occasion of its ninetieth anniversary, May 18, 1974, in the Bishop Bayne Library. Her painting *Warehouse* was sold.

Hyde lived life on her own terms, despite growing up in a less enlightened time for women. In all the press around her decades-long artistic career, she was always referred to as "Mrs. Robert Hyde," even after her husband's death. She never signed any of her work using her feminine first name and never sought out recognition from outside of her region, although she certainly had the talent to do so.

Beulah Loomis Hyde died January 19, 1983, at the age of ninety-six.

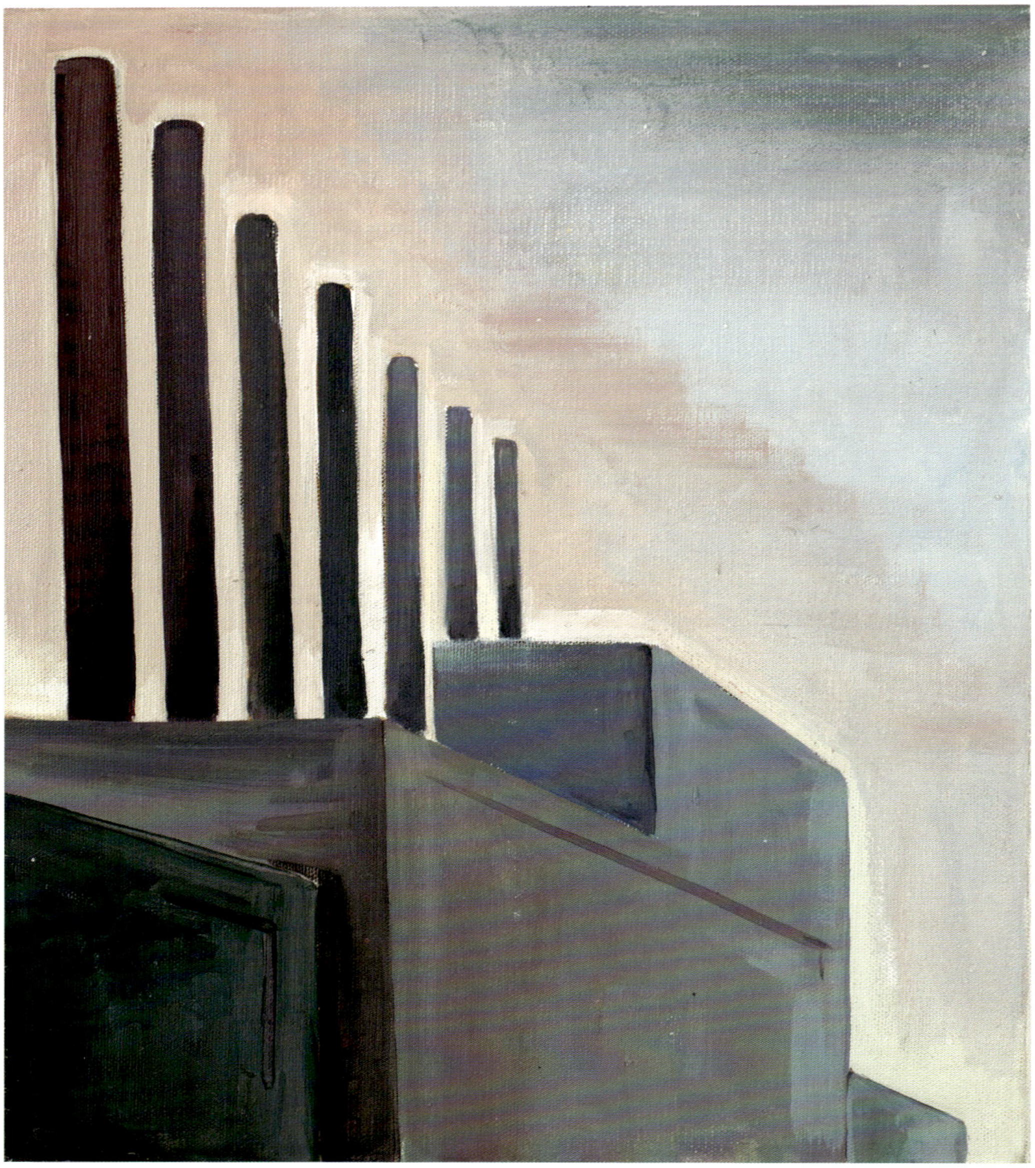

Beulah Loomis Hyde
(1886–1983)
Untitled, Lake Union Steam Plant, ca. 1955
Oil on canvas
13¾ × 12 in.
Collection of Pamela Hyde Smith

The Lake Union Steam Plant was within viewing distance from the Dusanne Gallery.

NOTES

1 Excerpt from Lizzie Beaton Loomis's journal, found by Ann Connell Whitehouse and transcribed by Pamela Hyde Smith, November 2022.

2 "The Ways of Society," *Tacoma Daily Ledger*, Sunday, May 7, 1893, p. 10.

3 According to Lizzie,

> My ranch was nine miles from town and two miles from a spur from the railroad which was my shipping point. Neighbors were, for the most part, thrifty Danish farmers who raised hay, grain and cattle. I had forty-five acres in fruit and fifty-five in hay, grain, gardens and the like, all irrigated. There were twenty acres in old orchard and twenty acres in young orchard—all apples. Five acres in a home orchard of all kinds of fruit, pears, plums, peaches, nectarines, apricots and all sorts of berries.
>
> I had ten acres of the young orchard planted in potatoes that year and the yield was tremendous, averaging ten tons to the acre. I got fourteen men, mostly transients, from town to work with my three regular men—(two had been with me two years; one, the foreman Borer, four years;

> they were all three good workers, faithful and loyal). The new men were to be paid the going wage by the day, board and lodging. We had three comfortable bunk houses and several sleeping tents in case of an overflow of workers during the harvesting season.

Lizzie Beaton's ranch journal, "That Was That" (ca. 1910), and Lizzie Beaton's Northeast Journal (undated), both transcribed by Pamela Hyde Smith.

4 E-mail correspondence with Paige Roberts, director of Archives and Special Collections, Phillips Academy, Andover, MA, April 16, 2024.

5 *Tacoma Daily Ledger*, Wednesday, August 14, 1901, p. 5.

6 *Tacoma Daily News*, Tuesday, April 5, 1904, p. 6; *Tacoma News Tribune*, Friday, June 3, 1927, p. 18.

7 *Philipsburg (MT) Mail*, Friday, October 22, 1915, p. 1.

8 For further information on Handforth, see David F. Martin, *The Lavender Palette: Gay Culture and the Art of Washington State* (Edmonds, WA: Cascadia Art Museum; Seattle: distributed by University of Washington Press, 2020).

9 E-mail correspondence from Pamela Hyde Smith, April 23, 2024.

10 For further information on Haffer, see Margaret E. Bullock, Christina S. Henderson, and David F. Martin, *A Turbulent Lens: The Photographic Art of Virna Haffer* (Tacoma, WA: Tacoma Art Museum; Seattle: distributed by University of Washington Press, 2011).

11 For further information on the SCC, see David F. Martin and Nicolette Bromberg, *Shadows of a Fleeting World: Pictorial Photography and the Seattle Camera Club* (Seattle: University of Washington Press, 2011).

12 Betty Bowen, introduction to *Tobey's 80: A Retrospective* (Seattle: Seattle Art Museum and University of Washington Press, 1970), unpaginated.

13 See Barbara Johns, *Kenjiro Nomura, American Modernist: An Issei Artist's Journey*, with a contributing chapter by David F. Martin (Edmonds, WA: Cascadia Art Museum; Seattle: distributed by University of Washington Press, 2021).

14 "Miss O'Keefe Described as All-American Modernist," *Seattle Daily Times*, February 9, 1938, p. 13.

15 For further information on Helder, see Margaret E. Bullock and David F. Martin, *Austere Beauty: The Art of Z. Vanessa Helder* (Tacoma, WA: Tacoma Art Museum, 2013).

16 For further information on Humber, see David F. Martin, "Yvonne Twining Humber: A Washington Painter of Renown and Obscurity," *Columbia: The Magazine of Northwest History*, Winter 2009–10, pp. 19–26.

17 For further information on Strong, see David F. Martin, "A Spirit Unbound: The Art of Peggy Strong," *Columbia: The Magazine of Northwest History*, Winter 2016–17, pp. 7–12.

18 "Daily Pedicure for Art Director," *Tacoma News Tribune*, April 7, 1945, p. 6.

19 Melvin Kohler, "Volume Stressed in Tacoman's Art," *Tacoma Times*, December 13, 1947, unpaginated.

20 *Tacoma News Tribune*, Friday, March 17, 1950, p. 19.

21 John Voorhees, "Tacoman's Paintings Draw 'Ha' and 'Ho,'" *Seattle Post-Intelligencer*, May 17, 1955, p. 6.

22 *Seattle Sunday Times*, May 8, 1955, p. 73.

23 John Voorhees, "Exhibit Features Work of Younger Painters," *Seattle Post-Intelligencer*, August 5, 1955, p. 6.

24 *Seattle Sunday Times*, May 8, 1955, p. 73.

25 Louis R. Guzzo, "Japanese Doll Speaks through Her Paintings," *Seattle Daily Times*, December 8, 1957, p. 63. For further information on Dusanne, see Richelle Munkhoff and Beth Ann Whittaker Williams, "'The Only One I Have': Zoe Dusanne in the Archive," Sam Francis Foundation, Archive Connection, essay no. 5, January 19, 2024, https://samfrancisfoundation.org/2024/01/19/archive-connection-essay-no-5-zoe-dusanne.

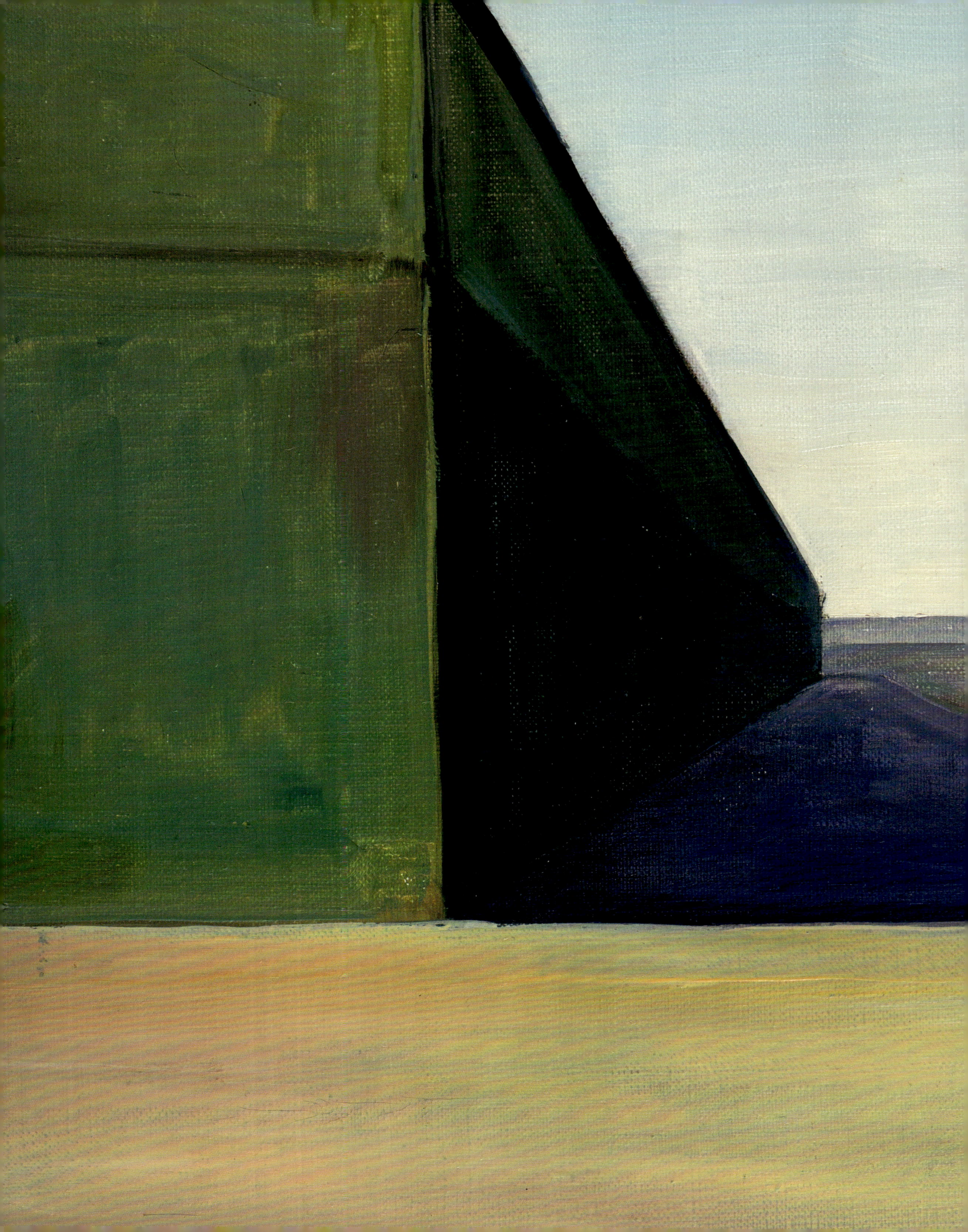

PLATES

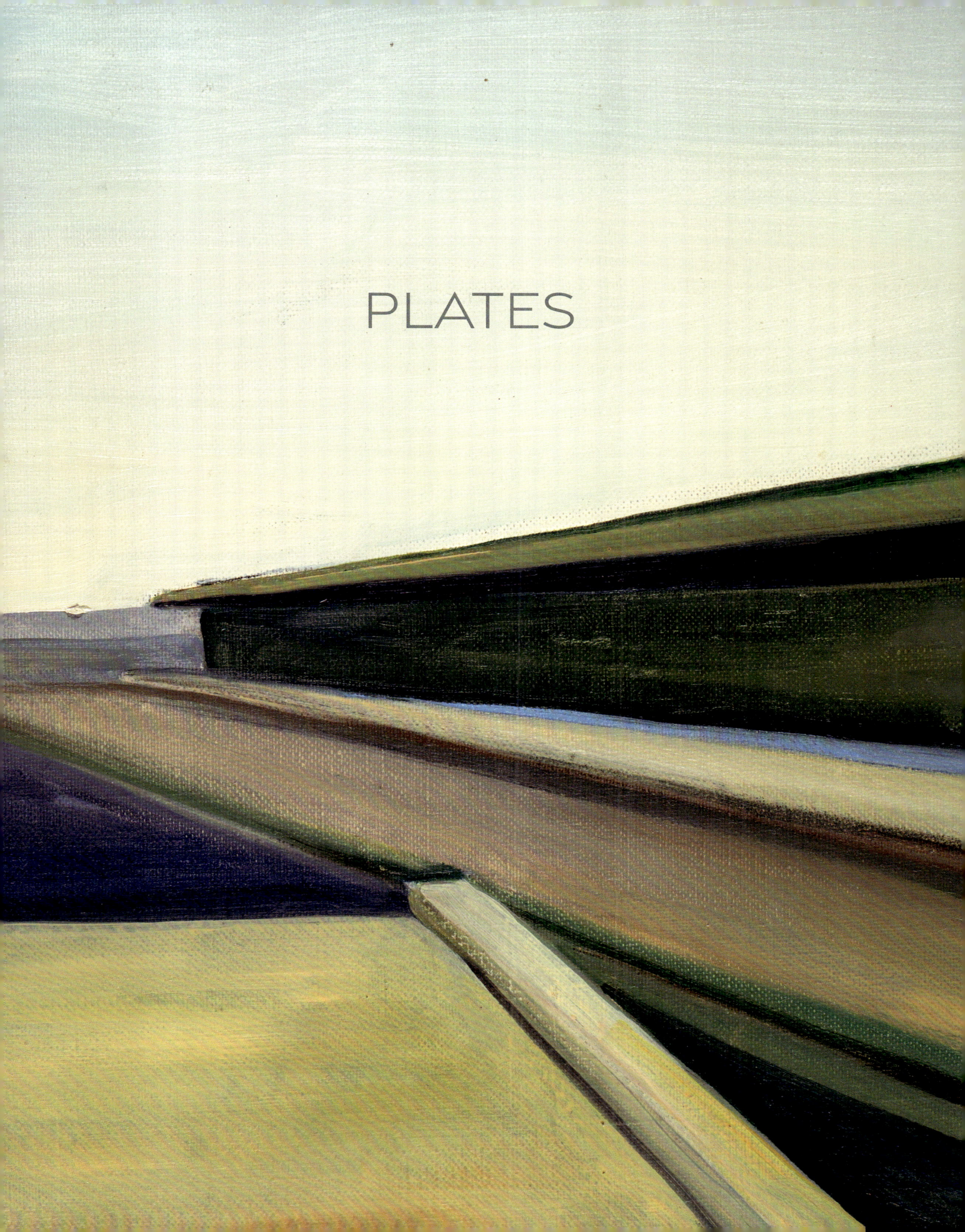

Beulah Loomis Hyde (1886–1983)
Self-portrait, ca. 1935–38
Oil on paper
23 × 18 in.
Collection of Pamela Hyde Smith

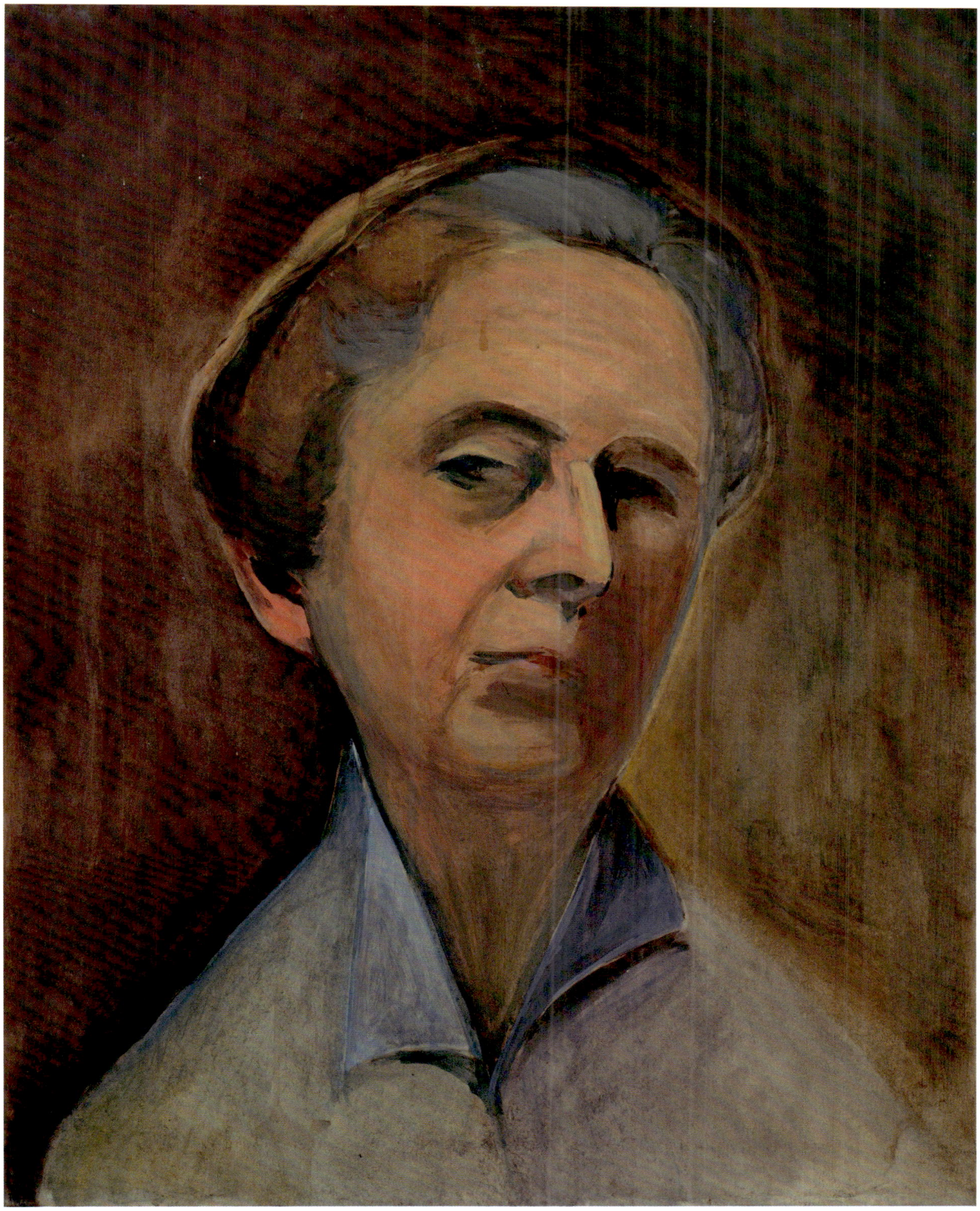

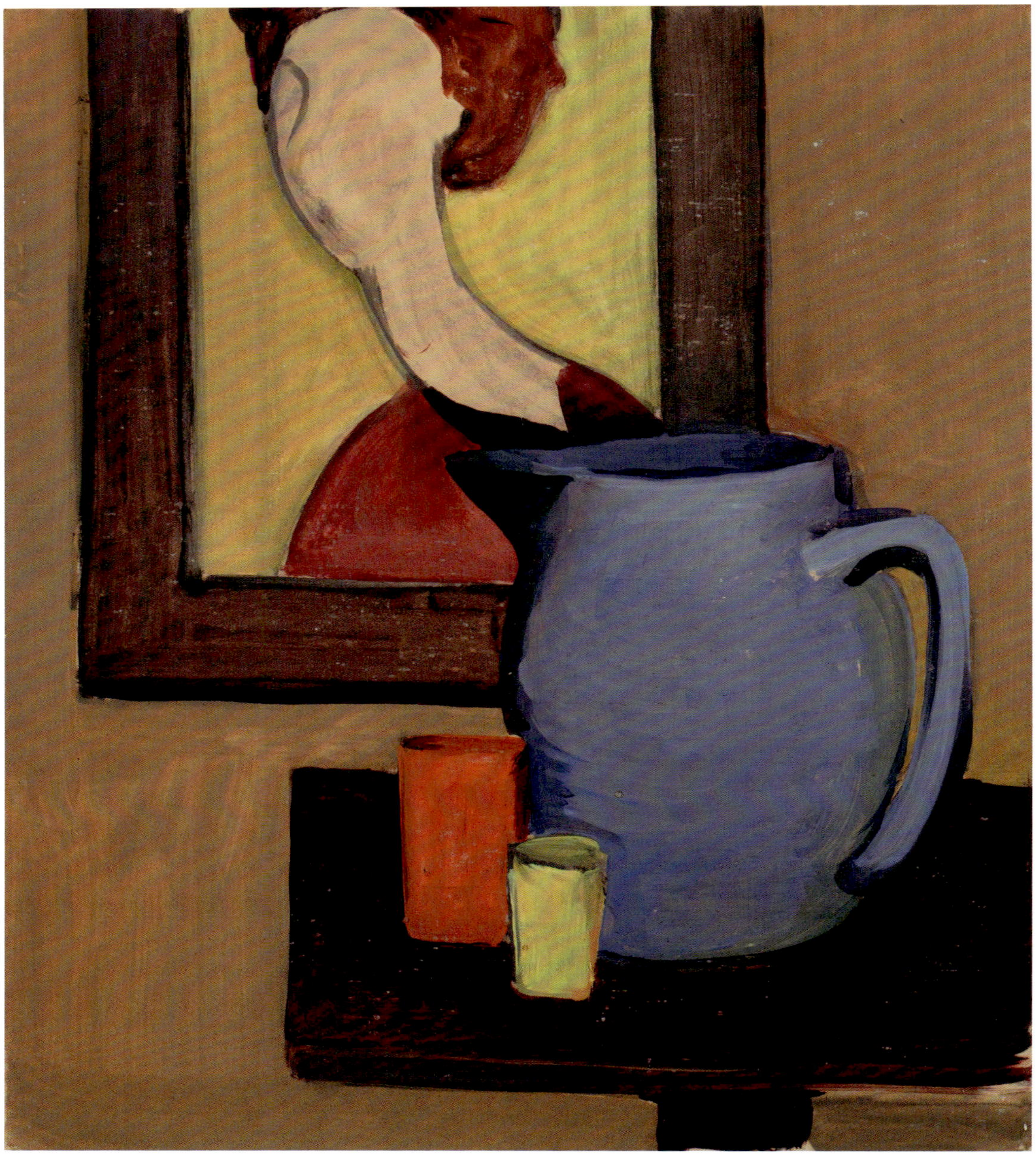

Beulah Loomis Hyde (1886–1983)
Untitled, still life,
ca. 1935–38
Oil on paper
14 × 13 in.
Collection of Pamela Hyde Smith

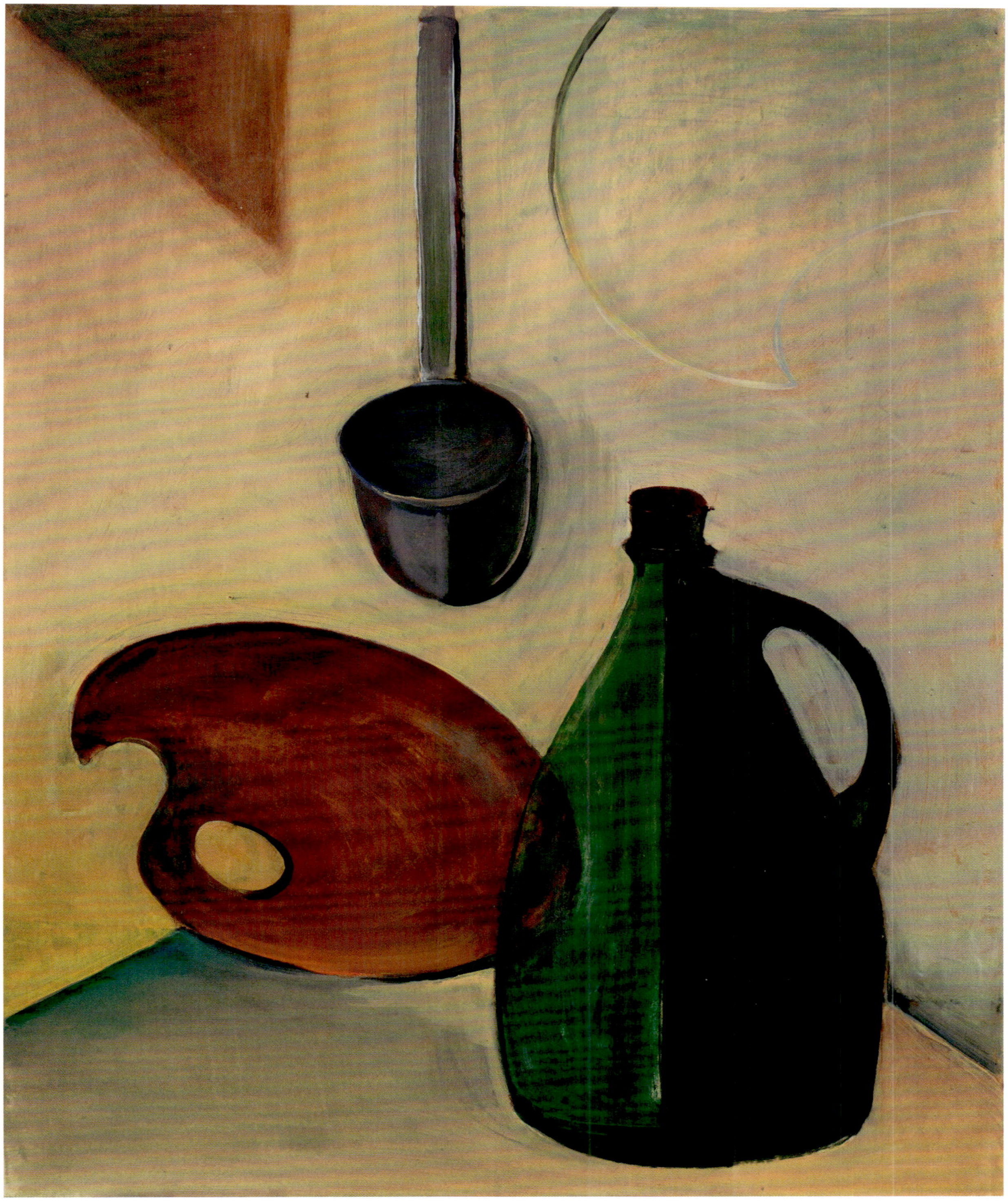

Beulah Loomis Hyde (1886–1983)
Untitled, still life,
ca. 1935–38
Oil on paper
20 × 16½ in.
Collection of Pamela Hyde Smith

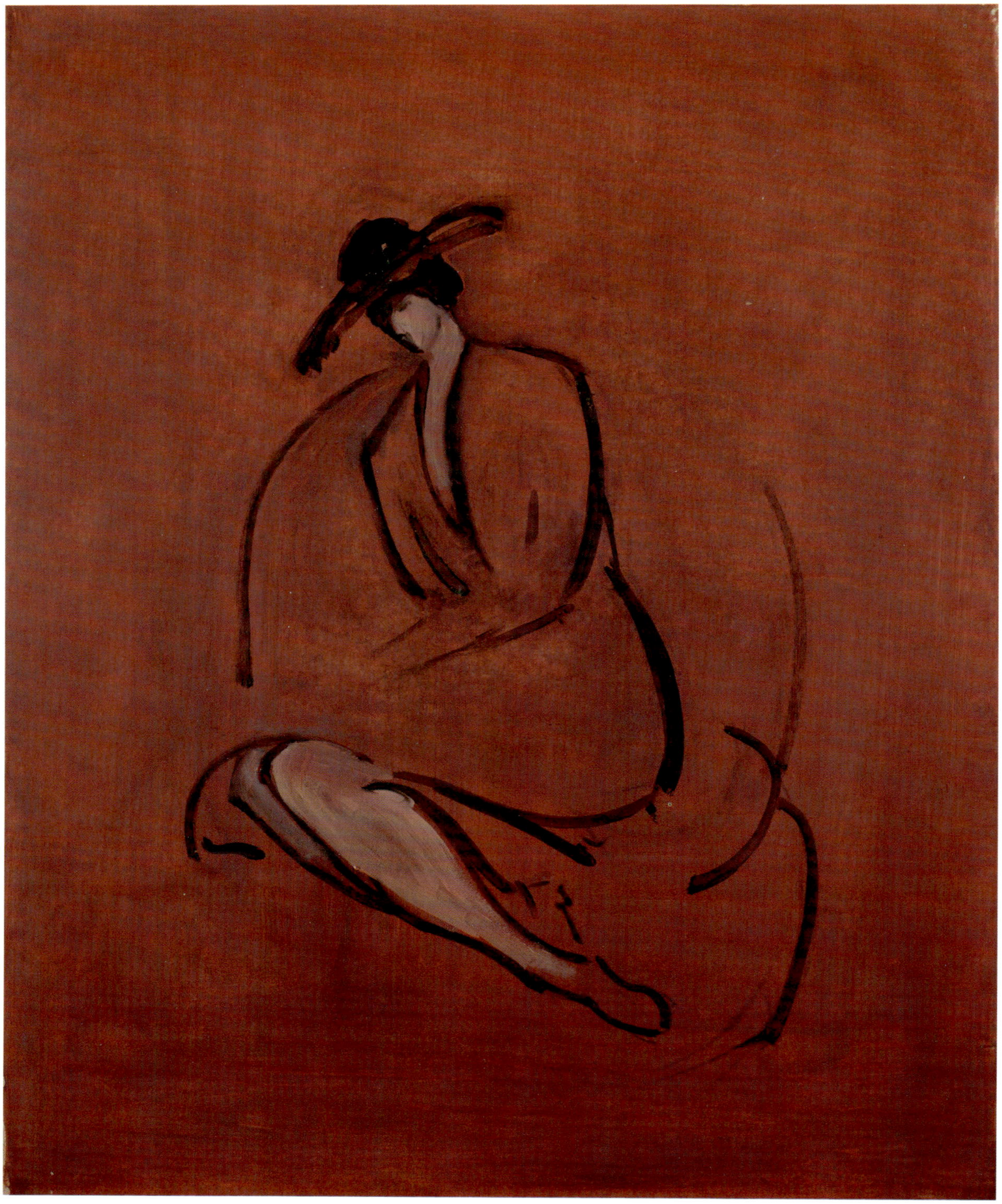

Beulah Loomis Hyde (1886–1983)
Untitled, ca. 1935–40
Oil on paper
21½ × 17½ in.
Collection of Pamela Hyde Smith

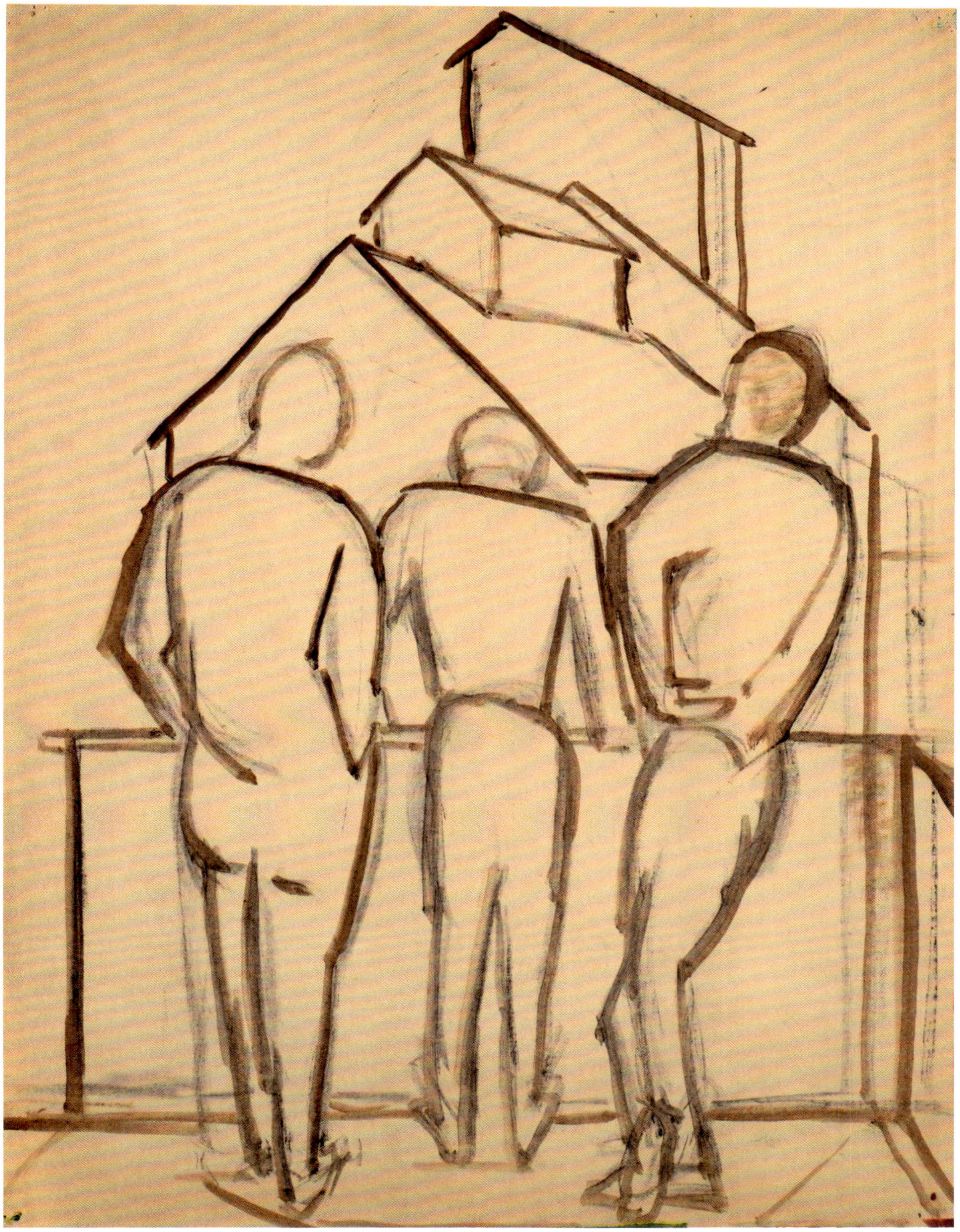

Beulah Loomis Hyde (1886–1983)
Untitled, ca. 1935–40
Oil and graphite on paper
20 × 15 in.
Collection of Pamela Hyde Smith

Beulah Loomis Hyde (1886–1983)
Untitled (Haystack Rock on the Oregon coast), ca. 1935–40
Oil on canvas
20 × 24 in.
Collection of Charles Henry Hyde III

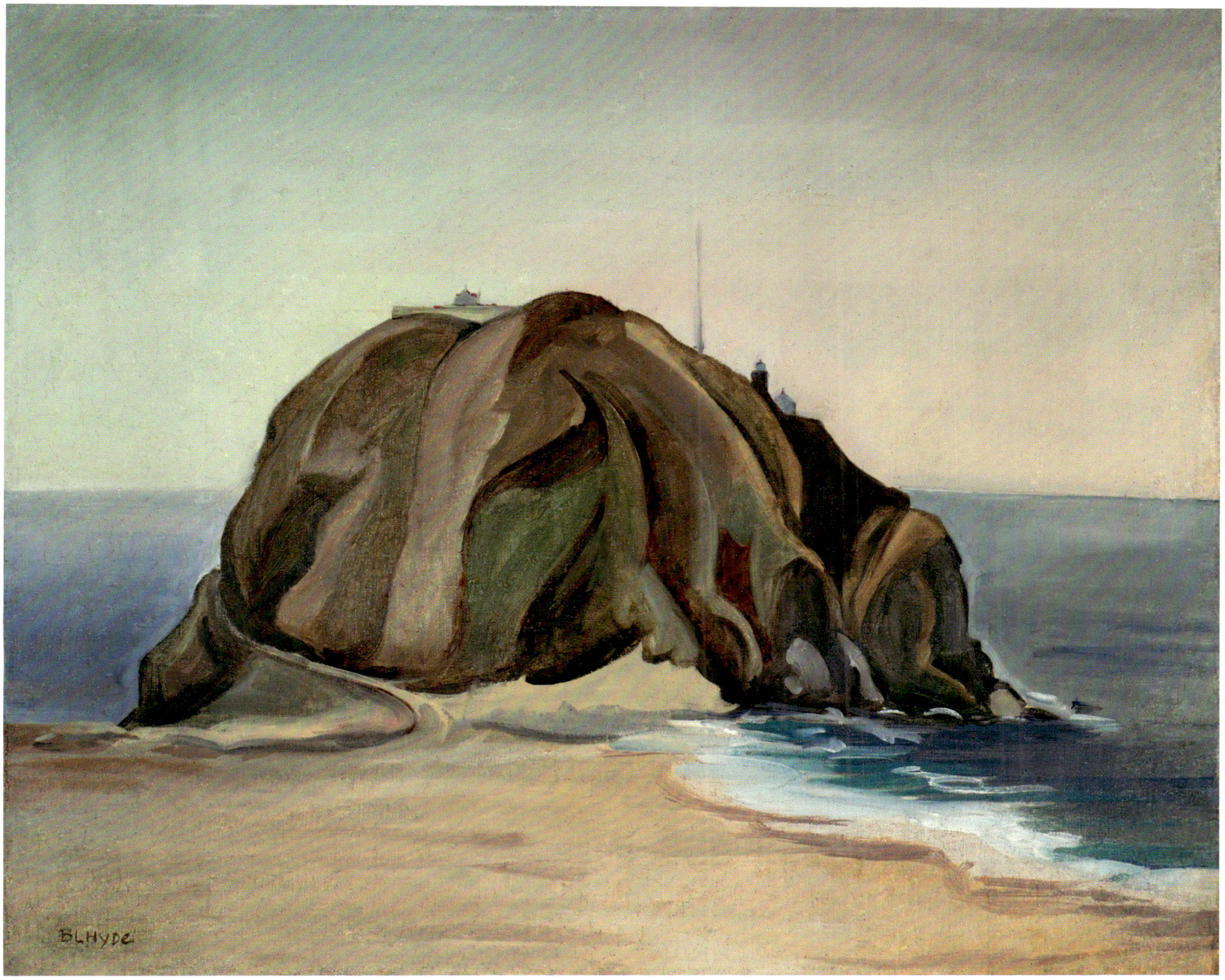
BLHYDE

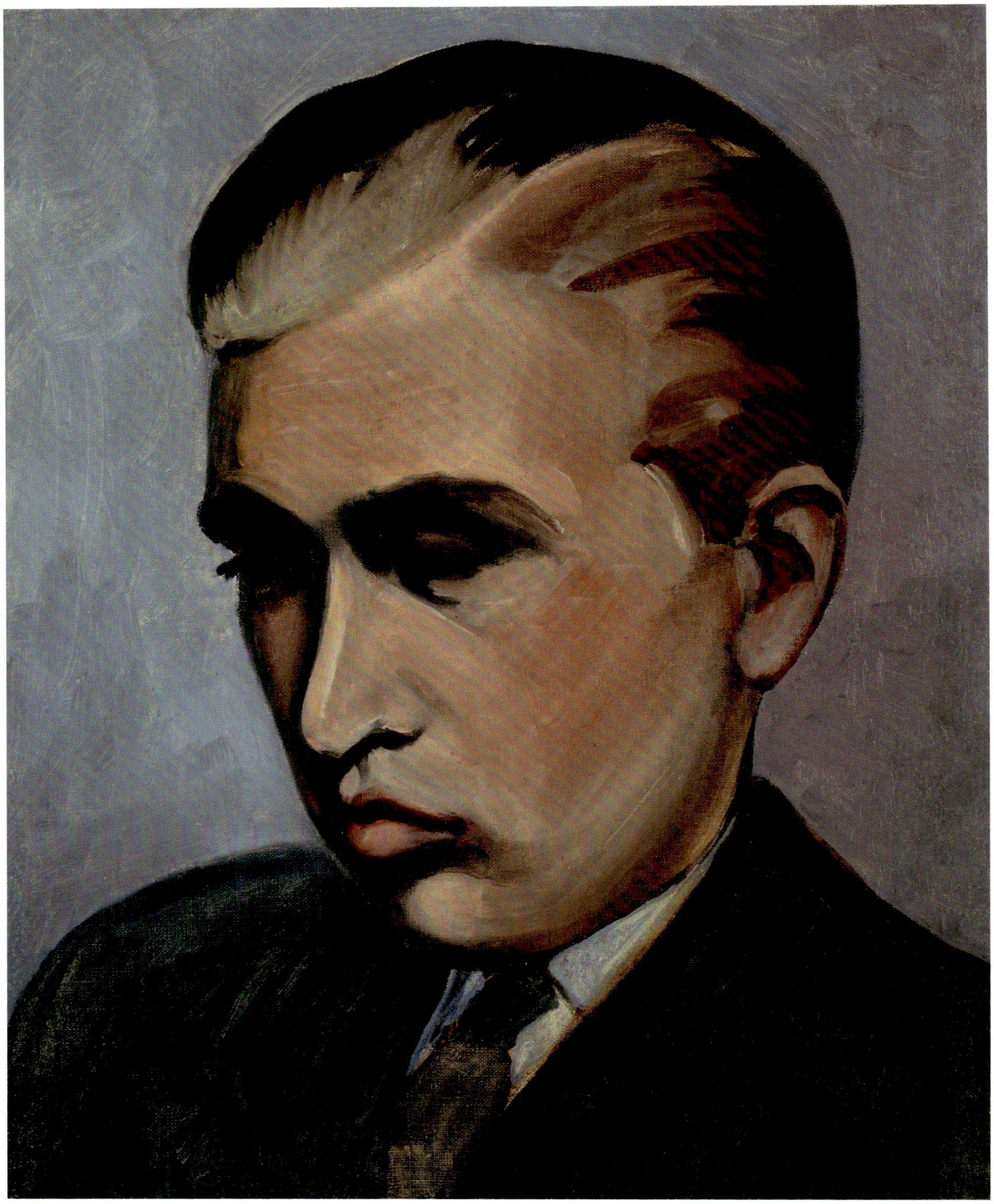

Beulah Loomis Hyde (1886–1983)
Untitled (portrait of the artist's son Robert H. Hyde), ca. 1935–40
Oil on canvas
20 × 16 in.
Collection of Charles H. Hyde IV

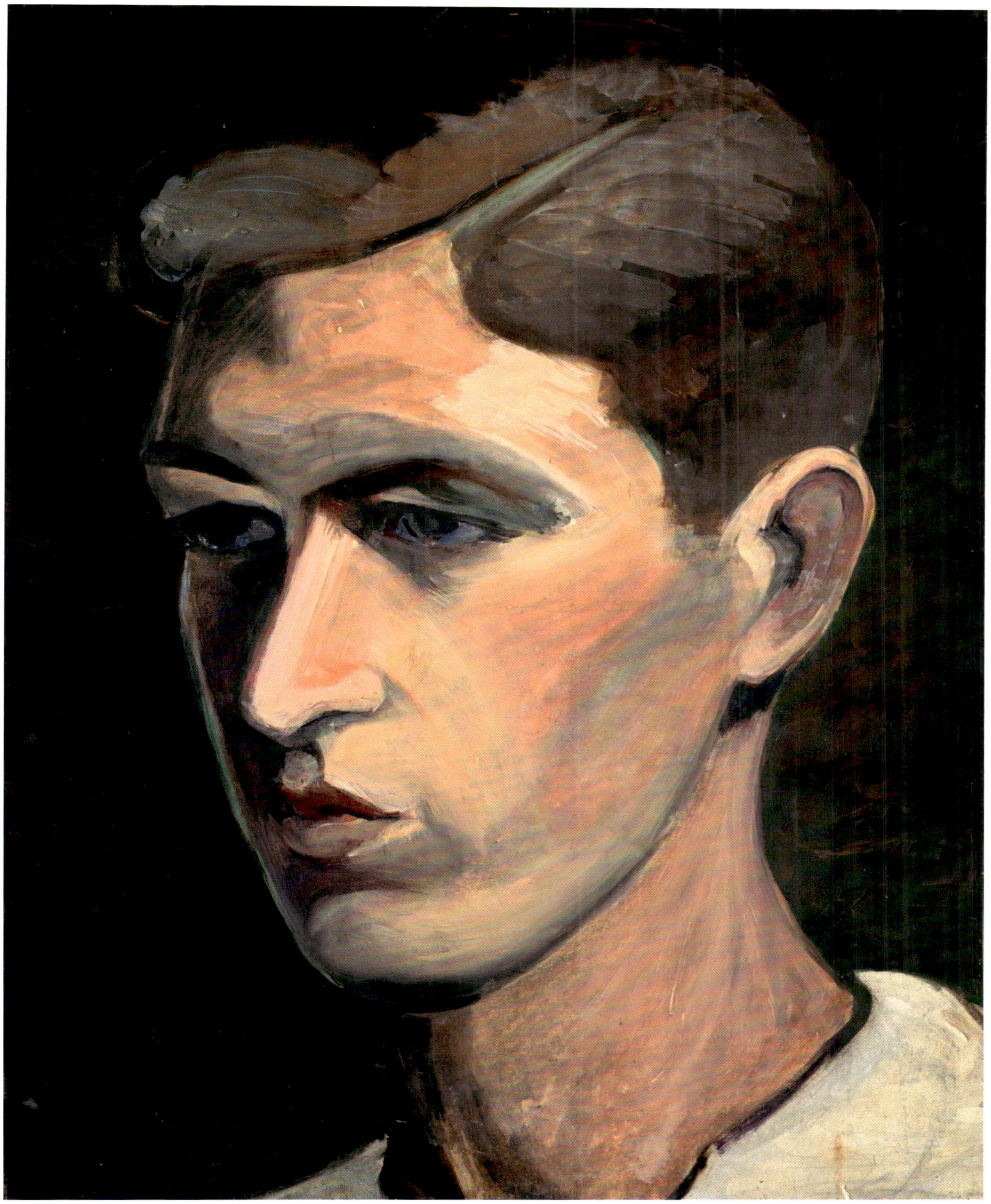

Beulah Loomis Hyde (1886–1983)
Untitled (portrait of the artist's son William B. Hyde), ca. 1935–40
Oil on paper
20 × 16 in.
Collection of Pamela Hyde Smith

Beulah Loomis Hyde (1886–1983)
Self-portrait, ca. 1935–40
Oil on paper
20 x 19 in.
Collection of Pamela Hyde Smith

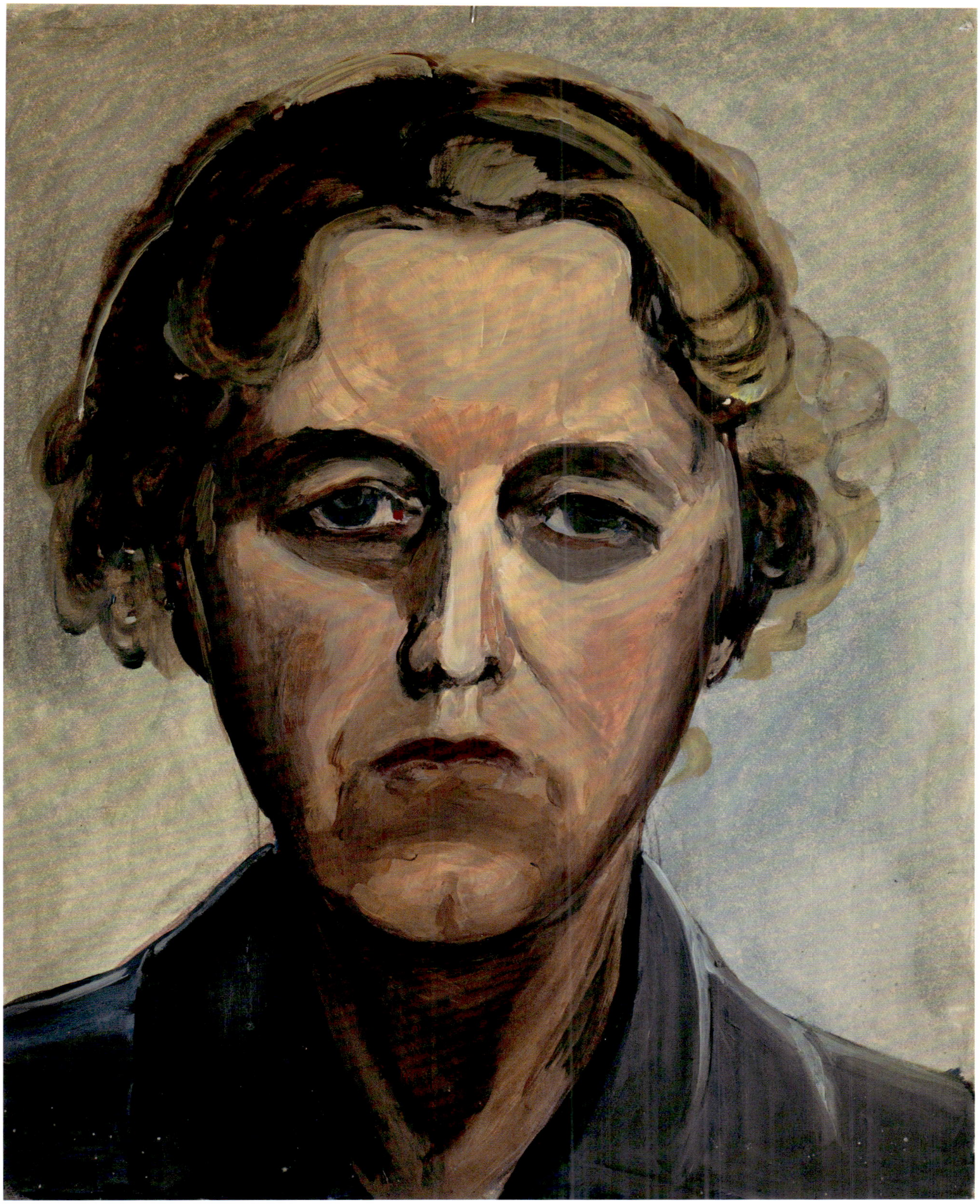

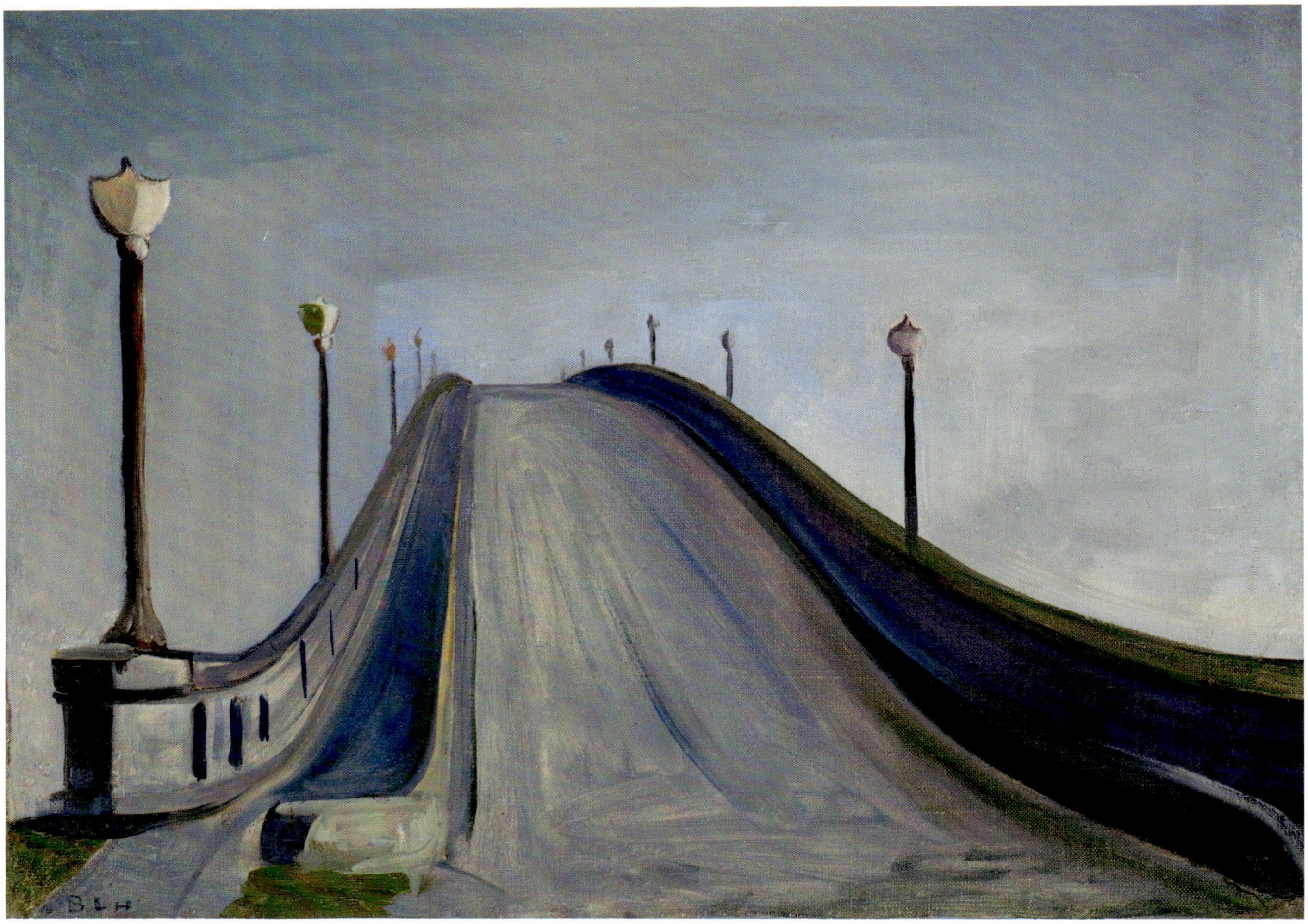

Beulah Loomis Hyde (1886–1983)
Untitled, ca. 1935–40
Oil on canvas
16 x 20 in.
Collection of Nicola M. Hyde

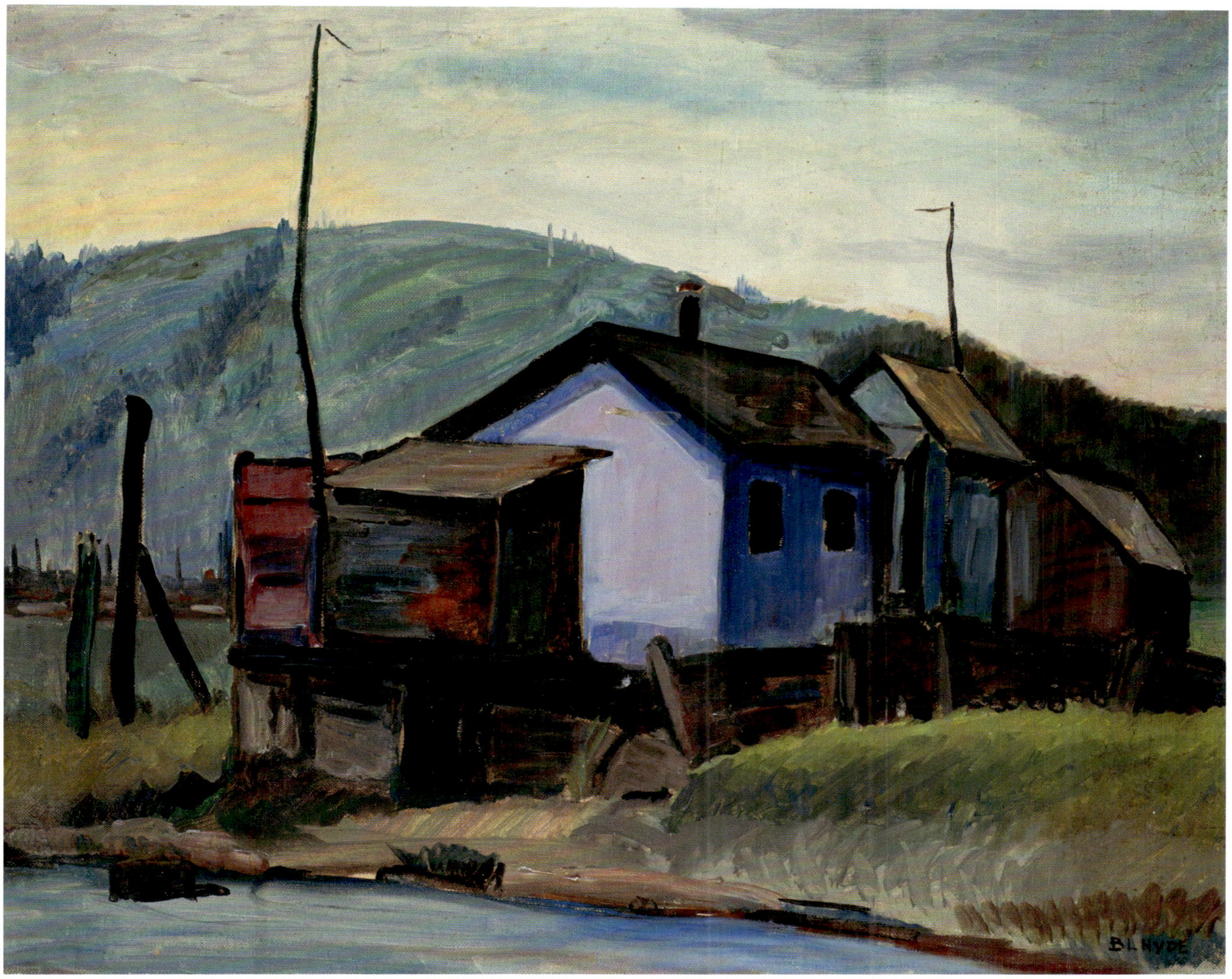

Beulah Loomis Hyde (1886–1983)
Hollywood on the Tideflats, ca. 1938
Oil on canvas
16 × 20 in.
Collection of Pamela Hyde Smith

This painting depicts some of the shacks in Tacoma's Hooverville, also known as Hollywood on the Tideflats. This large poverty-stricken community covered several acres until it was deliberately burned down by the Tacoma Fire Department under the direction of the US Coast Guard in May 1942. Hyde undoubtedly felt empathy for the inhabitants of these shacks, as she herself lived under such conditions as a young child.

Beulah Loomis Hyde (1886–1983)
Untitled, ca. 1935–40
Oil on canvas
16 × 20 in.
Collection of Charles Henry Hyde III

This painting depicts the Nelson Bennett Railroad Tunnel, just south of Point Defiance Park in Tacoma, with Mount Rainier visible in the background, dominating the landscape.

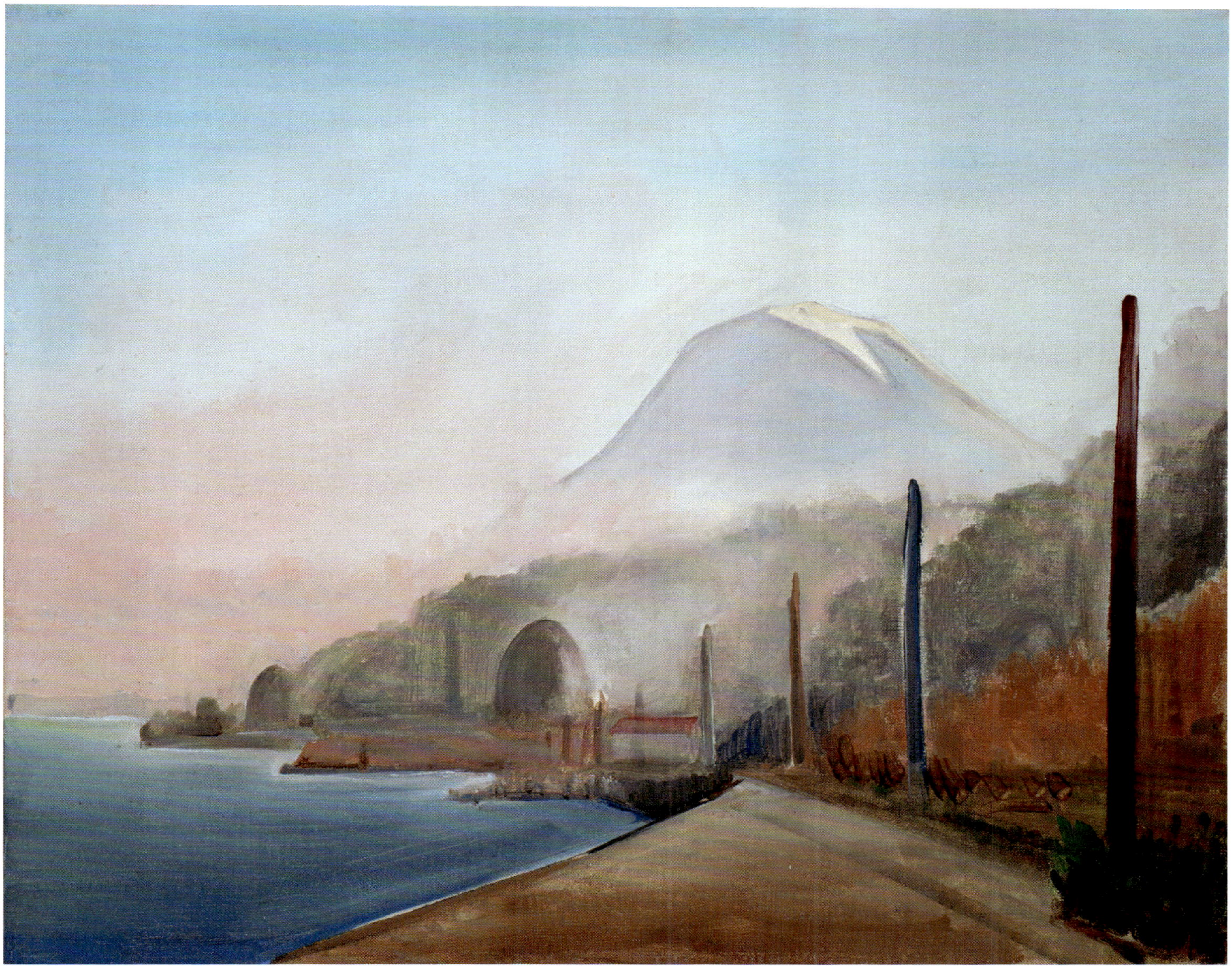

Beulah Loomis Hyde (1886–1983)
Untitled, ca. 1935–40
Oil on paper
16¼ × 20¼ in.
Collection of Pamela Hyde Smith

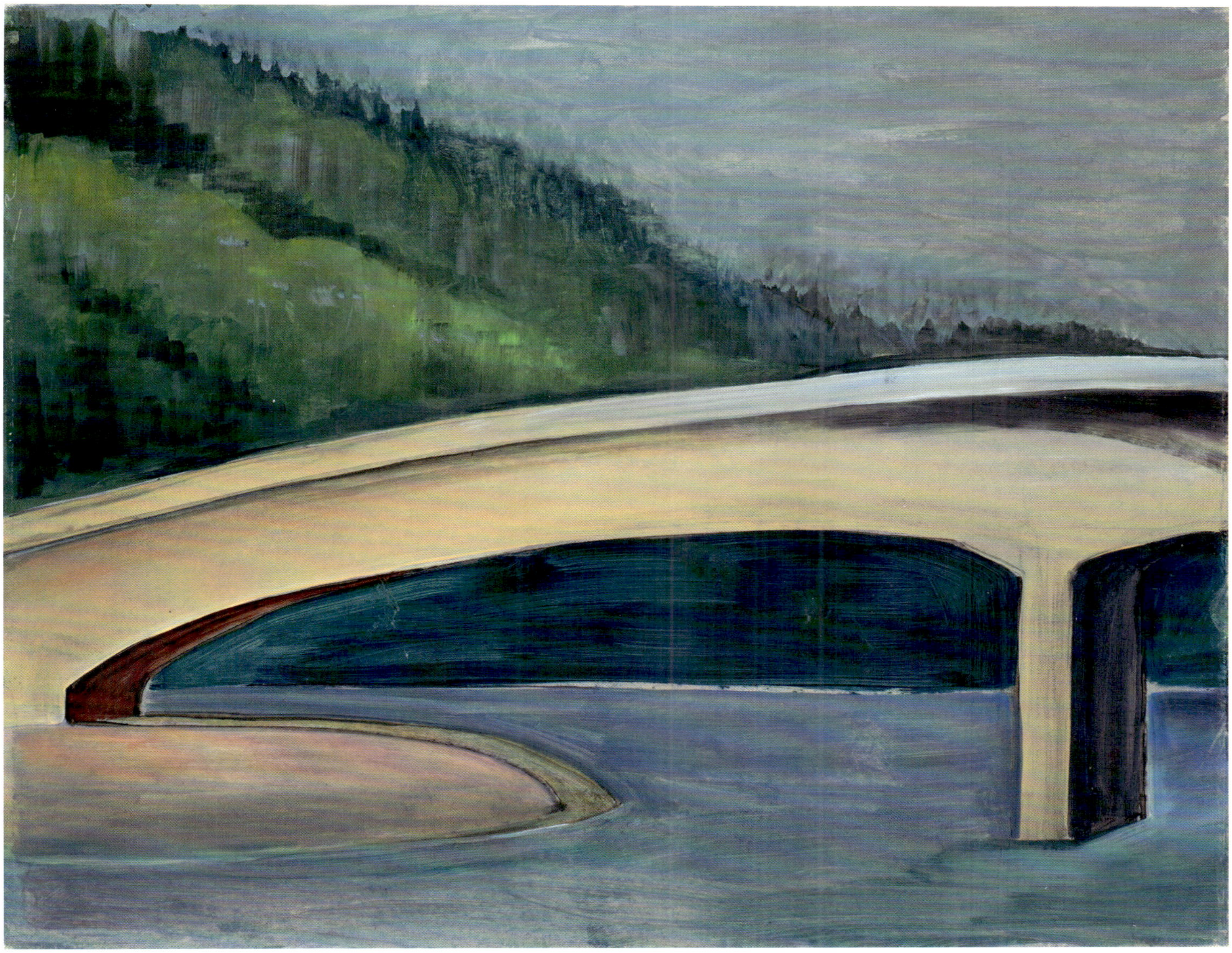

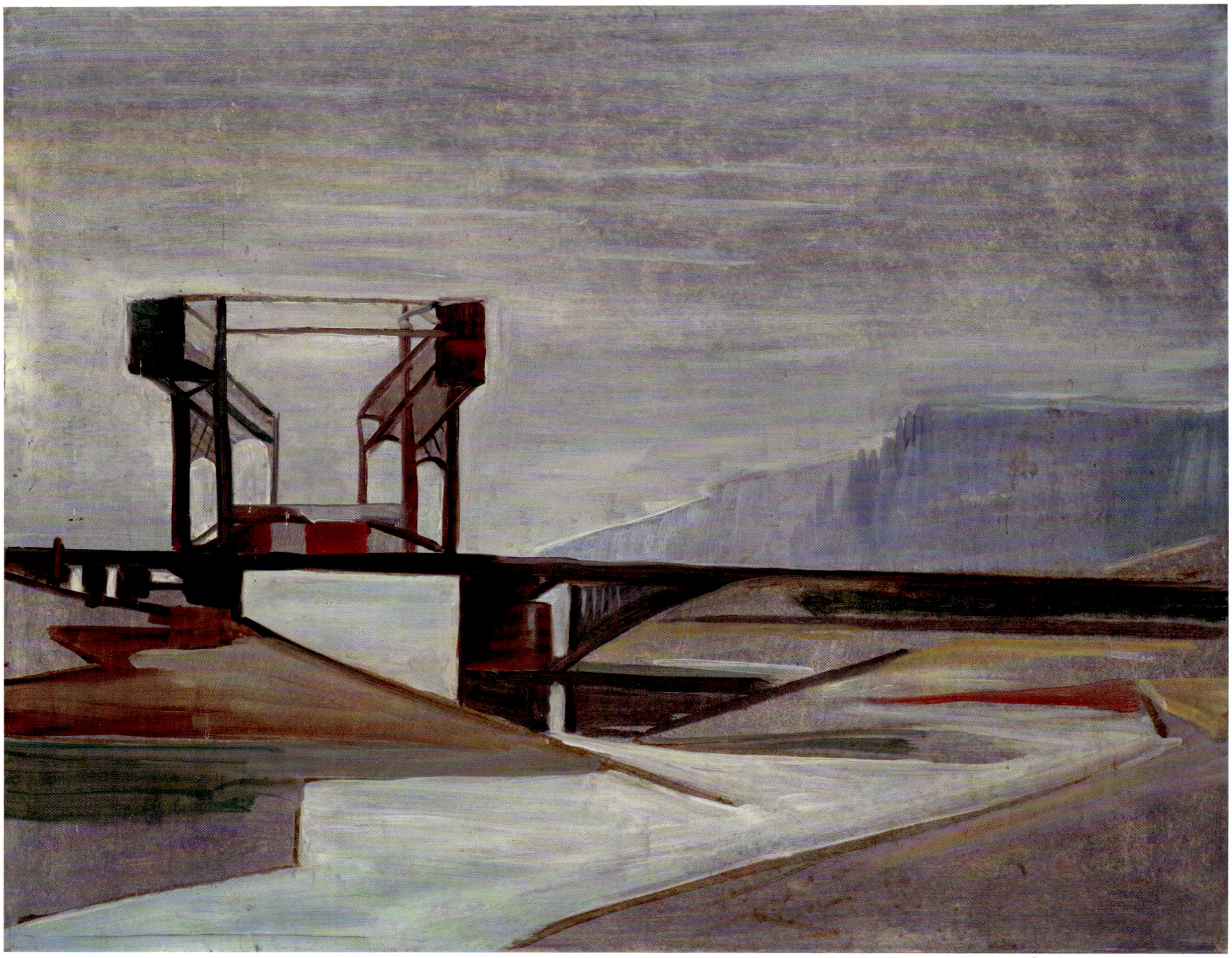

Beulah Loomis Hyde (1886–1983)
Untitled (Chambers Bay railroad bridge,
Steilacoom, WA), ca. 1935–40
Oil on paper
16 × 20¼ in.
Collection of Allison Hyde and Jake Nellis

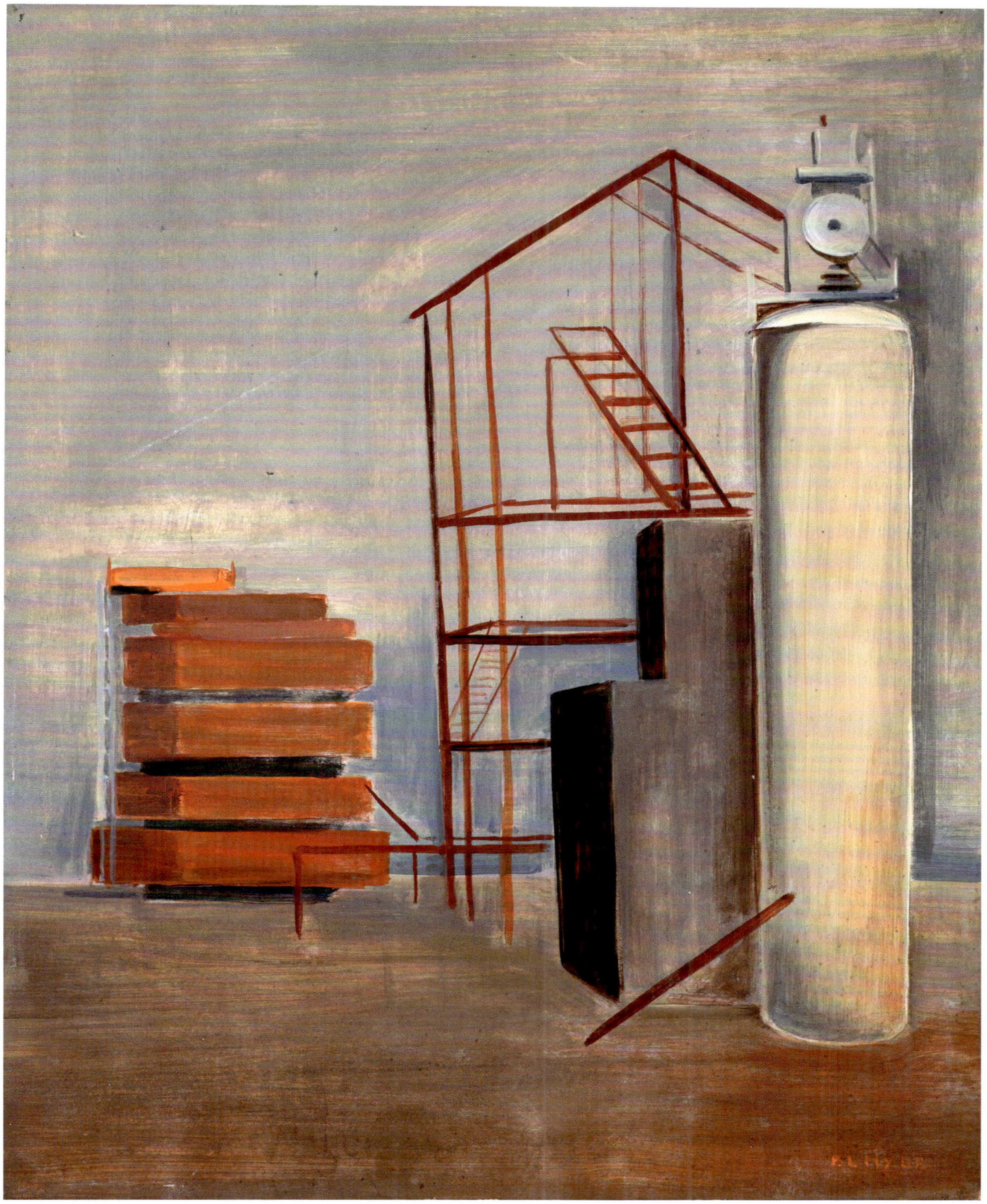

Beulah Loomis Hyde (1886–1983)
Untitled, ca. 1935–40
Oil on paper
20 × 16 in.
Collection of Allison Hyde and Jake Nellis

Beulah Loomis Hyde (1886–1983)
Self-portrait, ca. 1935–40
Oil on paper
21½ × 17 in.
Collection of Pamela Hyde Smith

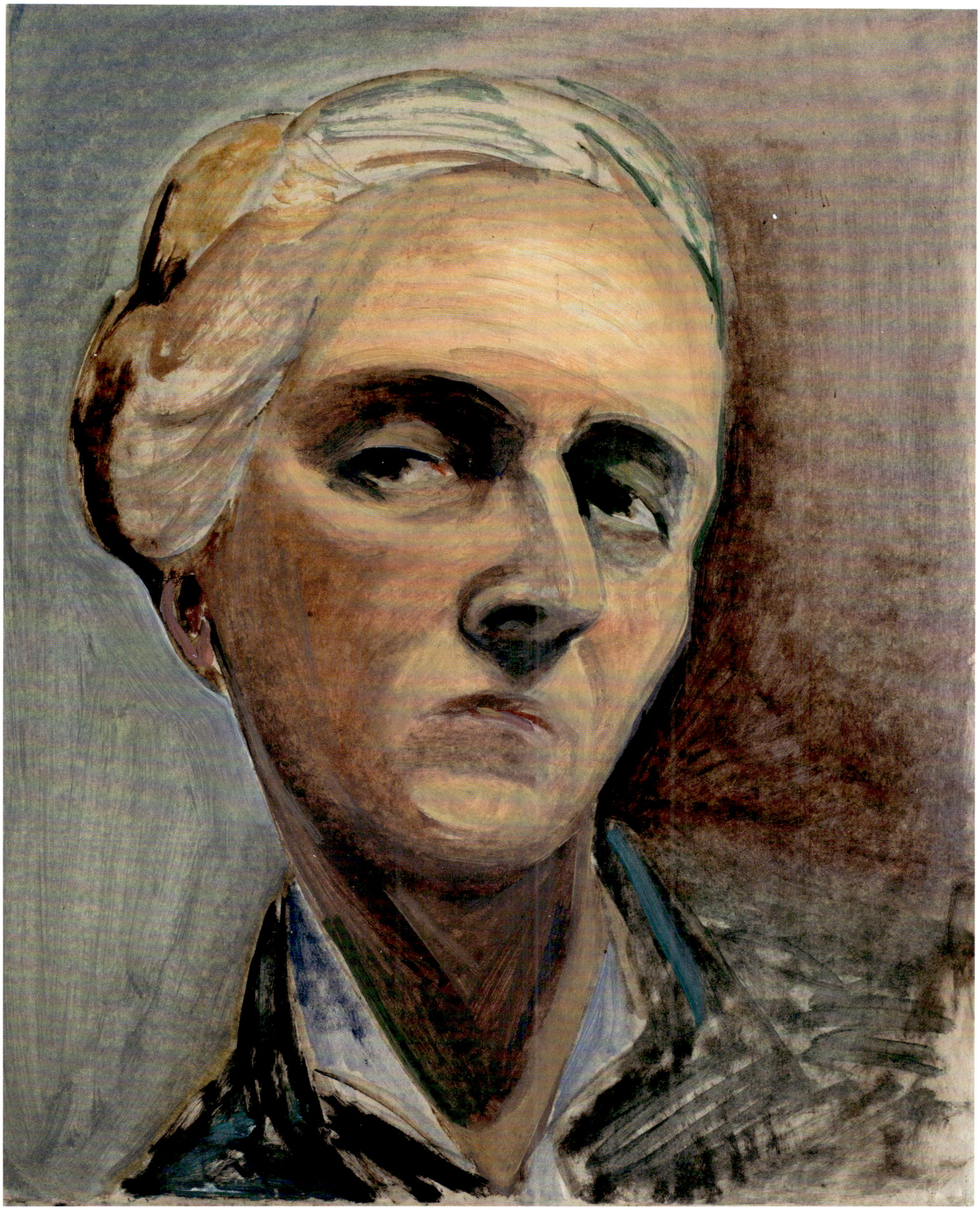

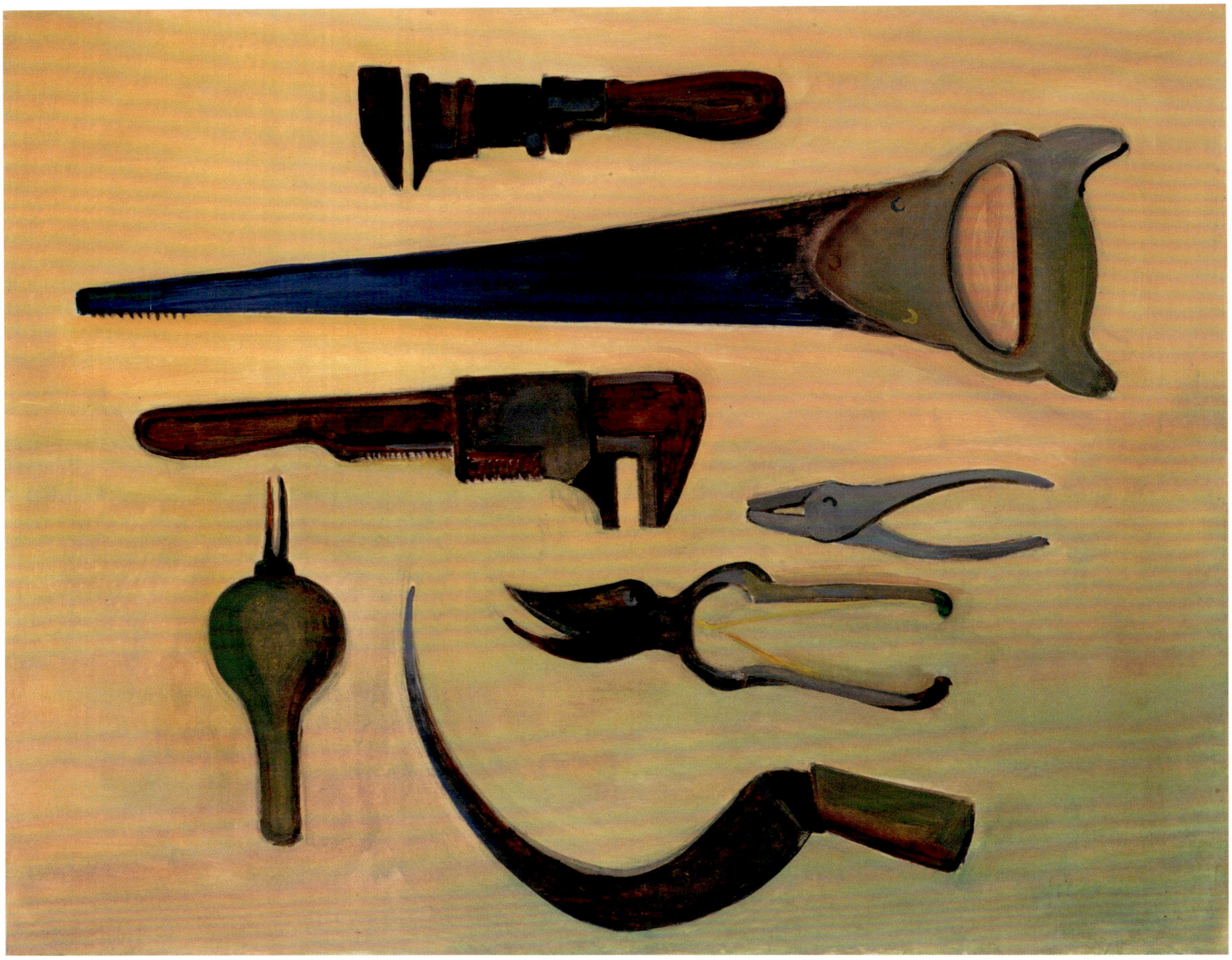

Beulah Loomis Hyde (1886–1983)
Untitled (tools), ca. 1935–40
Oil on paper
20 × 24 in.
Collection of Pamela Hyde Smith

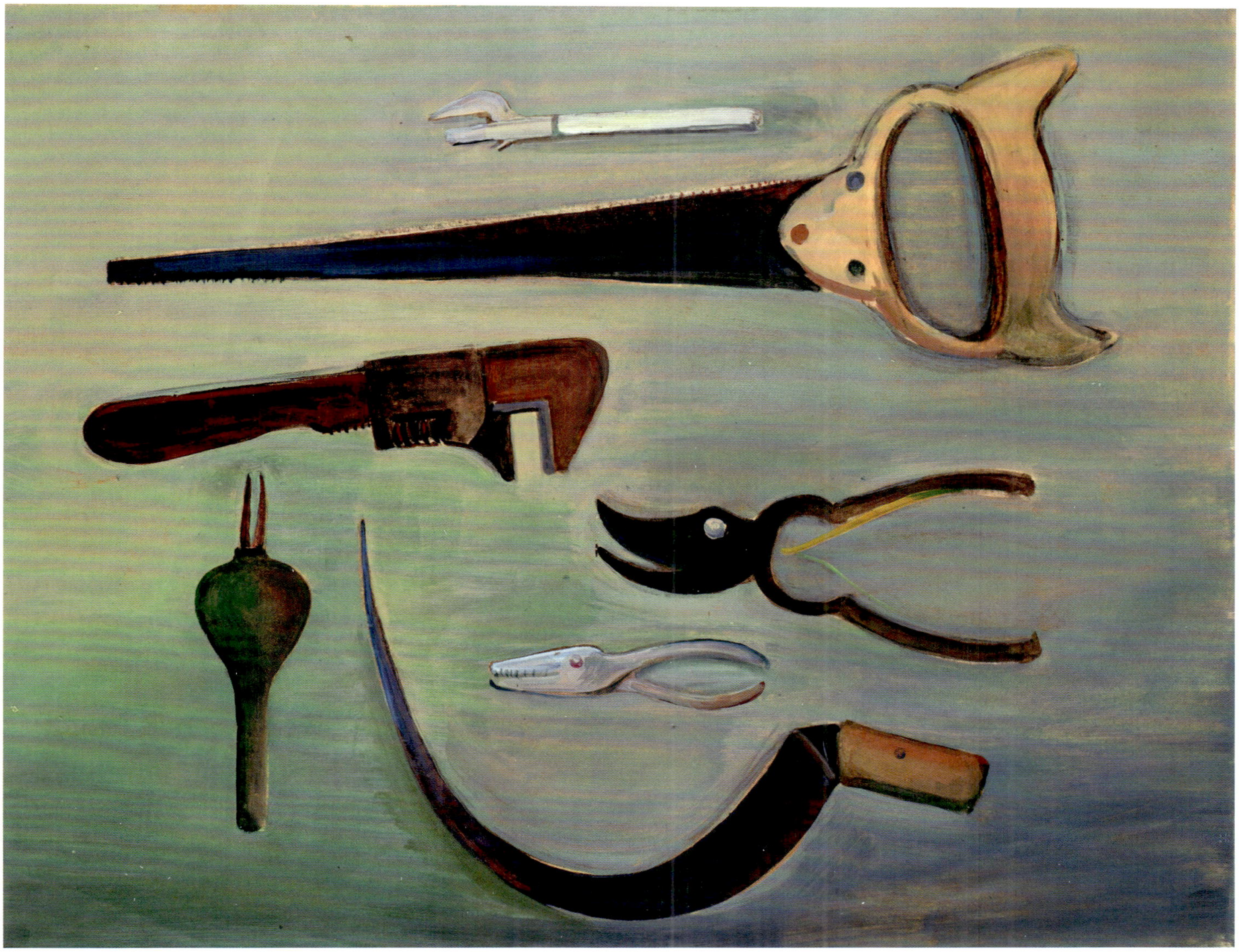

Beulah Loomis Hyde (1886–1983)
Untitled (tools, with color variation), ca. 1935–40
Oil on paper
20 × 24½ in.
Collection of Pamela Hyde Smith

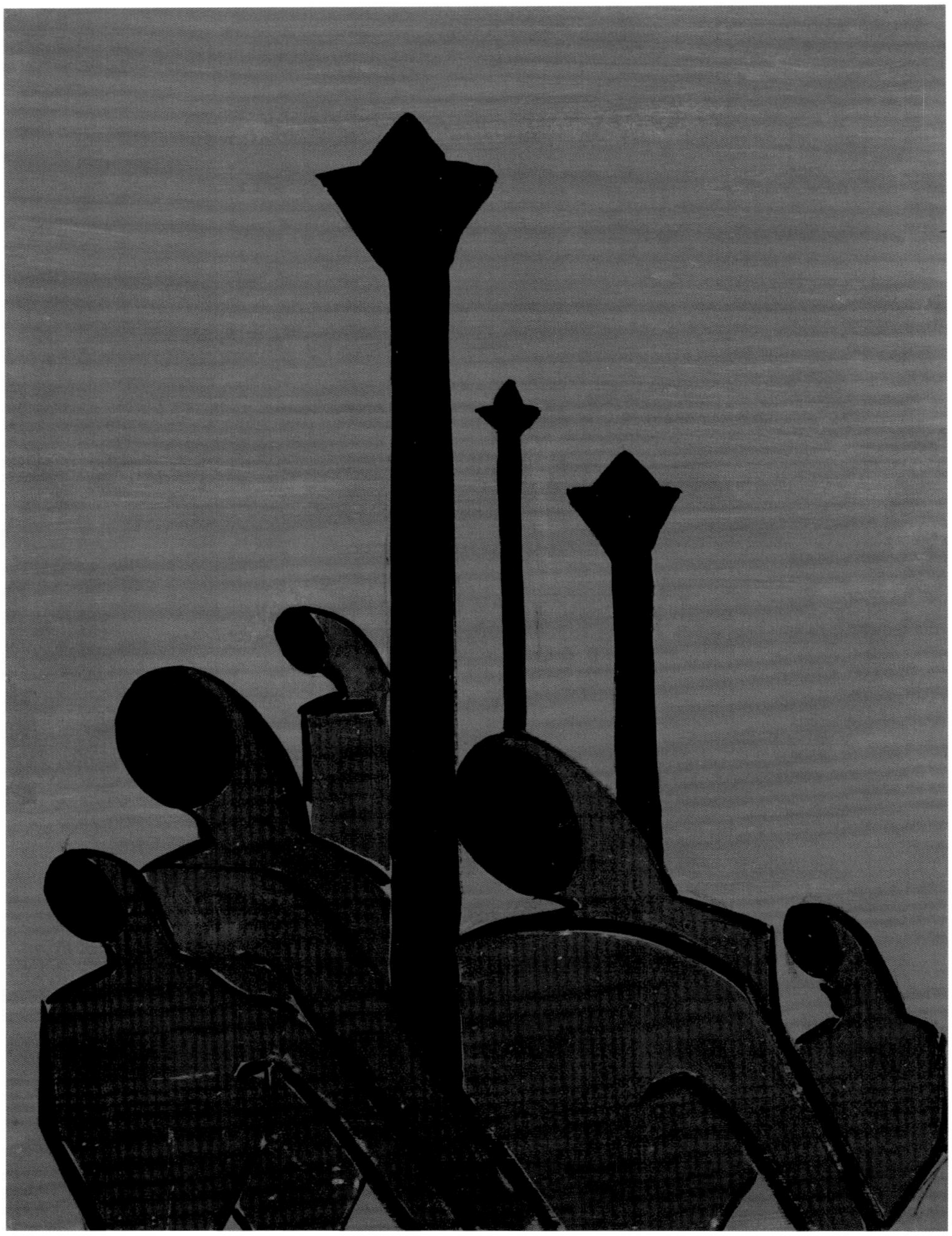

Beulah Loomis Hyde (1886–1983)
Untitled, ca. 1935–40
Oil on paper
19¾ × 14¾ in.
Collection of Pamela Hyde Smith

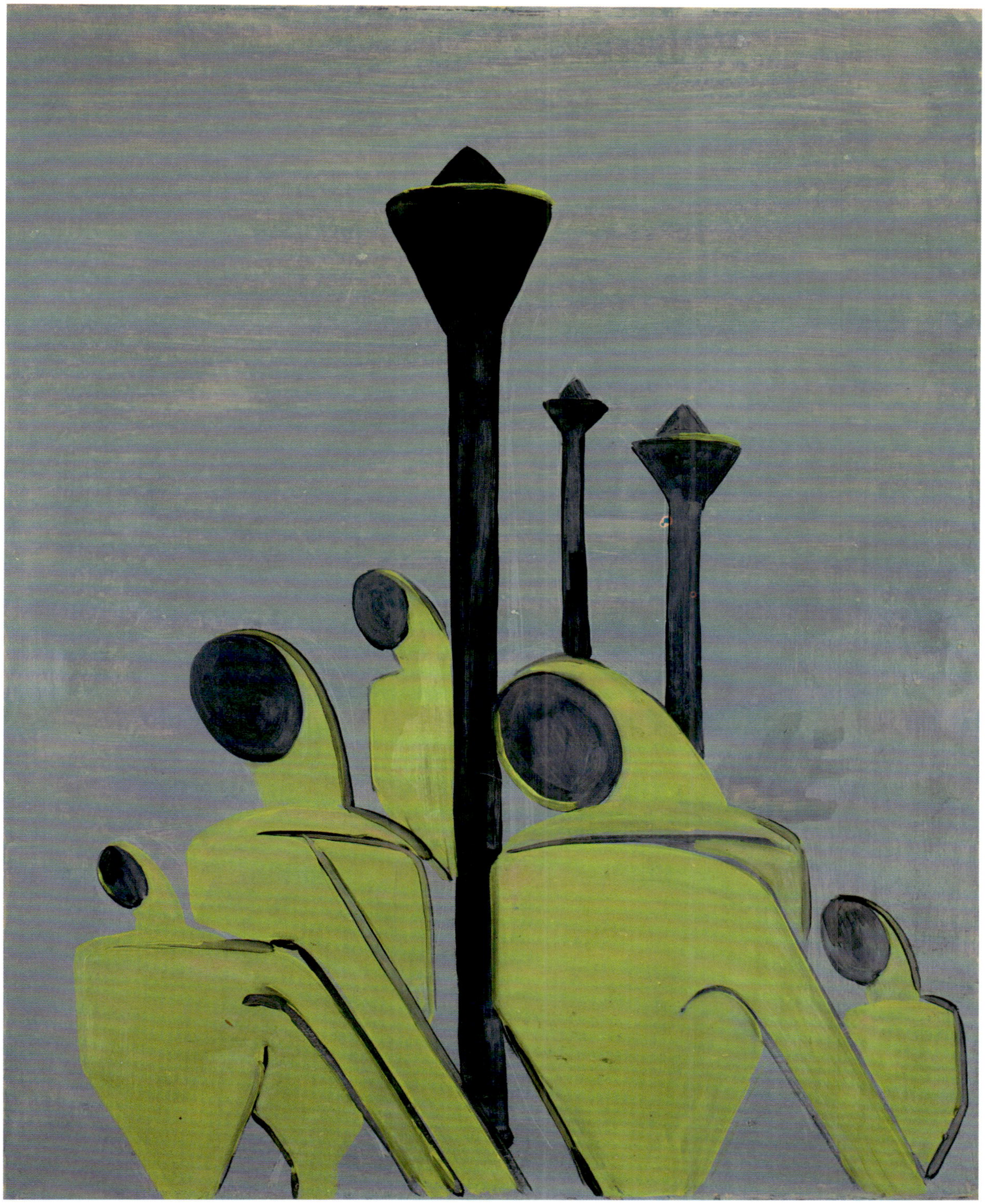

Beulah Loomis Hyde (1886–1983)
Untitled, ca. 1935–40
Oil on paper
23 × 19 in.
Collection of Pamela Hyde Smith

Both of these paintings were likely derived from the cyclone filters and capped smokestacks of the Wheeler-Osgood Plant in Tacoma.

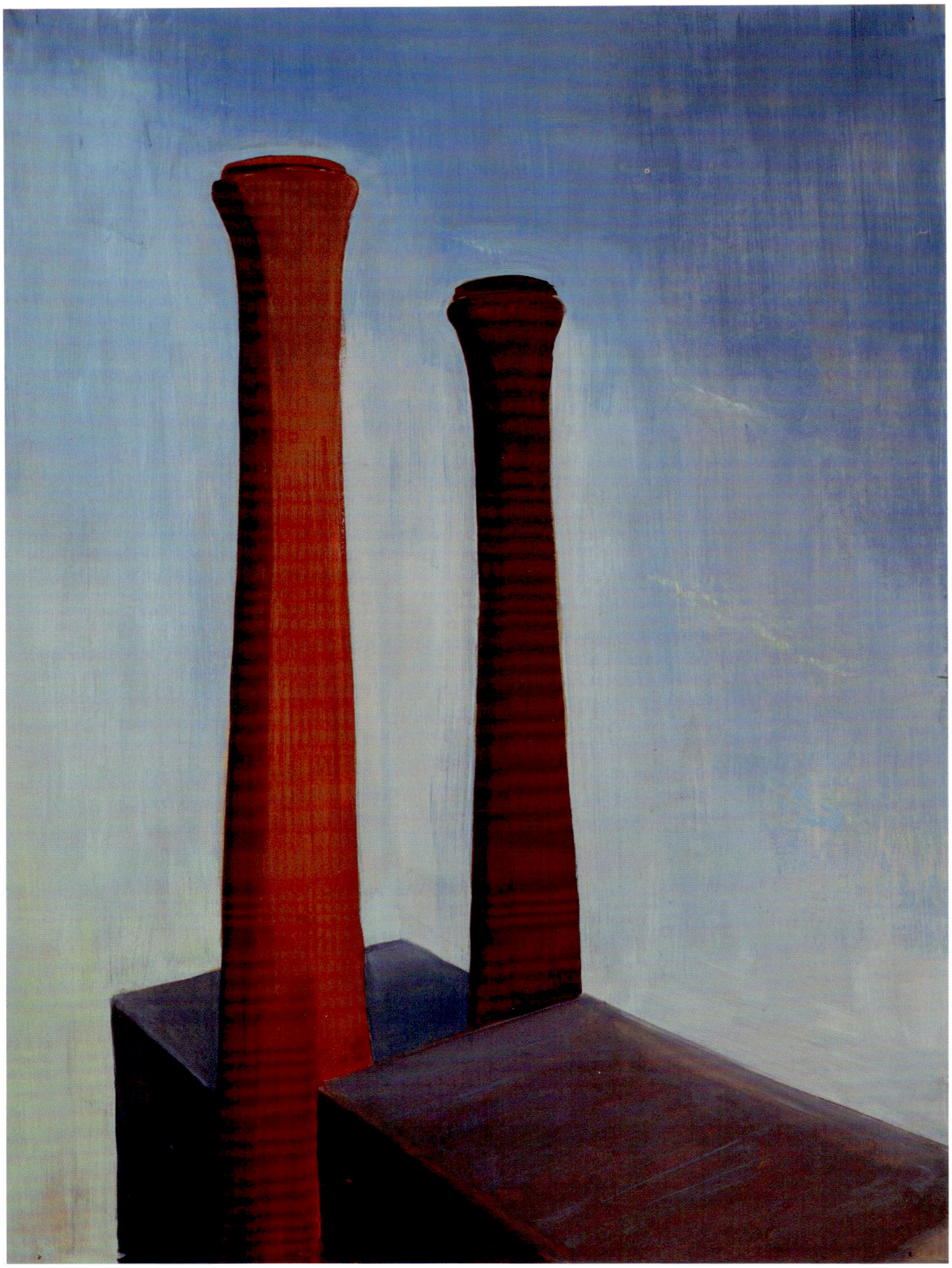

Beulah Loomis Hyde (1886–1983)
Untitled (smokestack forms), ca. 1935–40
Oil on paper
20 × 15 in.
Collection of Pamela Hyde Smith

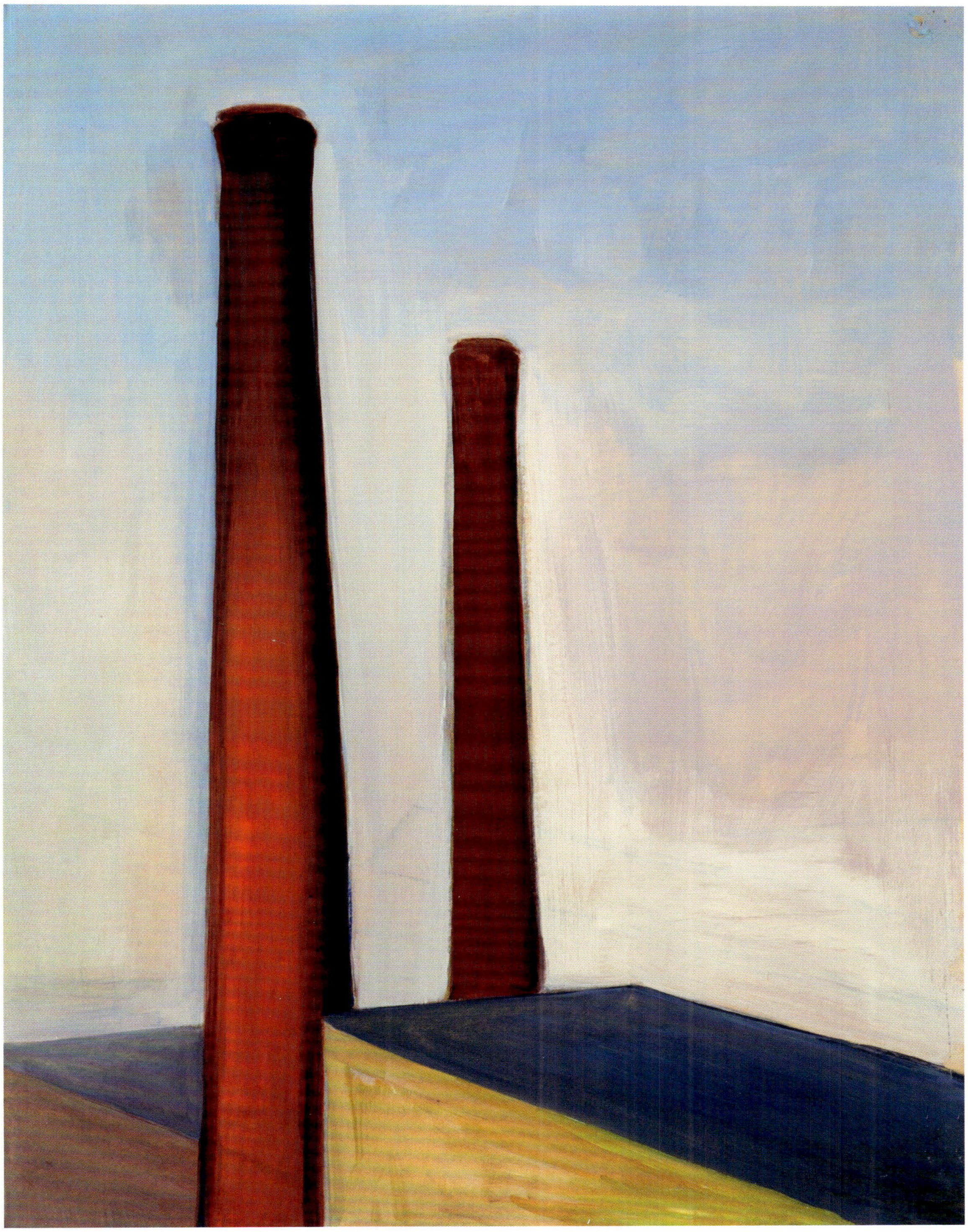

Beulah Loomis Hyde (1886–1983)
Untitled (smokestack forms with color variation), ca. 1935–40
Oil on paper
20 × 15 in.
Collection of Pamela Hyde Smith

Beulah Loomis Hyde (1886–1983)
Self-portrait, ca. 1935–40
Oil on canvas
18¼ × 16¼ in.
Collection of Catherine S. Ebert

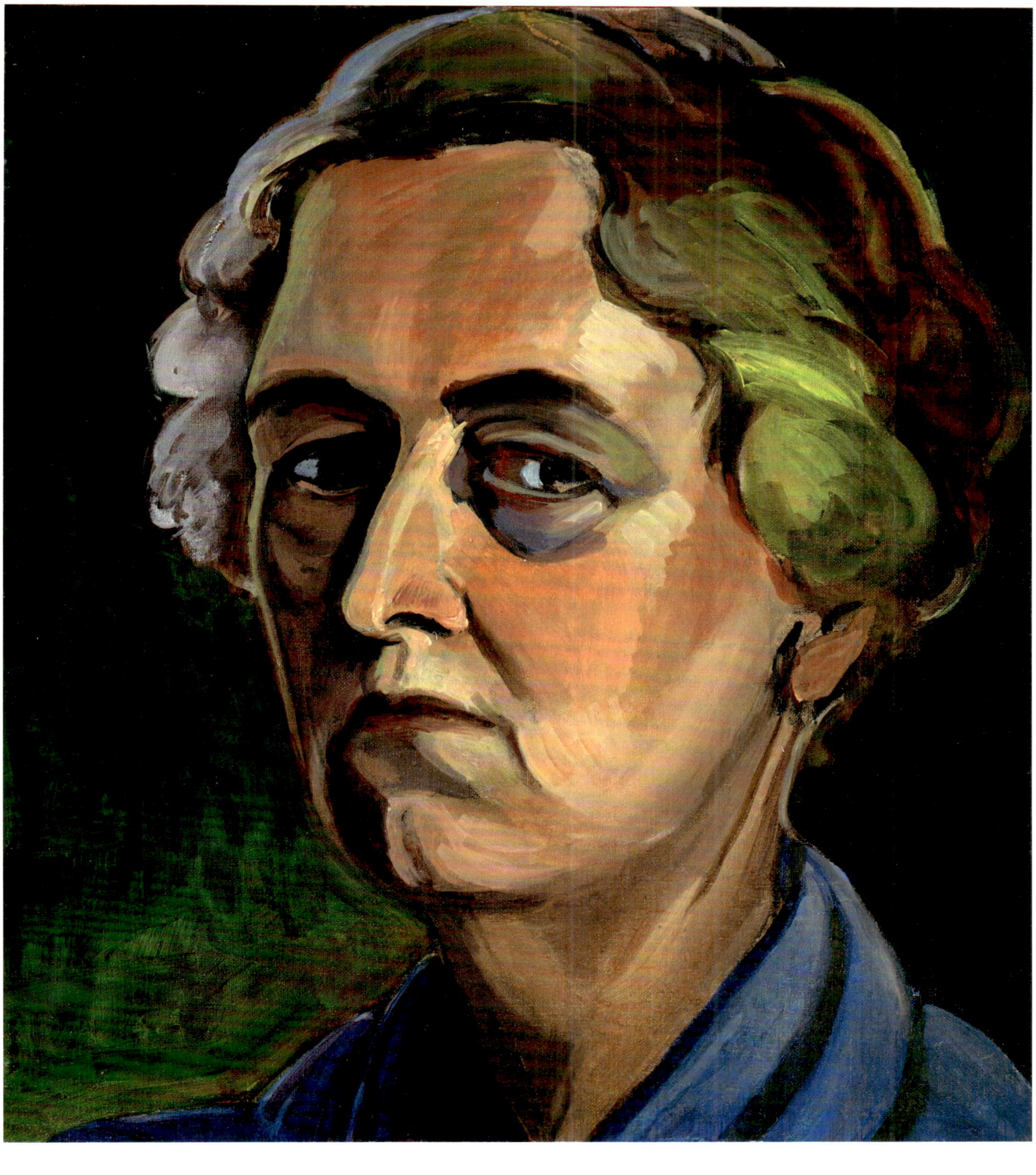

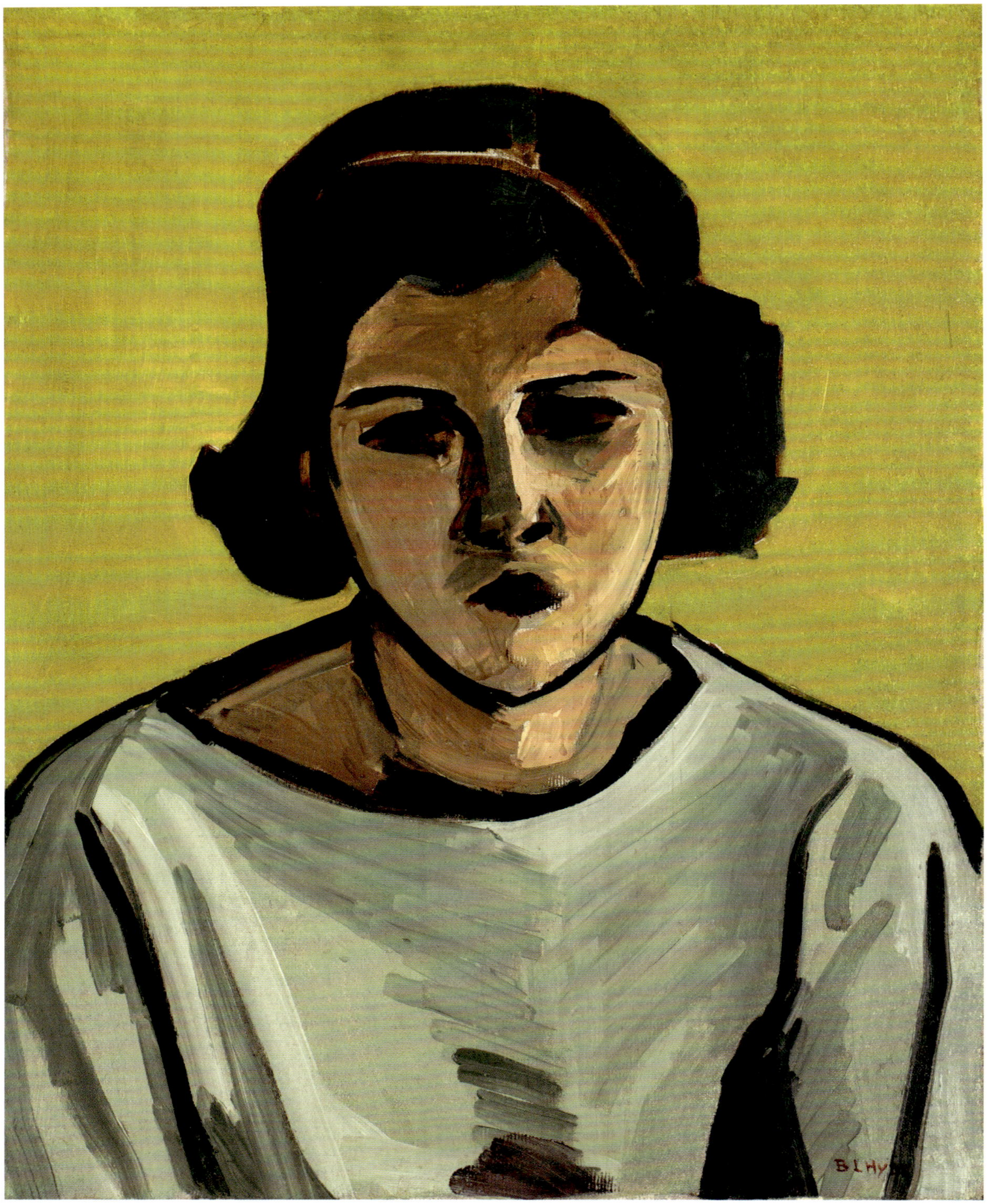

Beulah Loomis Hyde (1886–1983)
Untitled portrait, ca. 1935–40
Oil on canvas
20 × 16 in.
Collection of Pamela Hyde Smith

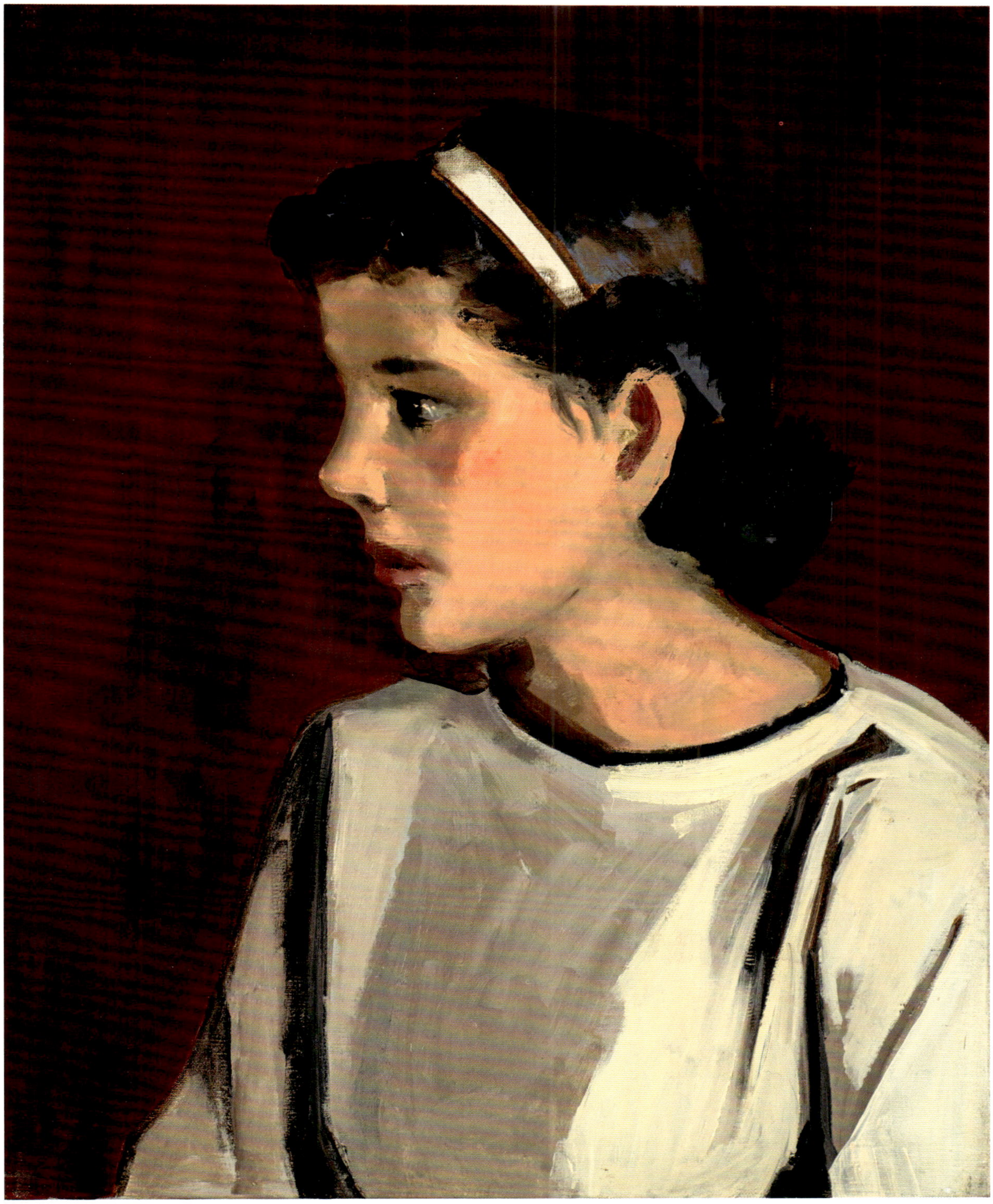

Beulah Loomis Hyde (1886–1983)
Untitled portrait (profile variation of painting on opposite page), ca. 1935–40
Oil on canvas
20 × 16¼ in.
Collection of Pamela Hyde Smith

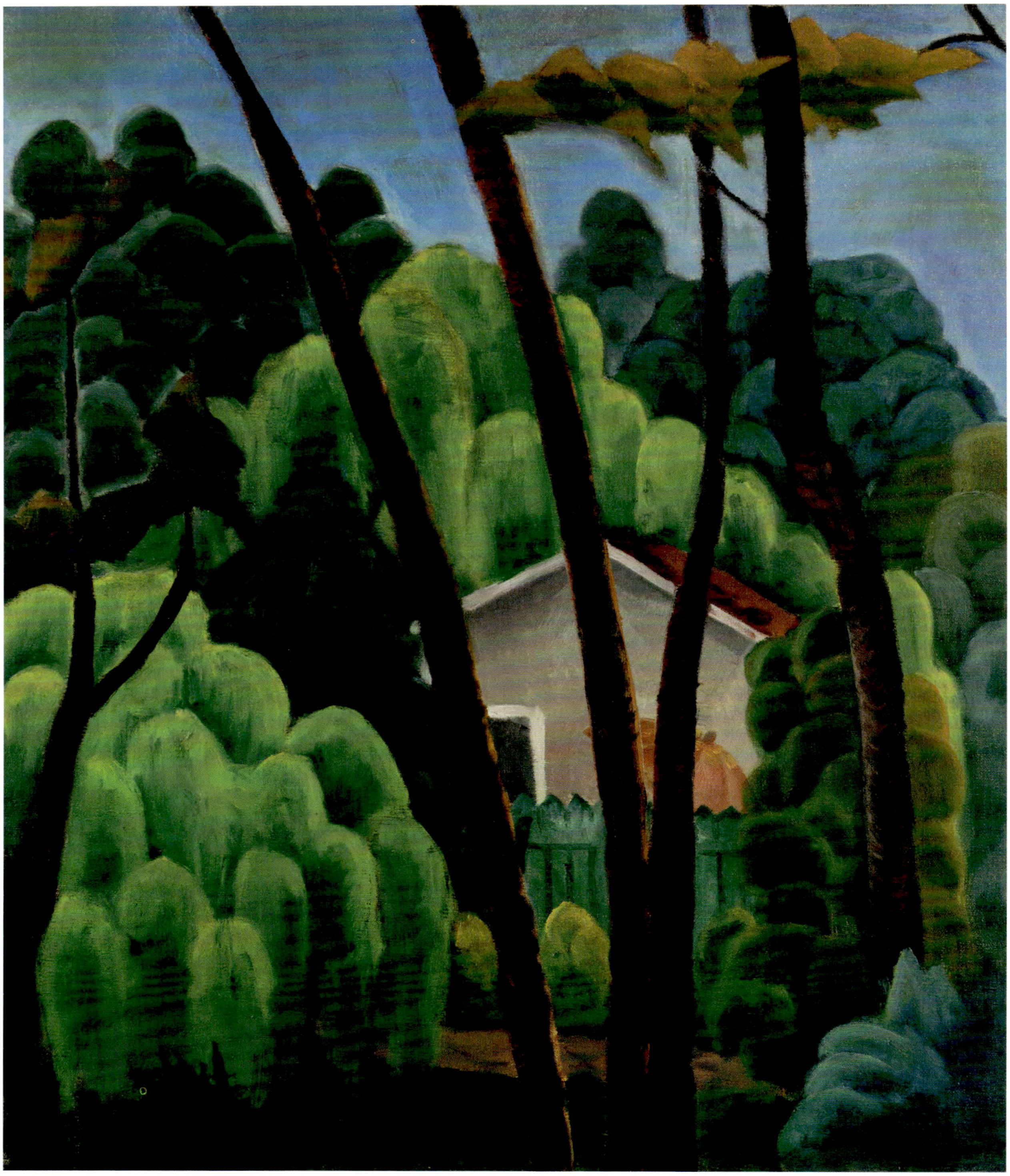

Beulah Loomis Hyde (1886–1983)
Untitled, ca. 1935–40
Oil on canvas
23¾ × 19¾ in.
Collection of Pamela Hyde Smith

This early work displays Hyde's interest in French Post-Impressionism and in particular the work of Henri Rousseau.

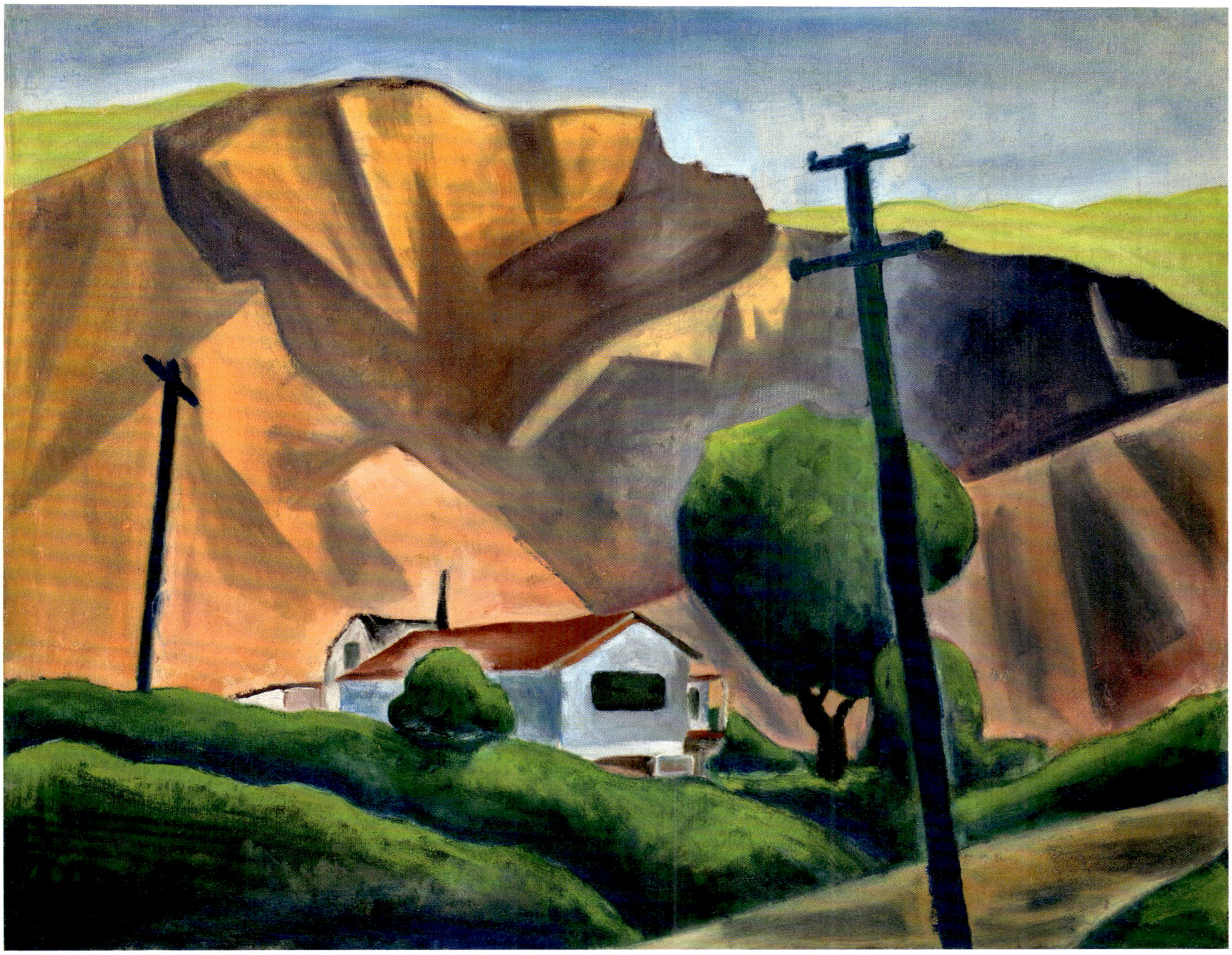

Beulah Loomis Hyde (1886–1983)
Untitled, ca. 1935–40
Oil on canvas
17½ × 22 in.
Collection of Pamela Hyde Smith

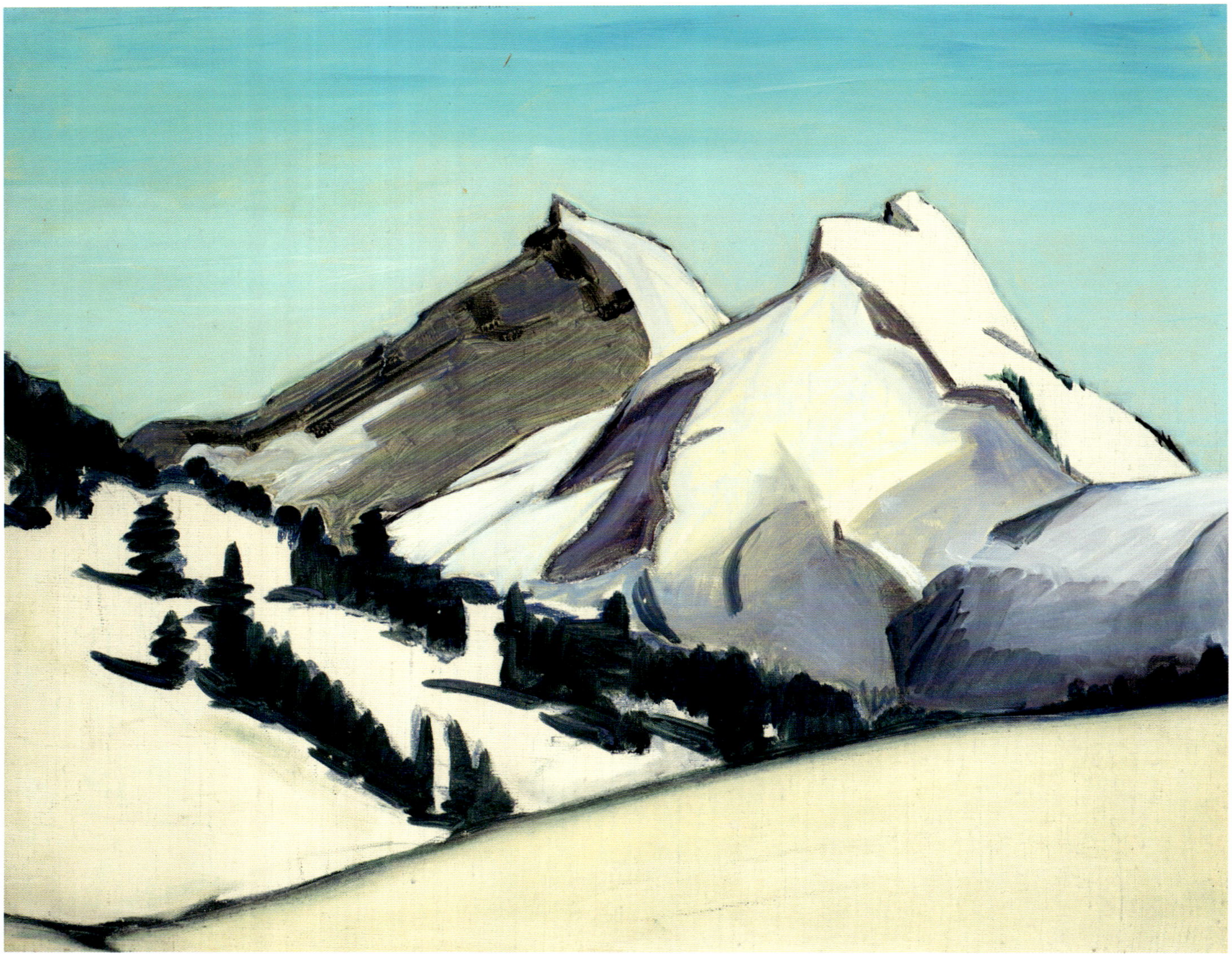

Beulah Loomis Hyde (1886–1983)
Untitled, ca. 1935–40
Oil on canvas
16 × 20 in.
Collection of Pamela Hyde Smith

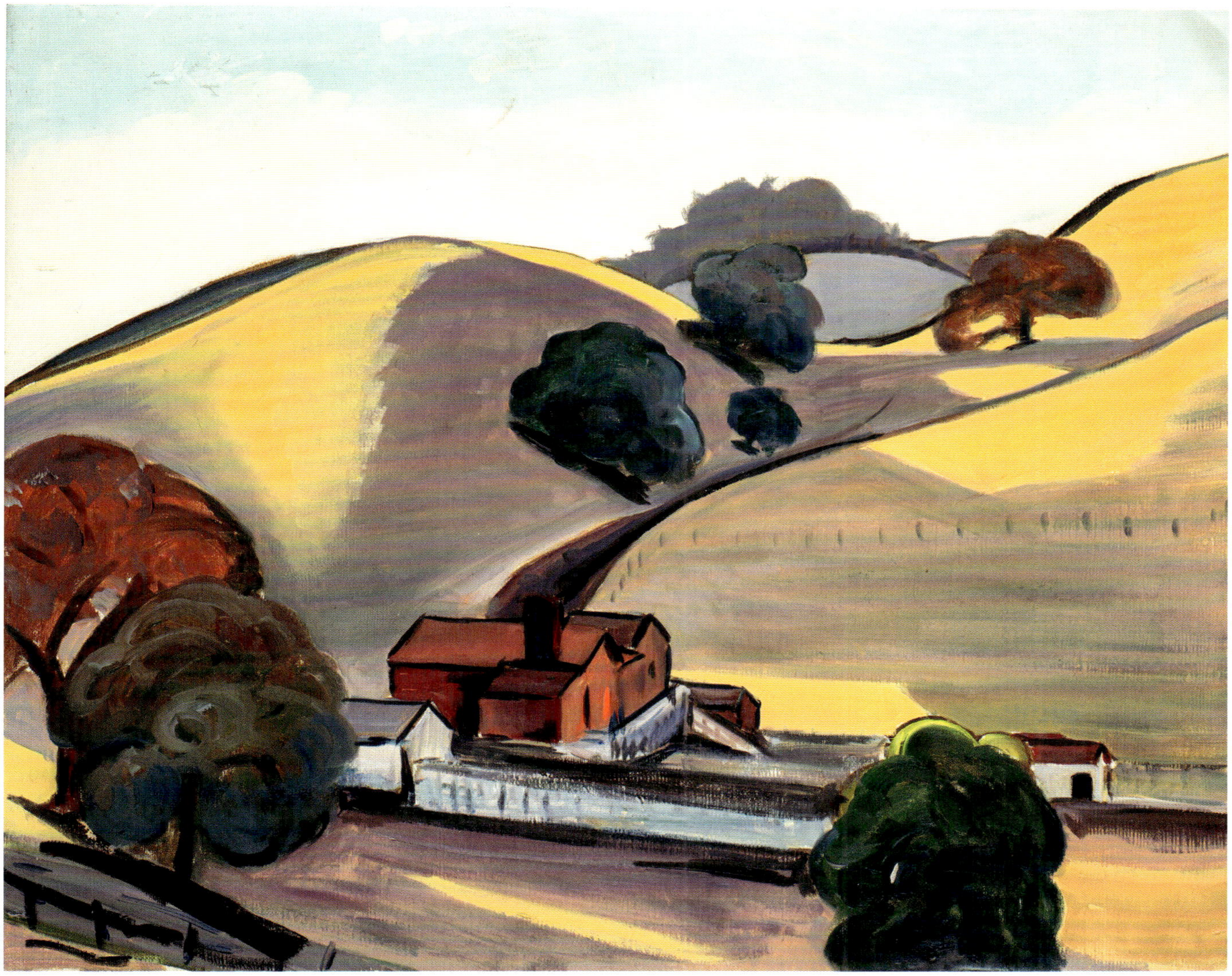

Beulah Loomis Hyde (1886–1983)
Untitled, ca. 1935–40
Oil on canvas
16 × 20 in.
Collection of Pamela Hyde Smith

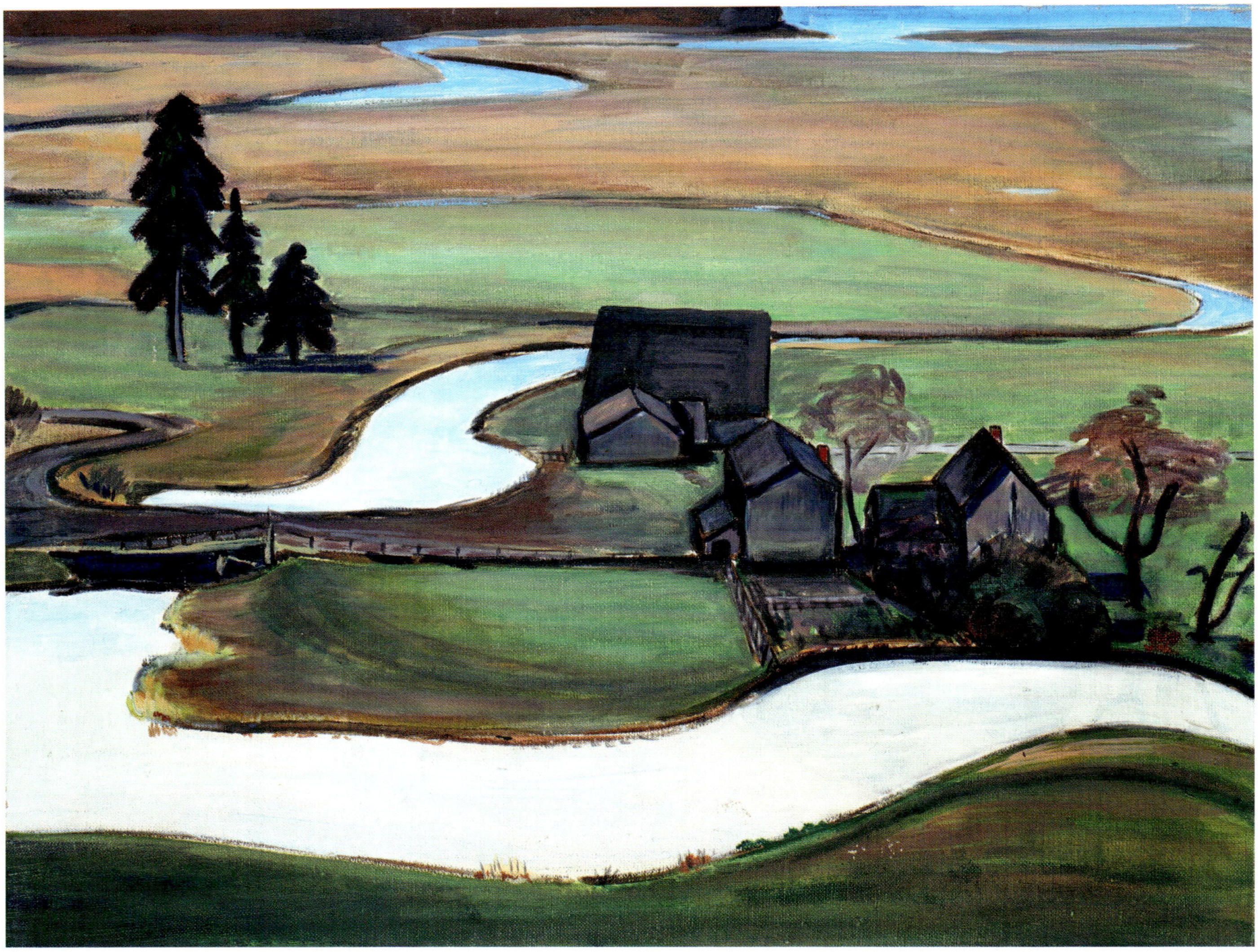

Beulah Loomis Hyde (1886–1983)
Untitled, ca. 1935–40
Oil on canvas
15½ × 19½ in.
Collection of Pamela Hyde Smith

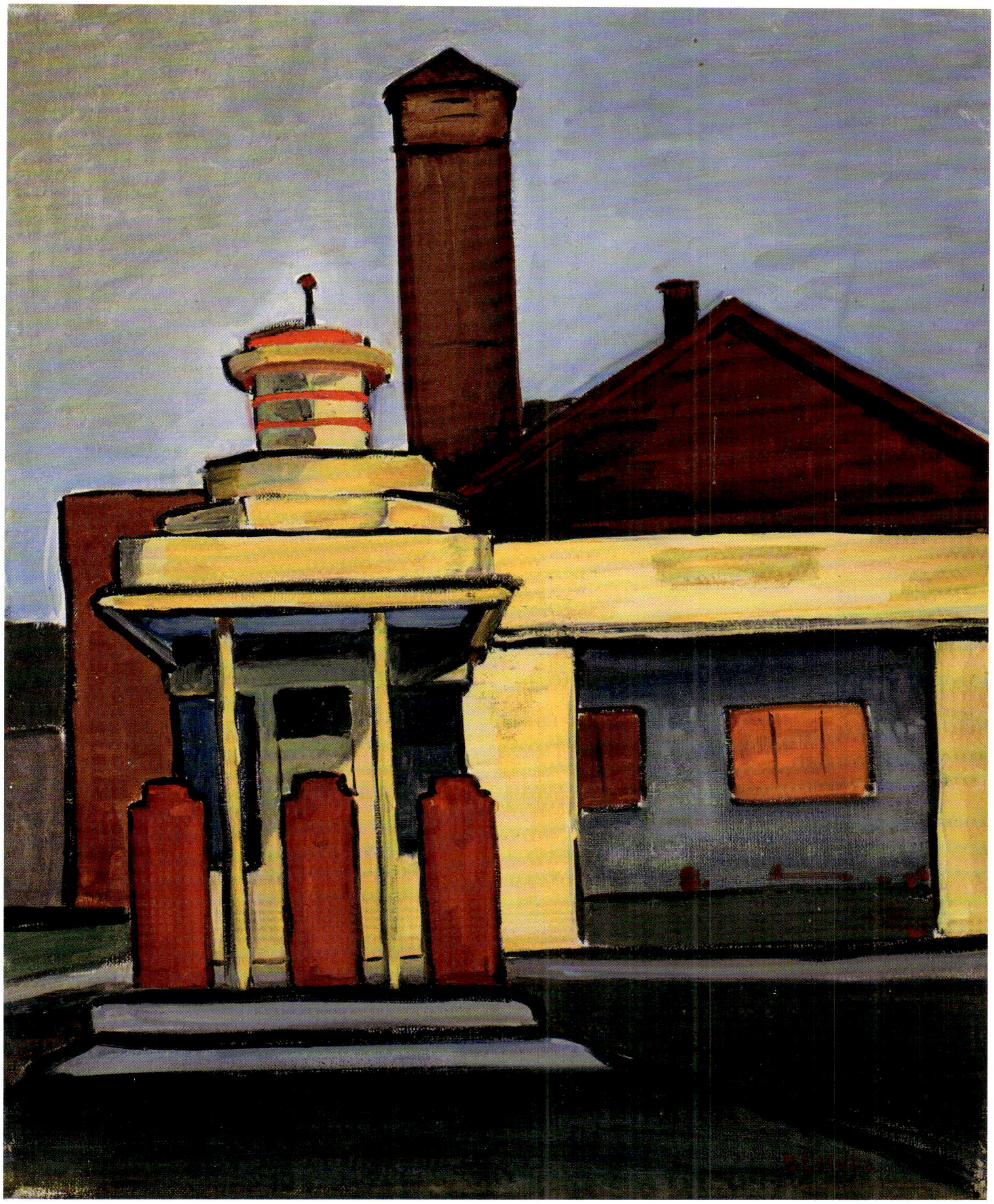

Beulah Loomis Hyde (1886–1983)
Untitled, ca. 1935–40
Oil on canvas
20 × 16 in.
Collection of Pamela Hyde Smith

This may be the Hyde painting titled *Gas Station*, which won second prize at the *Contemporary American Art* exhibition, Western Washington Fair Art Galleries, Puyallup, WA, in 1941. However, Hyde produced several other untitled paintings depicting vernacular streamlined architecture in Tacoma including gas stations and retail stores.

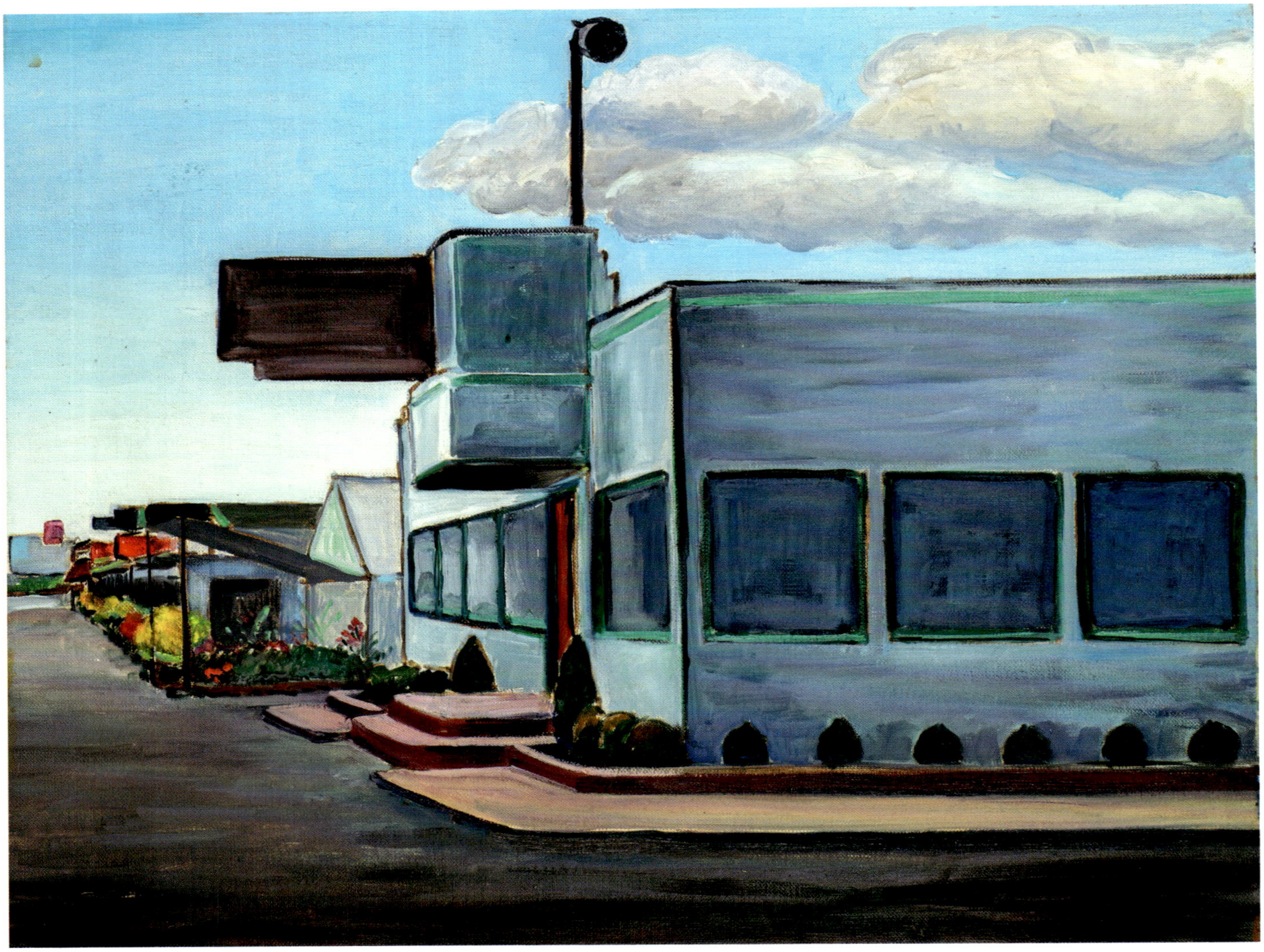

Beulah Loomis Hyde (1886–1983)
Untitled, ca. 1935–40
Oil on canvas
15½ × 20 in.
Collection of Pamela Hyde Smith

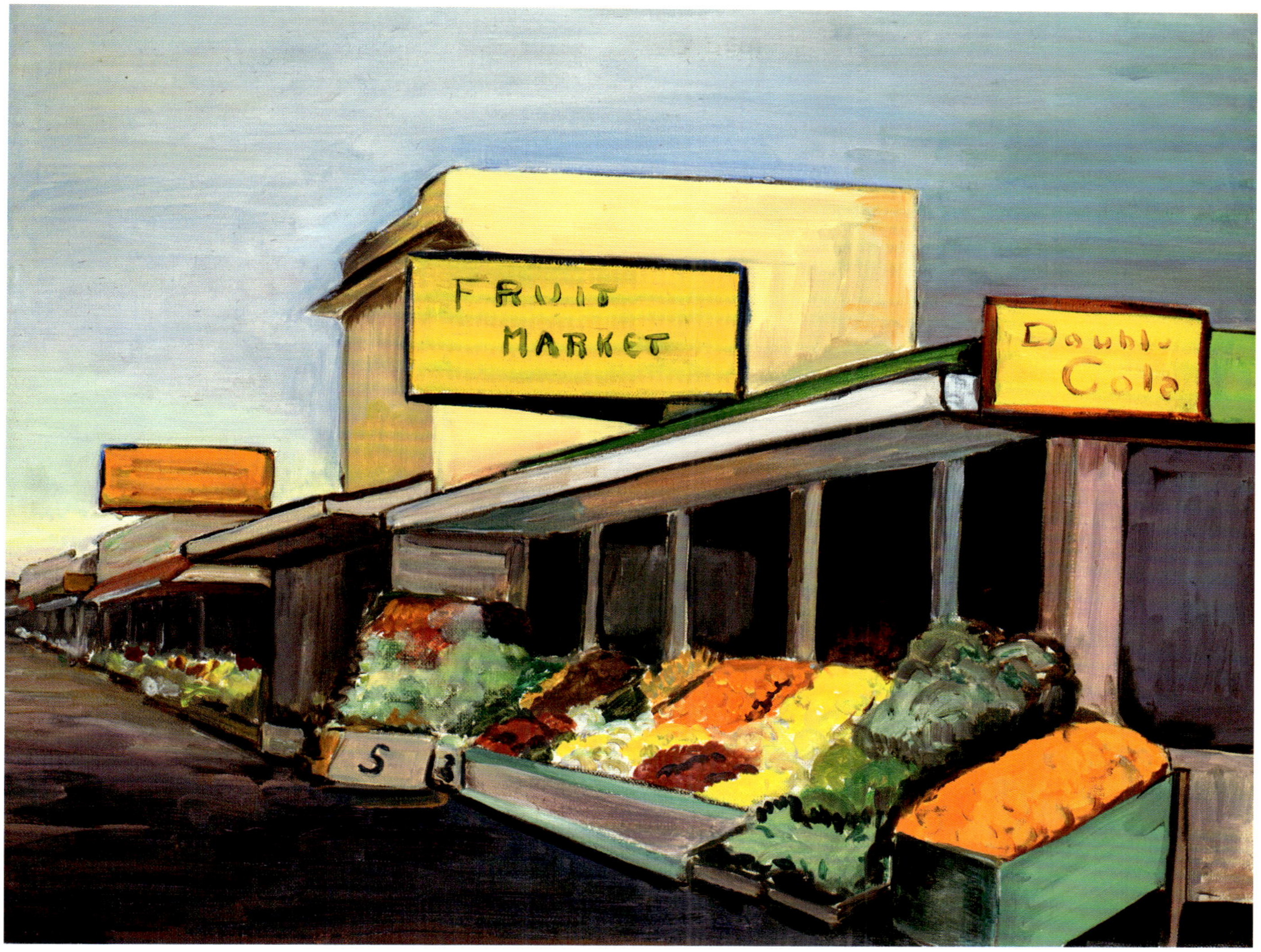

Beulah Loomis Hyde (1886–1983)
Untitled, ca. 1935–40
Oil on canvas
15½ × 20 in.
Collection of Pamela Hyde Smith

Beulah Loomis Hyde (1886–1983)
Untitled, ca. 1935–40
Oil on canvas
20 × 16 in.
Collection of Pamela Hyde Smith

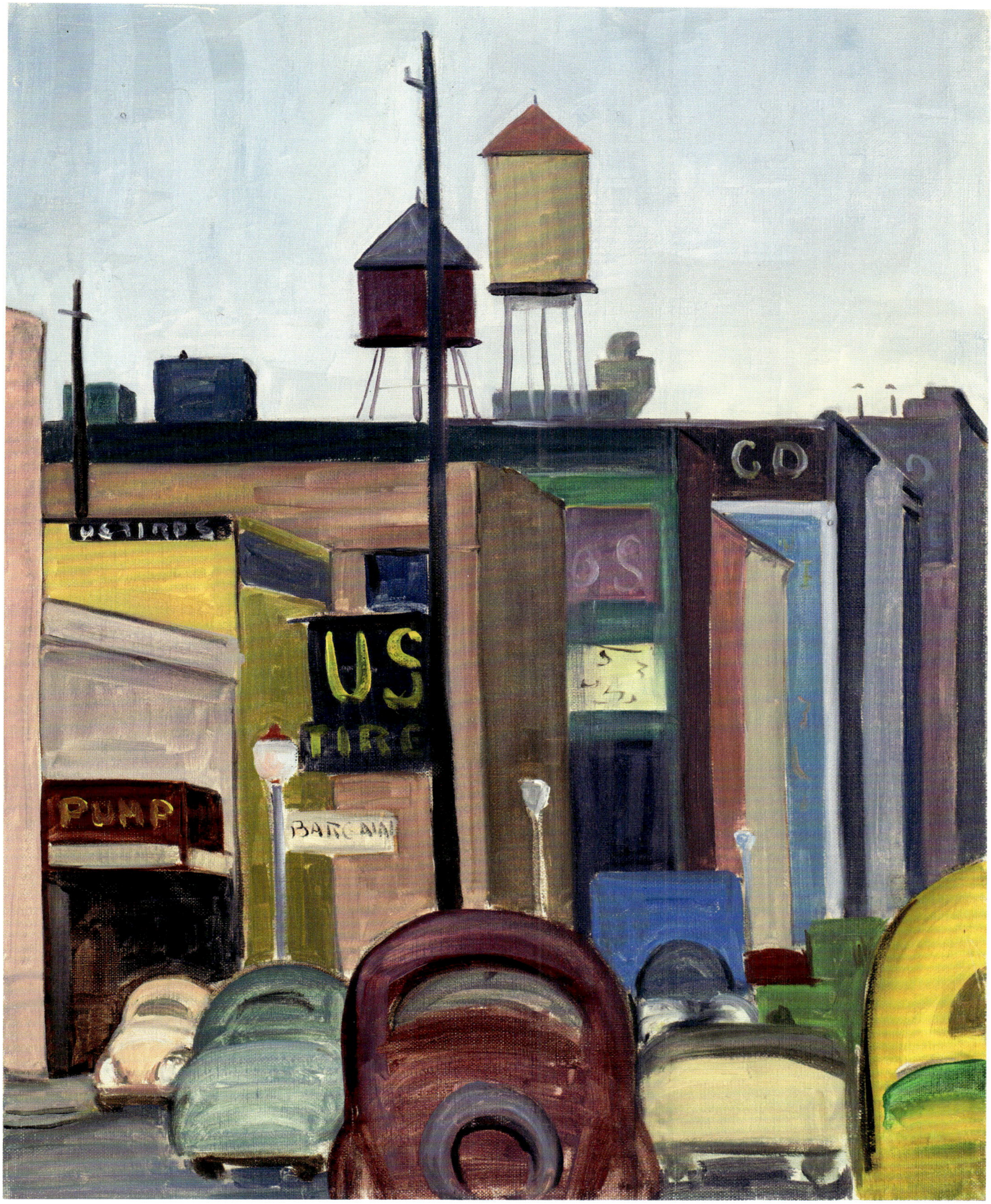

US
TIRE
PUMP
BARGAIN
CD

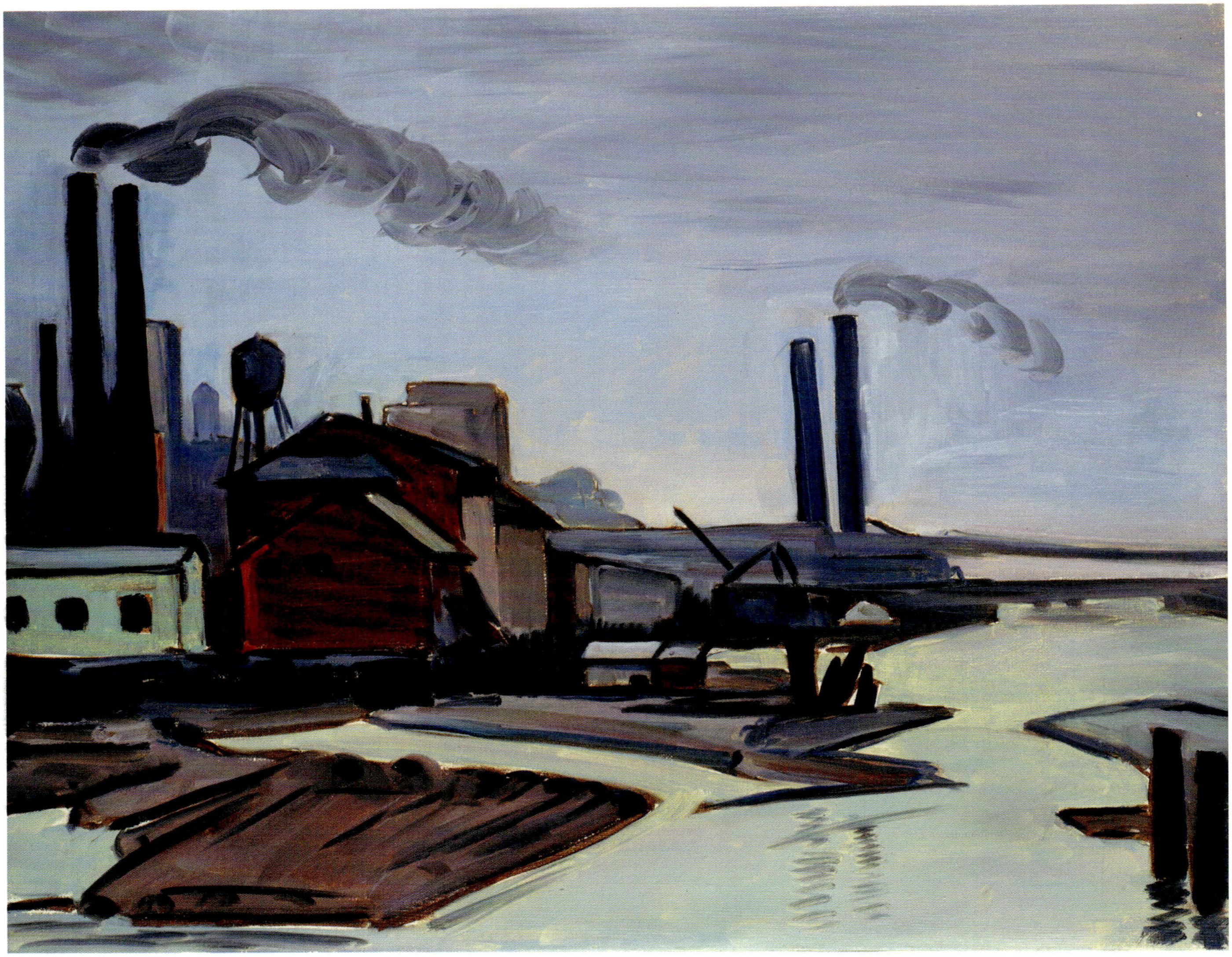

Beulah Loomis Hyde (1886–1983)
Untitled, ca. 1935–40
Oil on canvas
16 × 20 in.
Collection of Pamela Hyde Smith

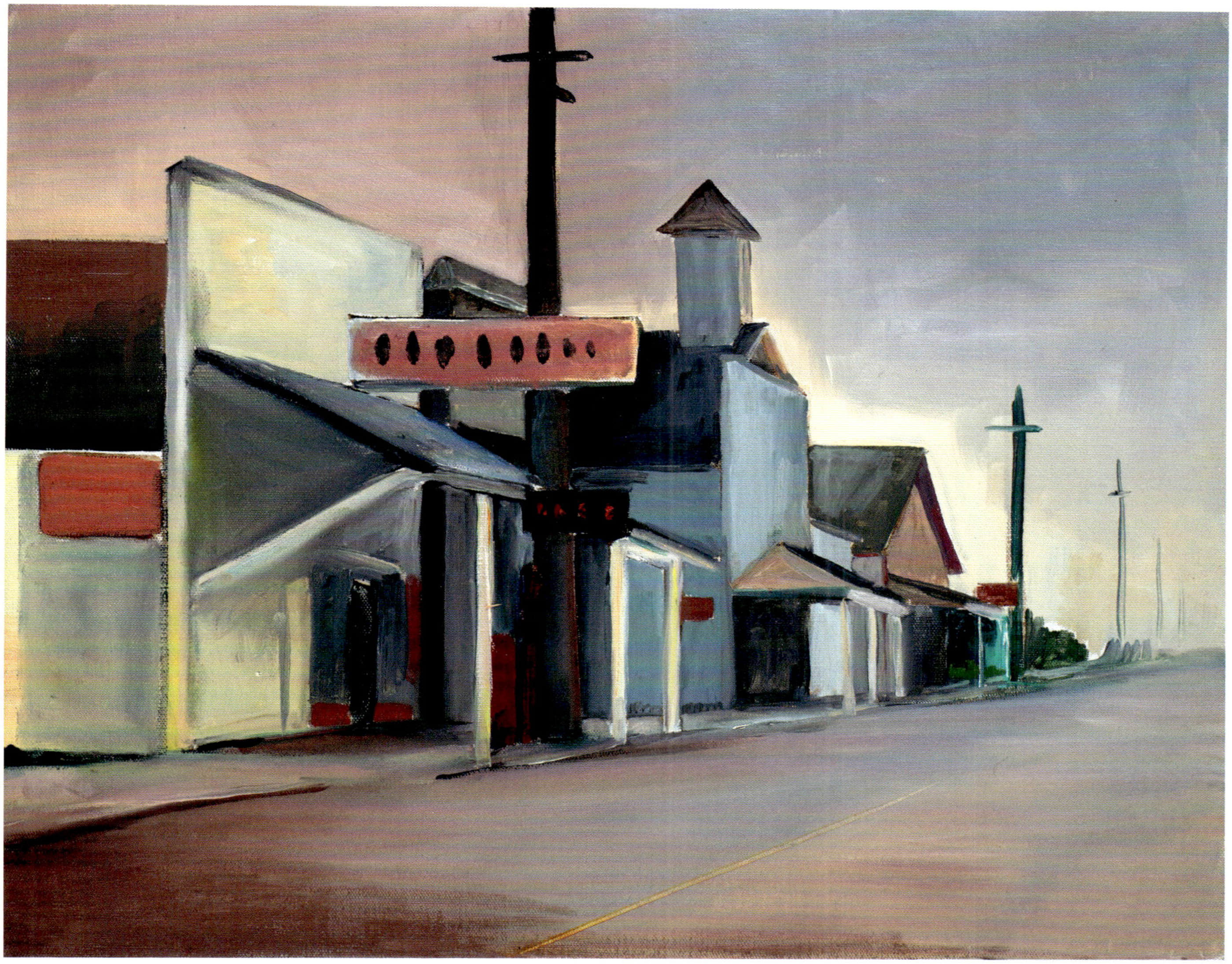

Beulah Loomis Hyde (1886–1983)
Untitled, ca. 1935–40
Oil on canvas
16 × 20 in.
Collection of Pamela Hyde Smith

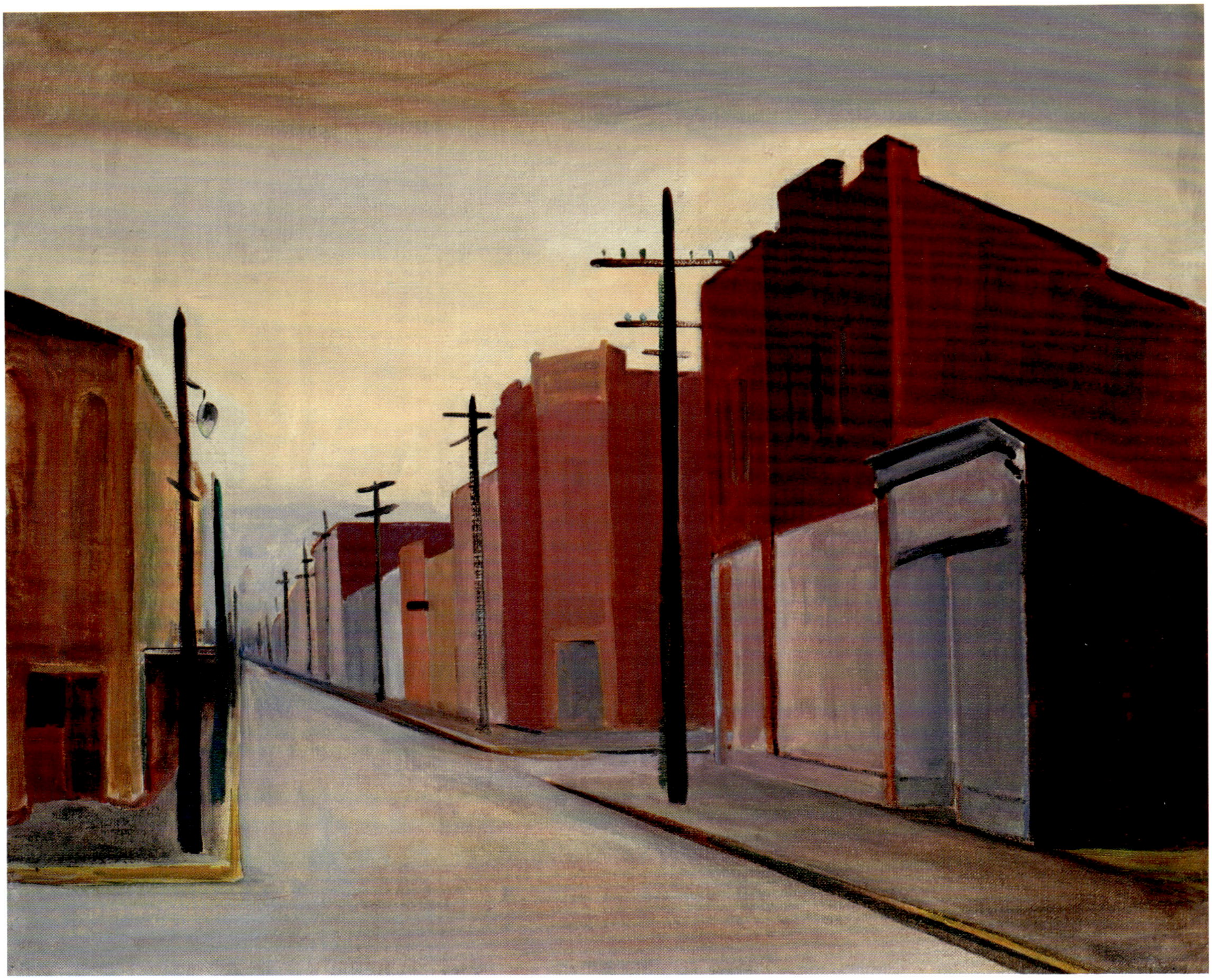

Beulah Loomis Hyde (1886–1983)
Untitled, ca. 1935–42
Oil on canvas
20 × 24 in.
Collection of Pamela Hyde Smith

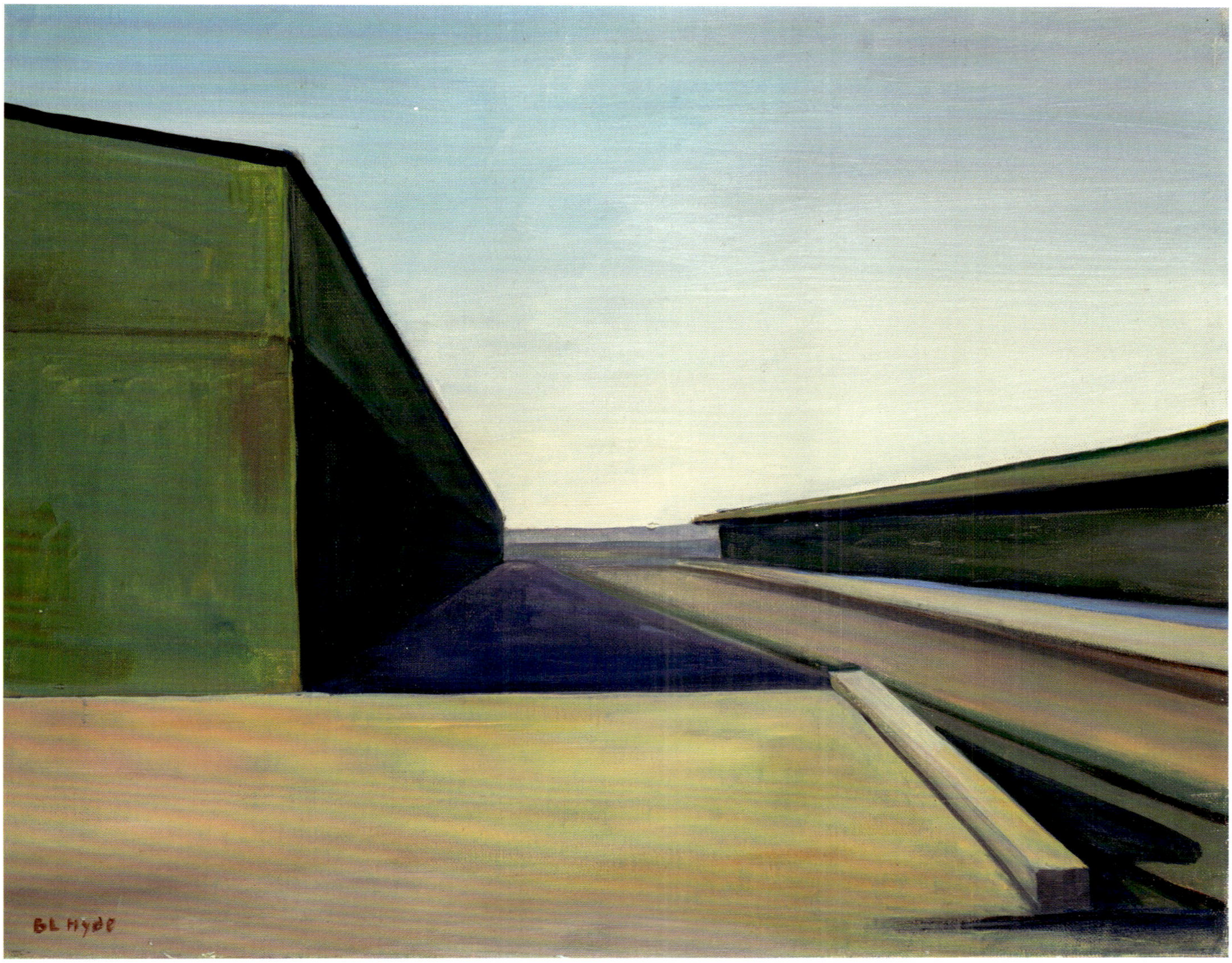

Beulah Loomis Hyde (1886–1983)
Untitled, ca. 1935–40
Oil on canvas
16 × 20 in.
Collection of Pamela Hyde Smith

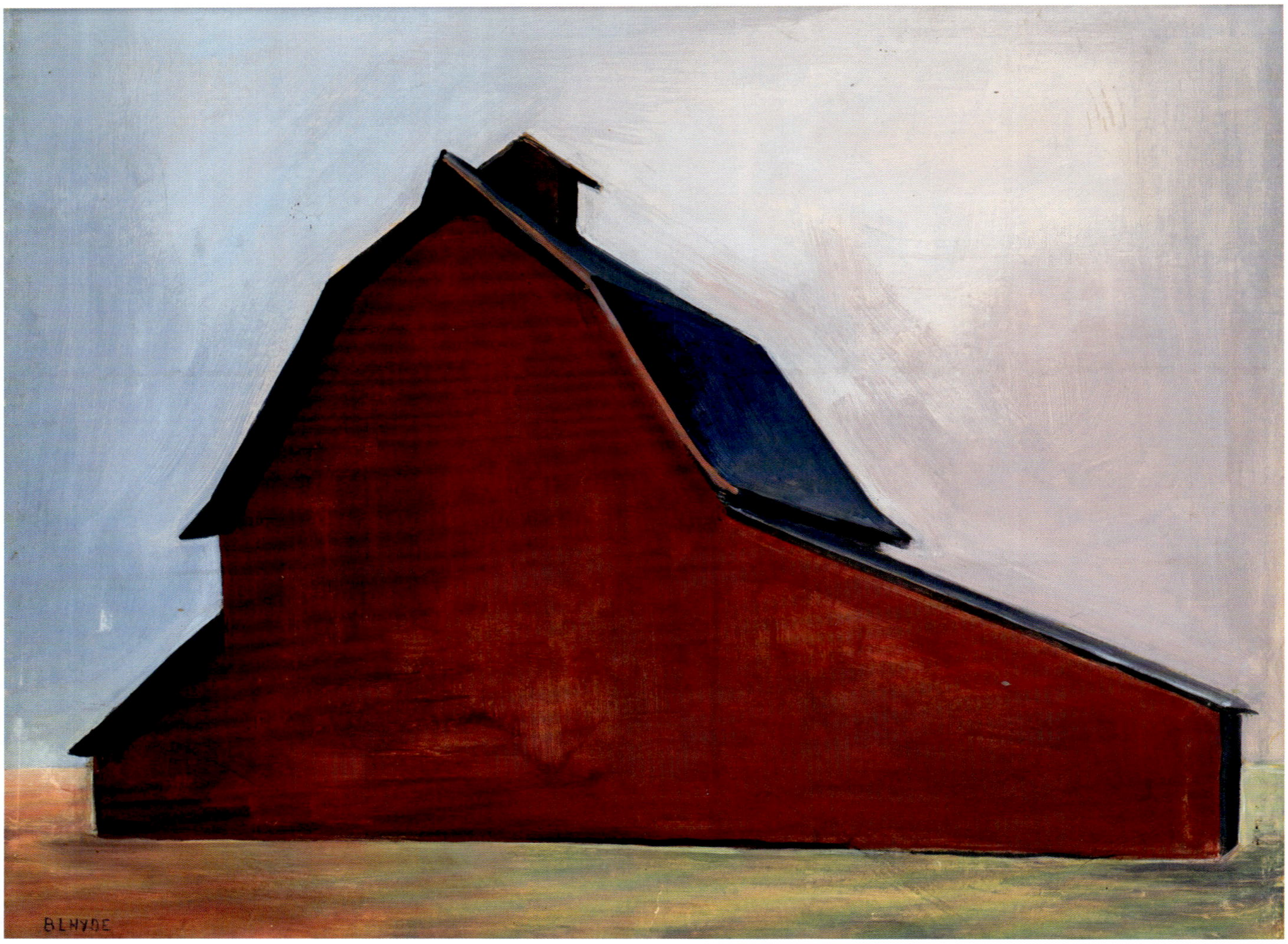

Beulah Loomis Hyde (1886–1983)
Untitled, ca. 1935–40
Oil on paper
16 × 20 in.
Collection of Douglas Hyde Land

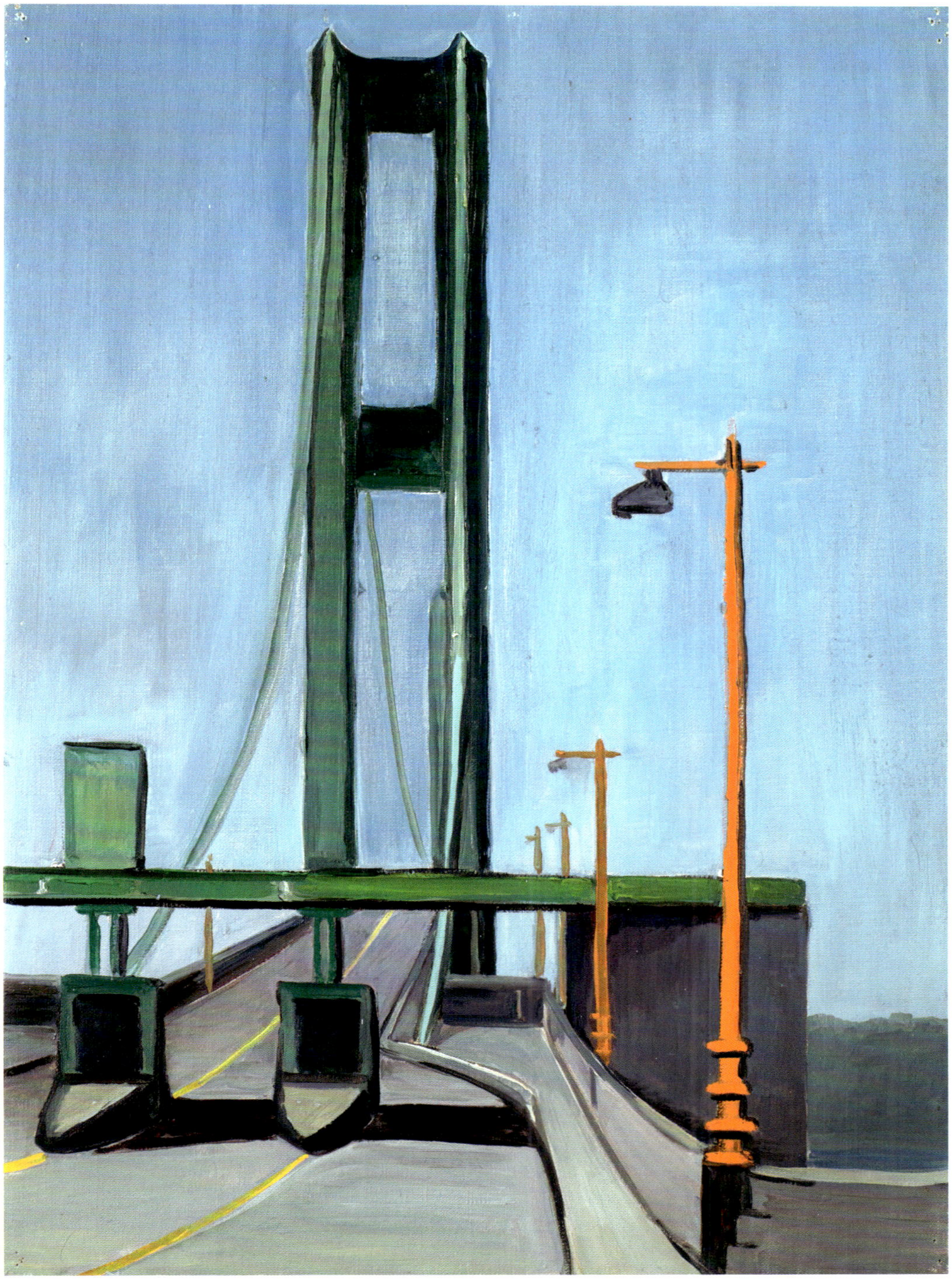

Beulah Loomis Hyde (1886–1983)
Untitled (Tacoma Narrows Bridge), 1940
Oil on canvas
20 × 14¼ in.
Collection of Pamela Hyde Smith

The Tacoma Narrows Bridge was a short-lived suspension bridge that connected Tacoma with Kitsap County in Washington State. It opened to traffic on July 1, 1940, but because of structural problems, the bridge collapsed into the Tacoma Narrows Strait of Puget Sound just four months later. Due to the bridge's dramatic movements before its collapse, it has gone down in history as "Galloping Gertie."

Beulah Loomis Hyde (1886–1983)
Untitled, ca. 1940–45
Oil on canvas
16 × 20 in.
Collection of Heide Fernandez-Llamazares

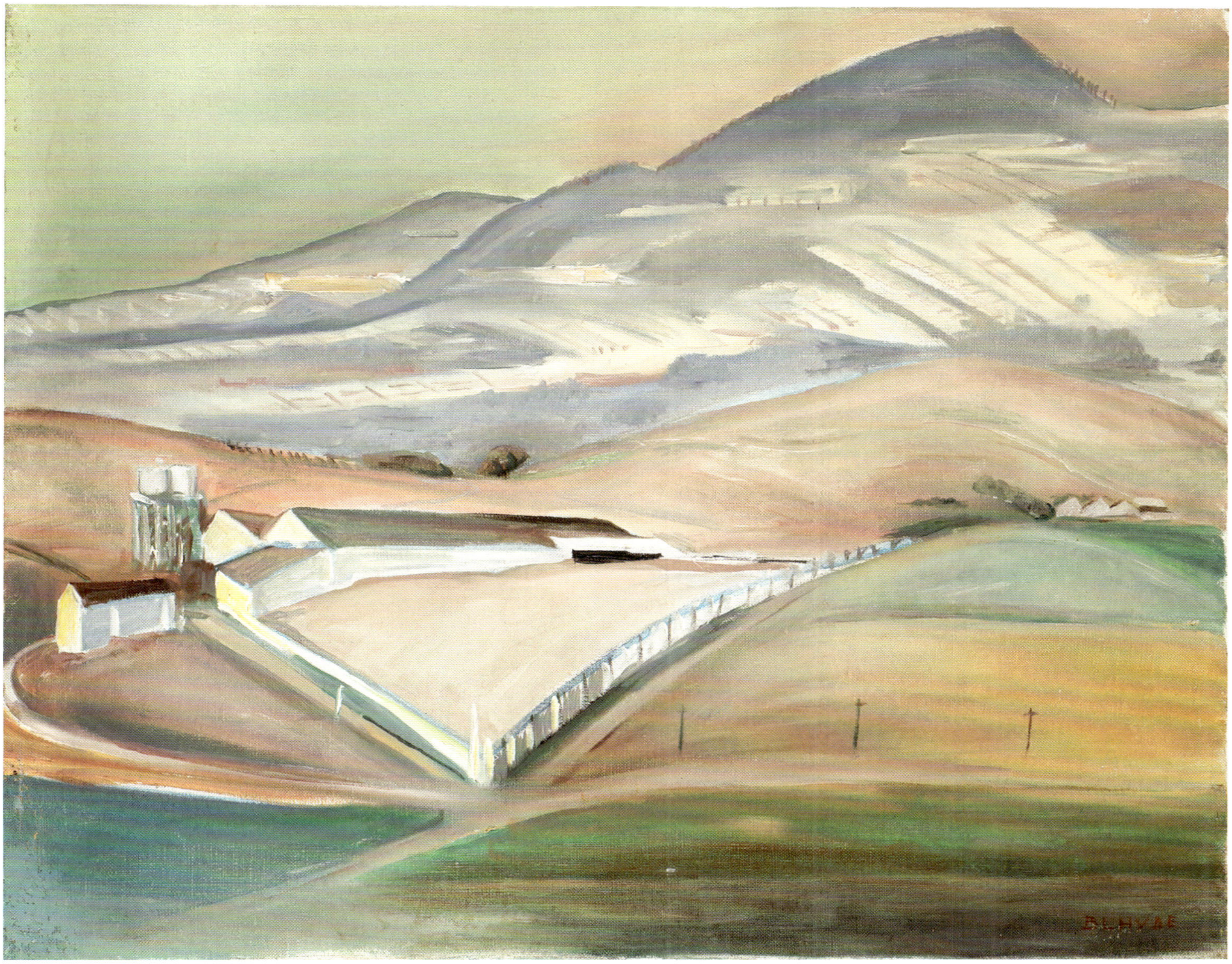

Beulah Loomis Hyde (1886–1983)
Untitled, ca. 1940–45
Oil on paper
20 × 16 in.
Collection of Pamela Hyde Smith

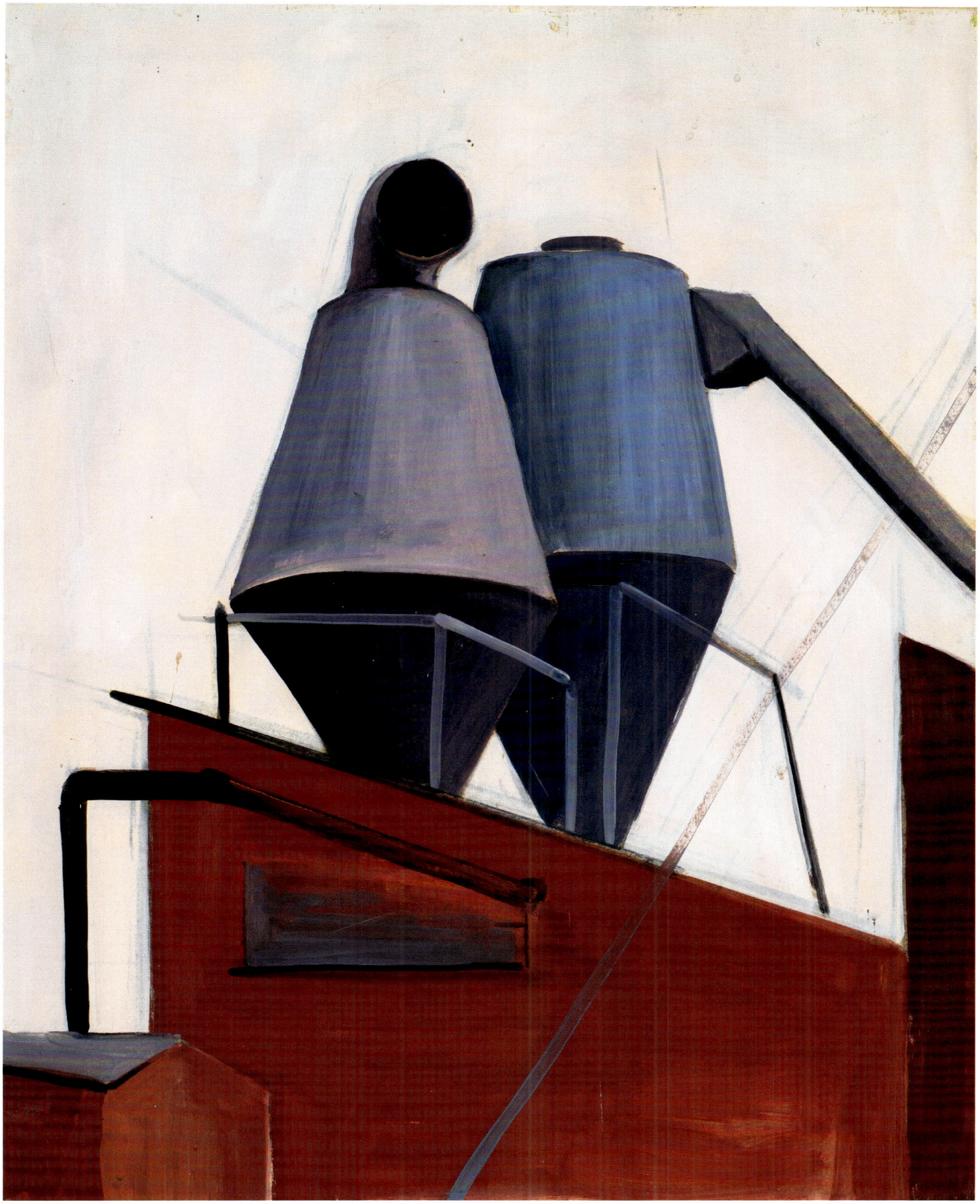

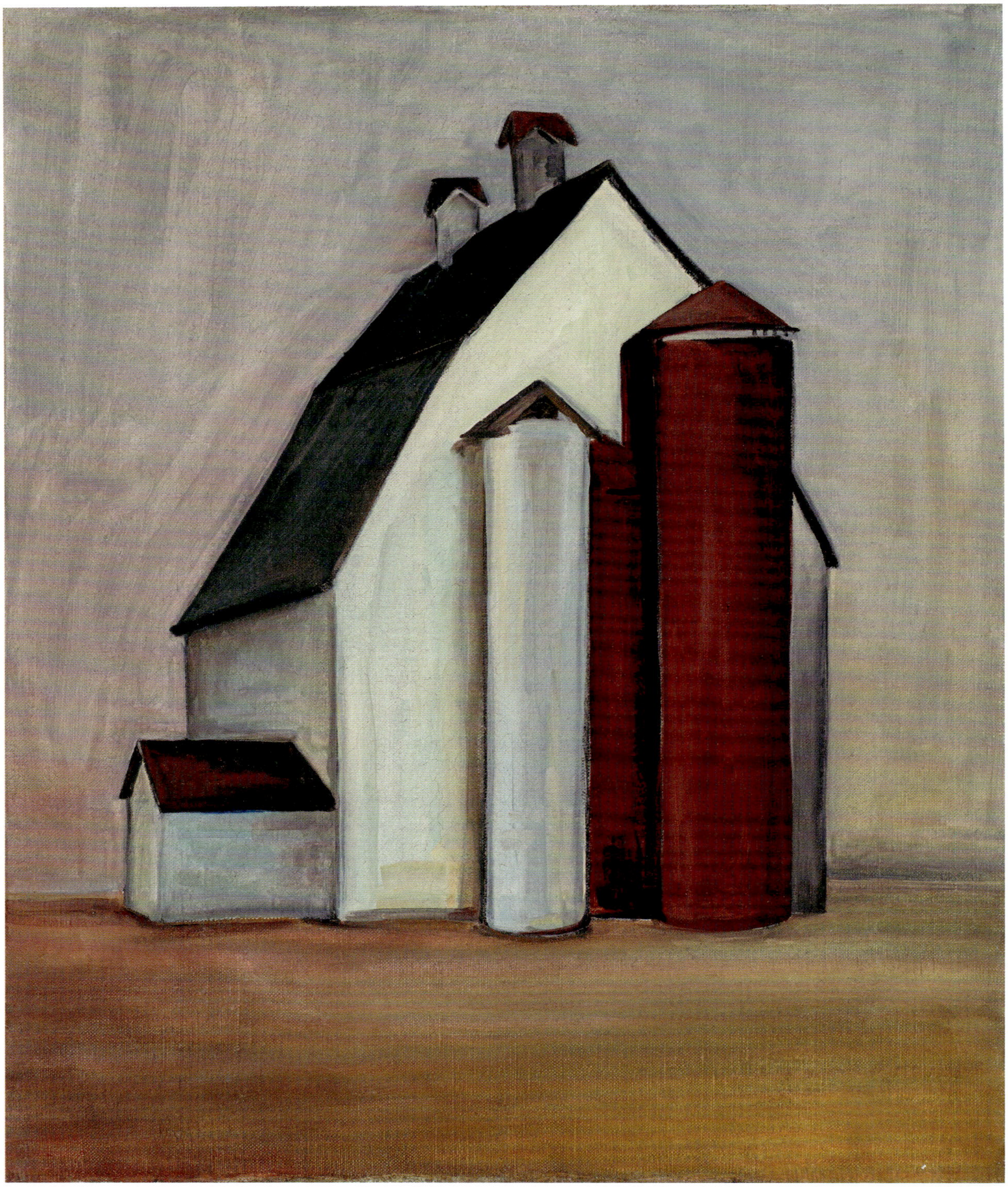

Beulah Loomis Hyde (1886–1983)
Untitled, ca. 1940–45
Oil on canvas
24 × 20 in.
Collection of Charles Henry Hyde III

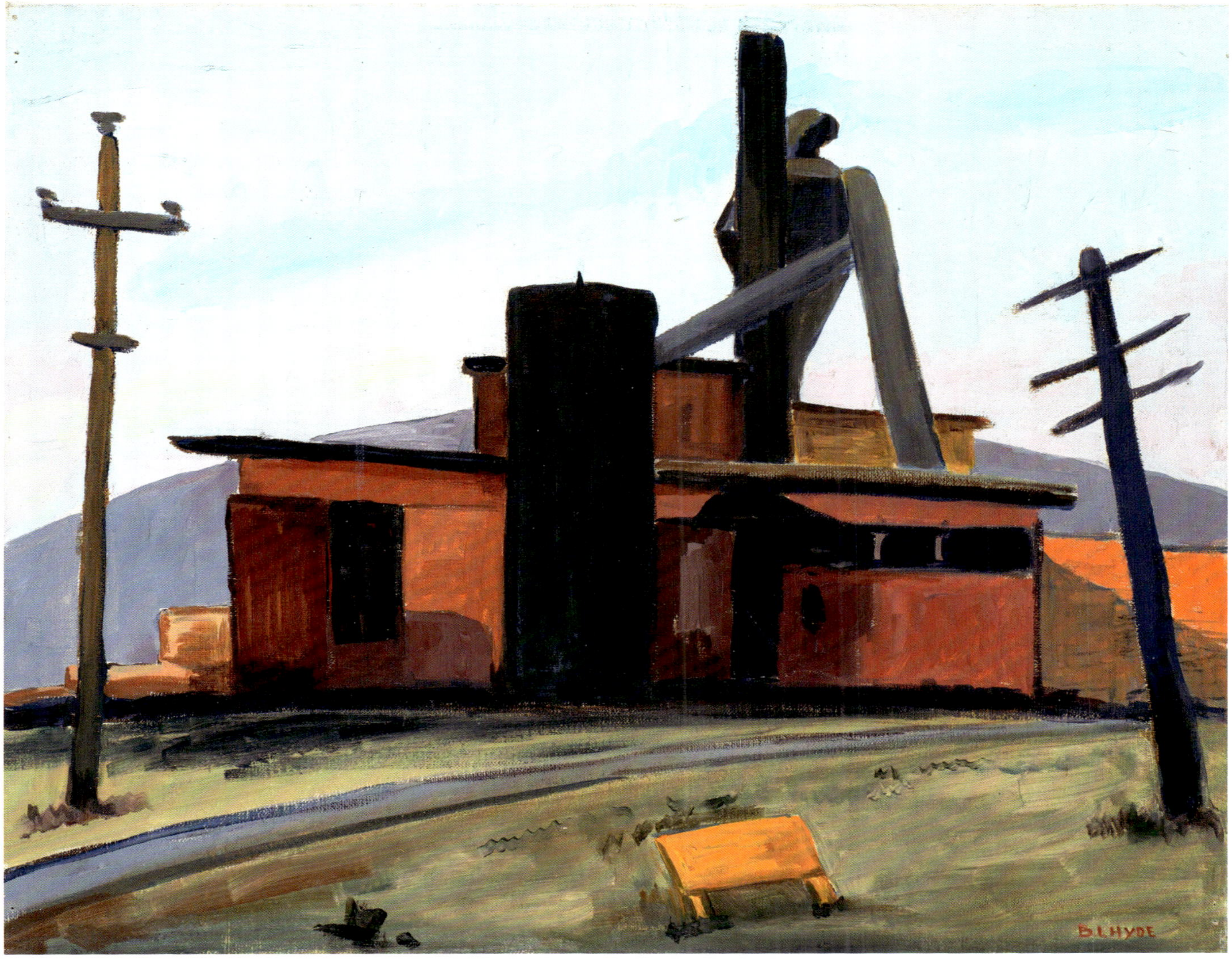

Beulah Loomis Hyde (1886–1983)
Untitled, ca. 1940–45
Oil on canvas
16 × 20 in.
Collection of Pamela Hyde Smith

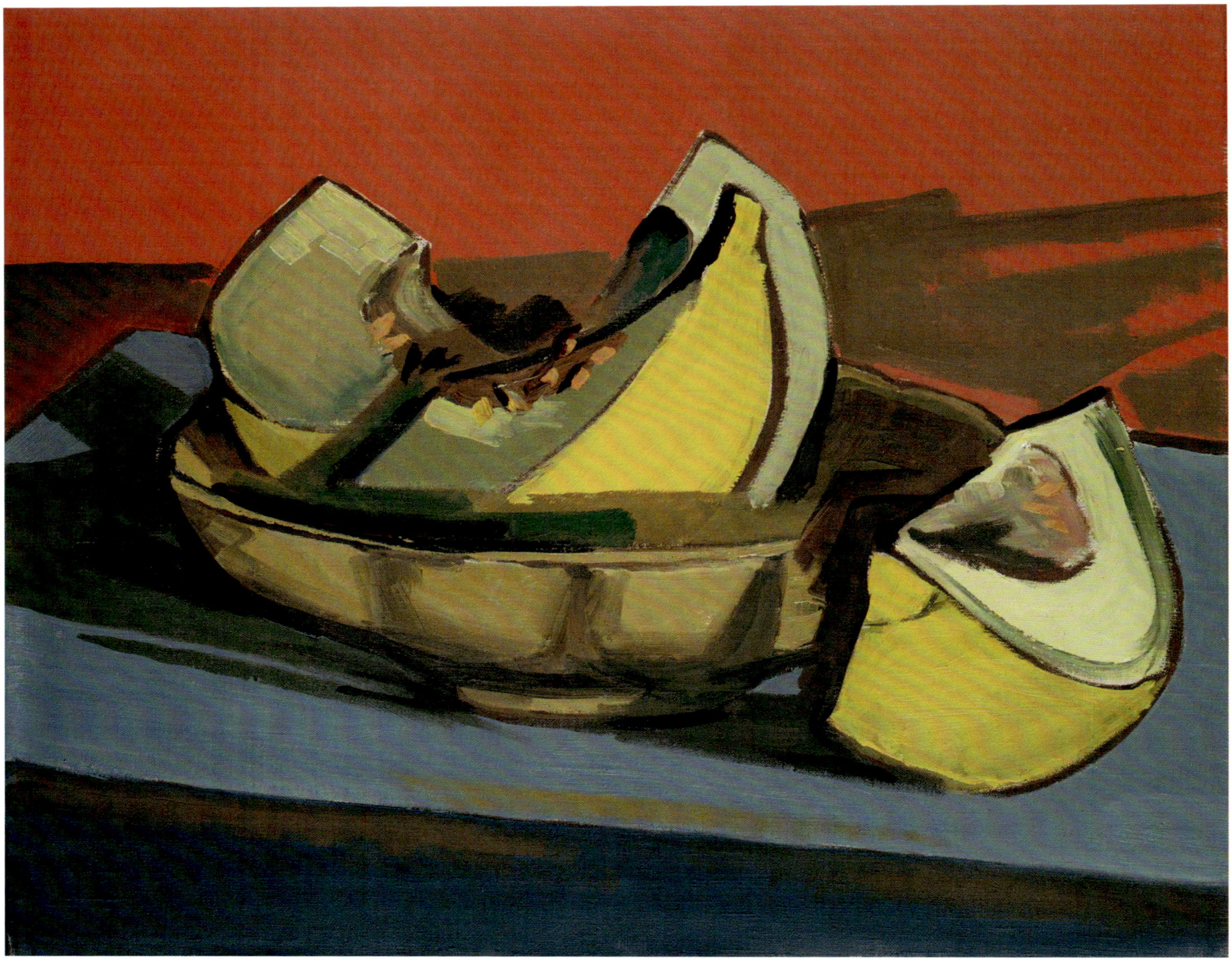

Beulah Loomis Hyde (1886–1983)
Untitled, ca. 1940–45
Oil on canvas
16 × 20 in.
Collection of Pamela Hyde Smith

Influenced by sources found in the works of Cezanne and Van Gogh, Hyde's extant still lifes emphasize the underlying geometric structure of the fruit. The sophisticated compositions and lush color palette continue her exploration into structure and form over literal representation.

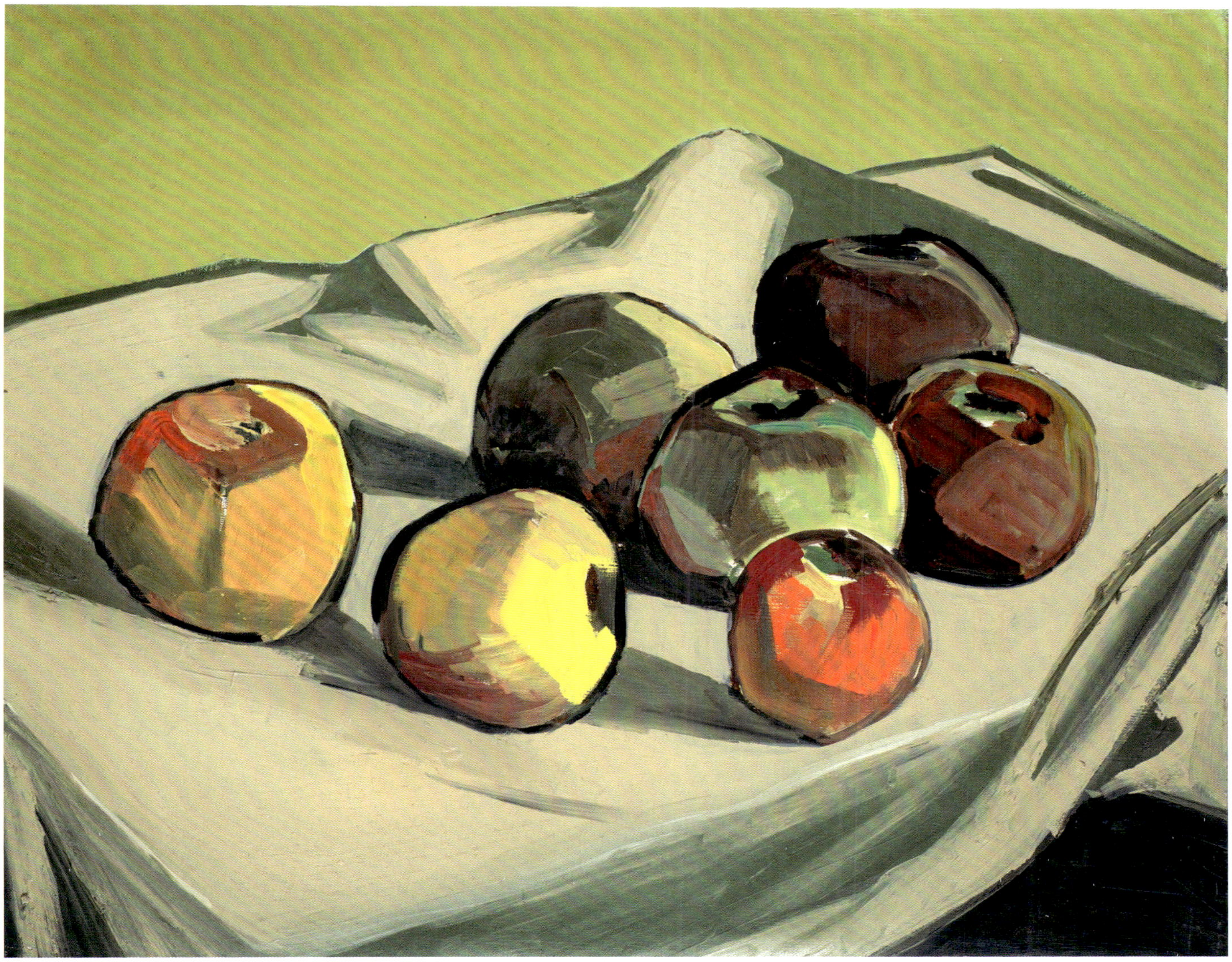

Beulah Loomis Hyde (1886–1983)
Untitled, ca. 1940–45
Oil on canvas
16 × 20 in.
Collection of Pamela Hyde Smith

Beulah Loomis Hyde (1886–1983)
Untitled, ca. 1940–45
Oil on canvas
16 × 20 in.
Collection of Pamela Hyde Smith

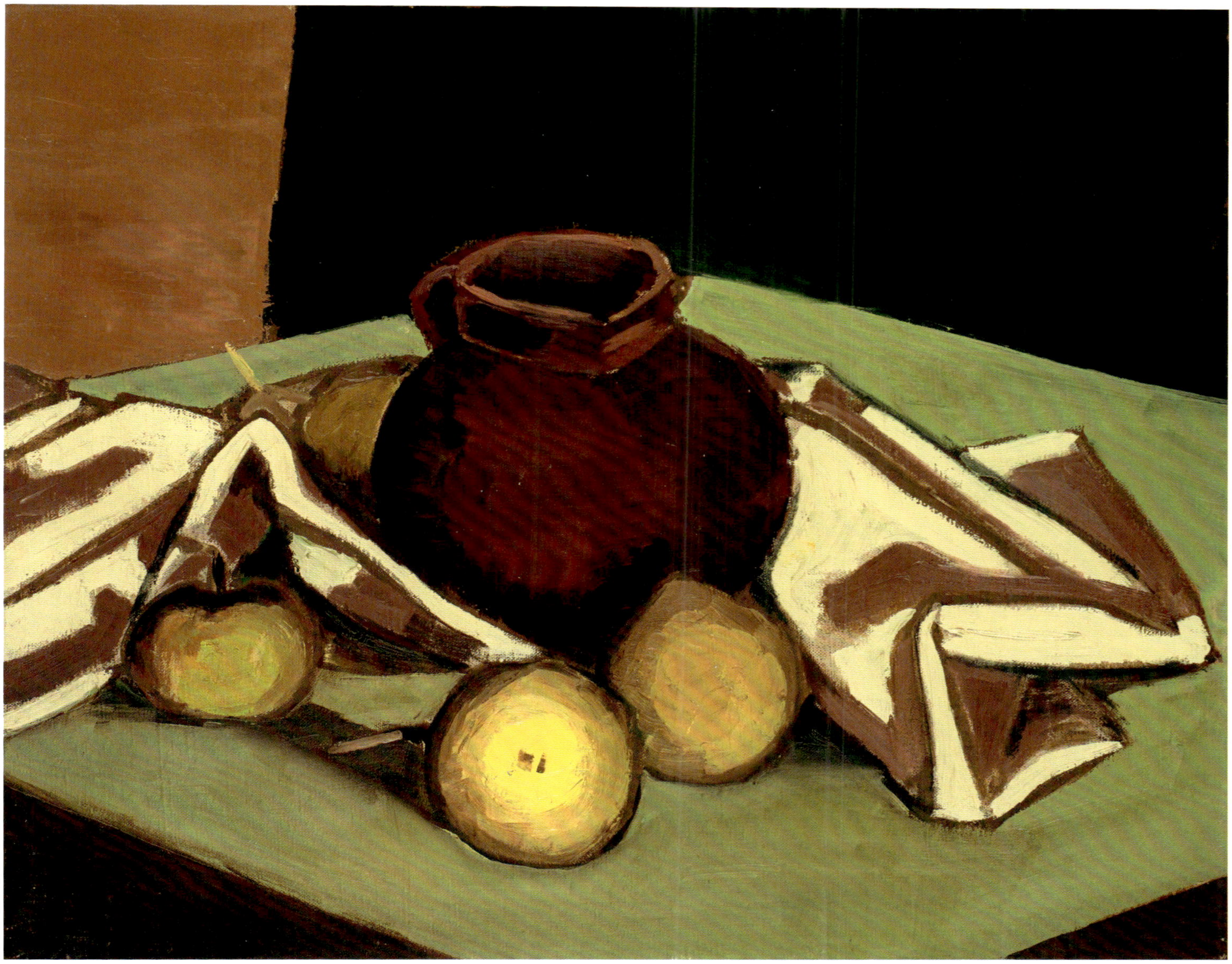

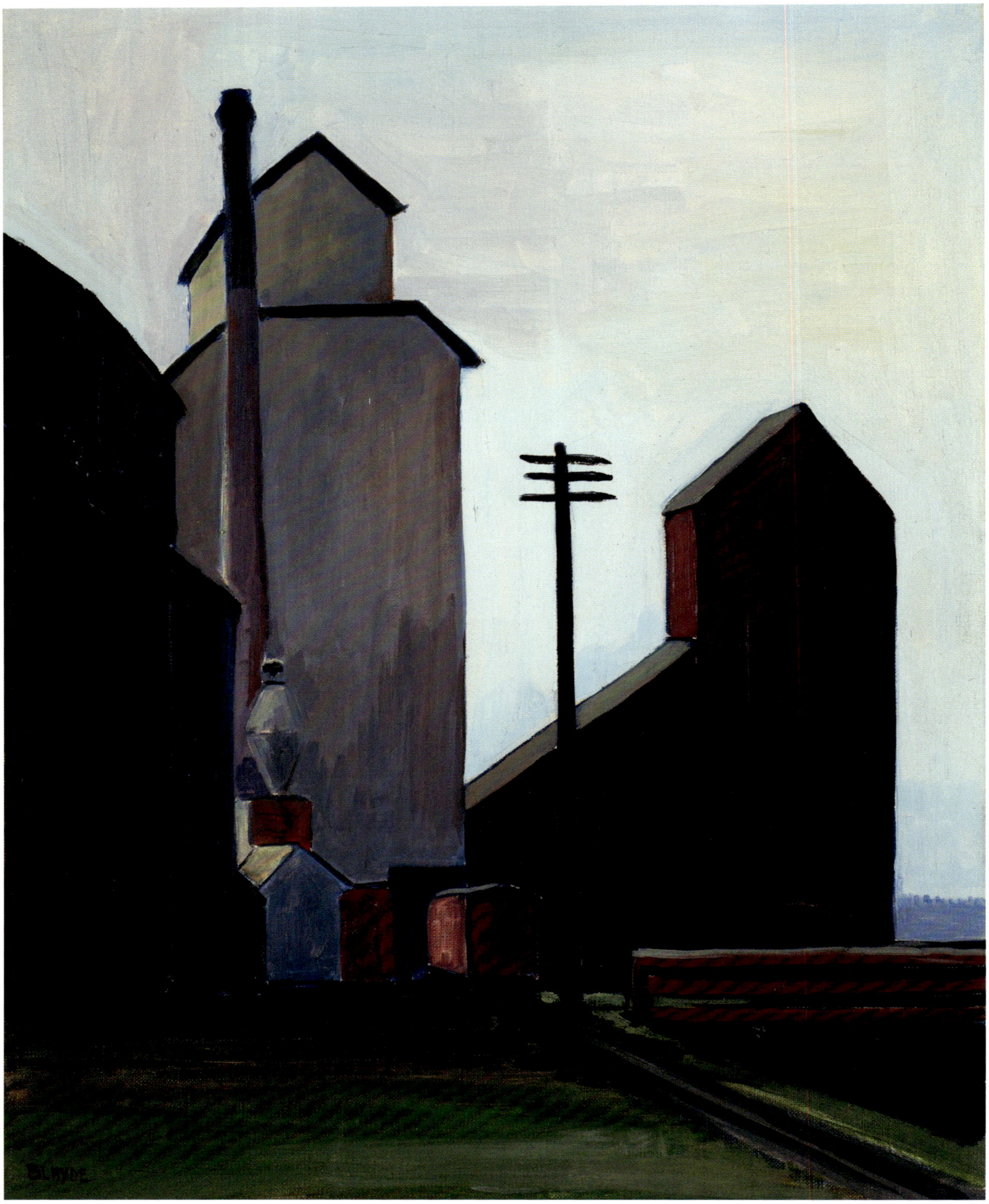

Beulah Loomis Hyde (1886–1983)
Untitled, ca. 1940–45
Oil on canvas
20 × 16 in.
Collection of Pamela Hyde Smith

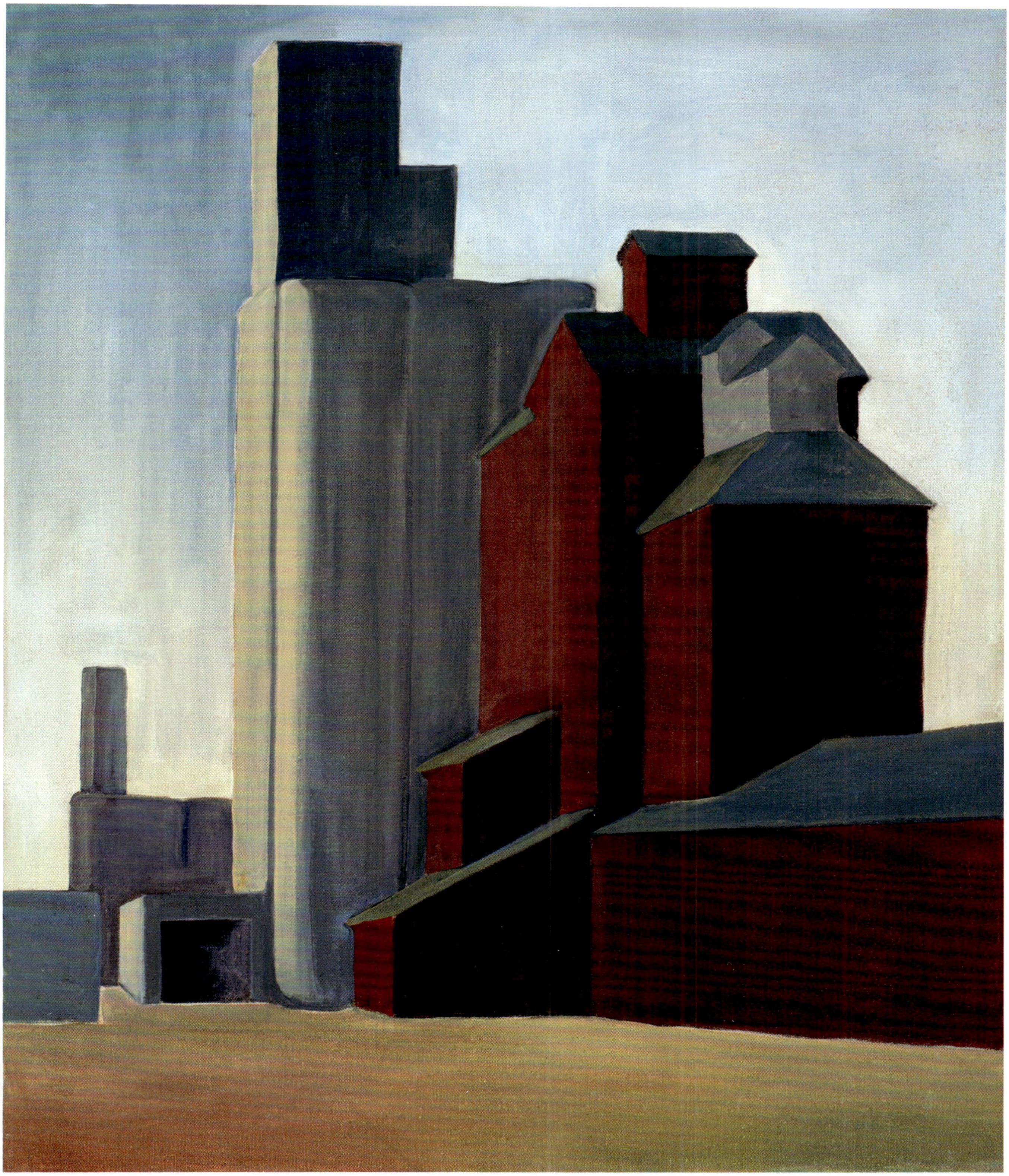

Beulah Loomis Hyde (1886–1983)
Untitled, ca. 1940–45
Oil on canvas
24 × 20 in.
Collection of Charles Henry Hyde III

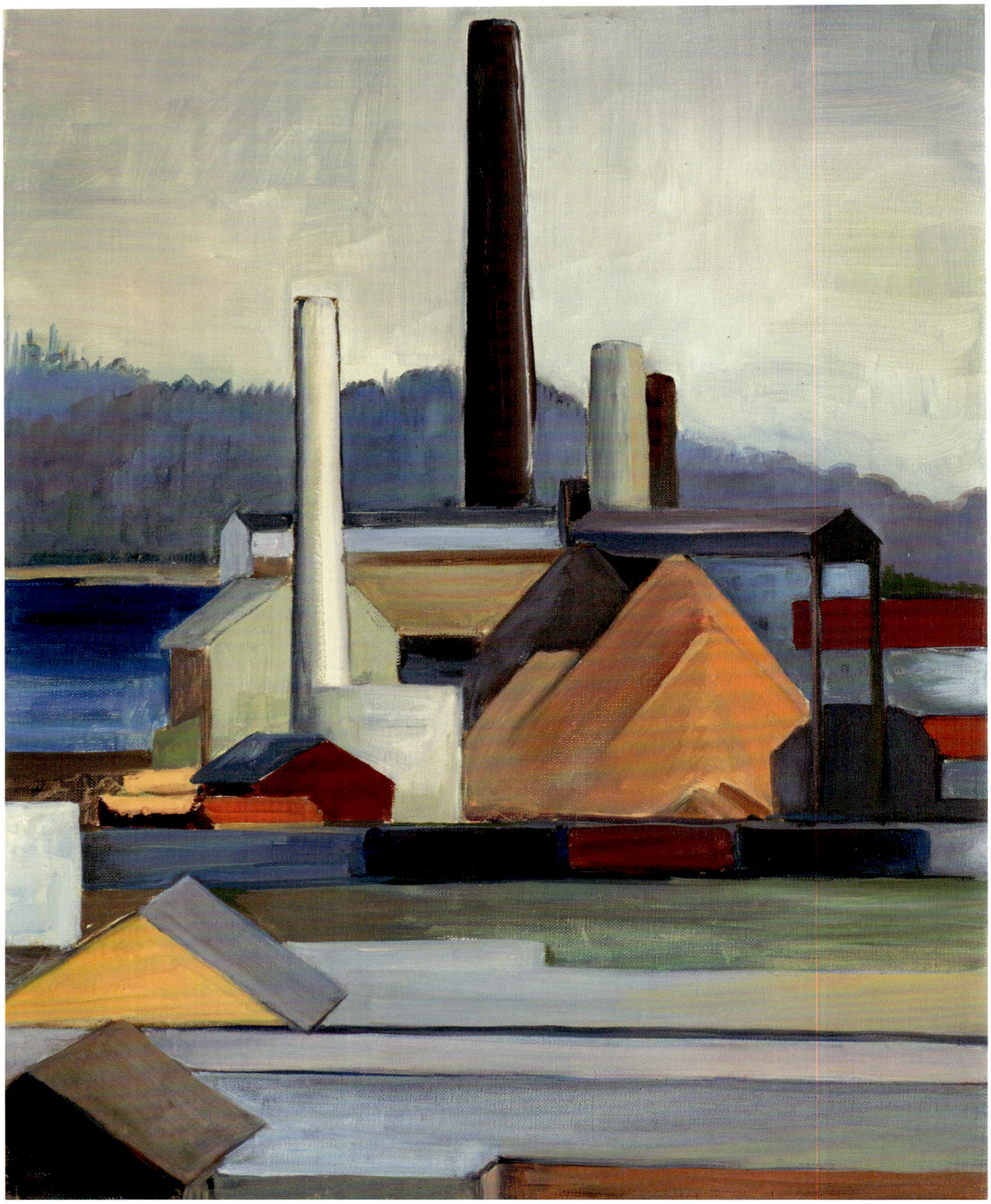

Beulah Loomis Hyde (1886–1983)
Untitled, ca. 1940–45
Oil on canvas
20 × 16 in.
Collection of Pamela Hyde Smith

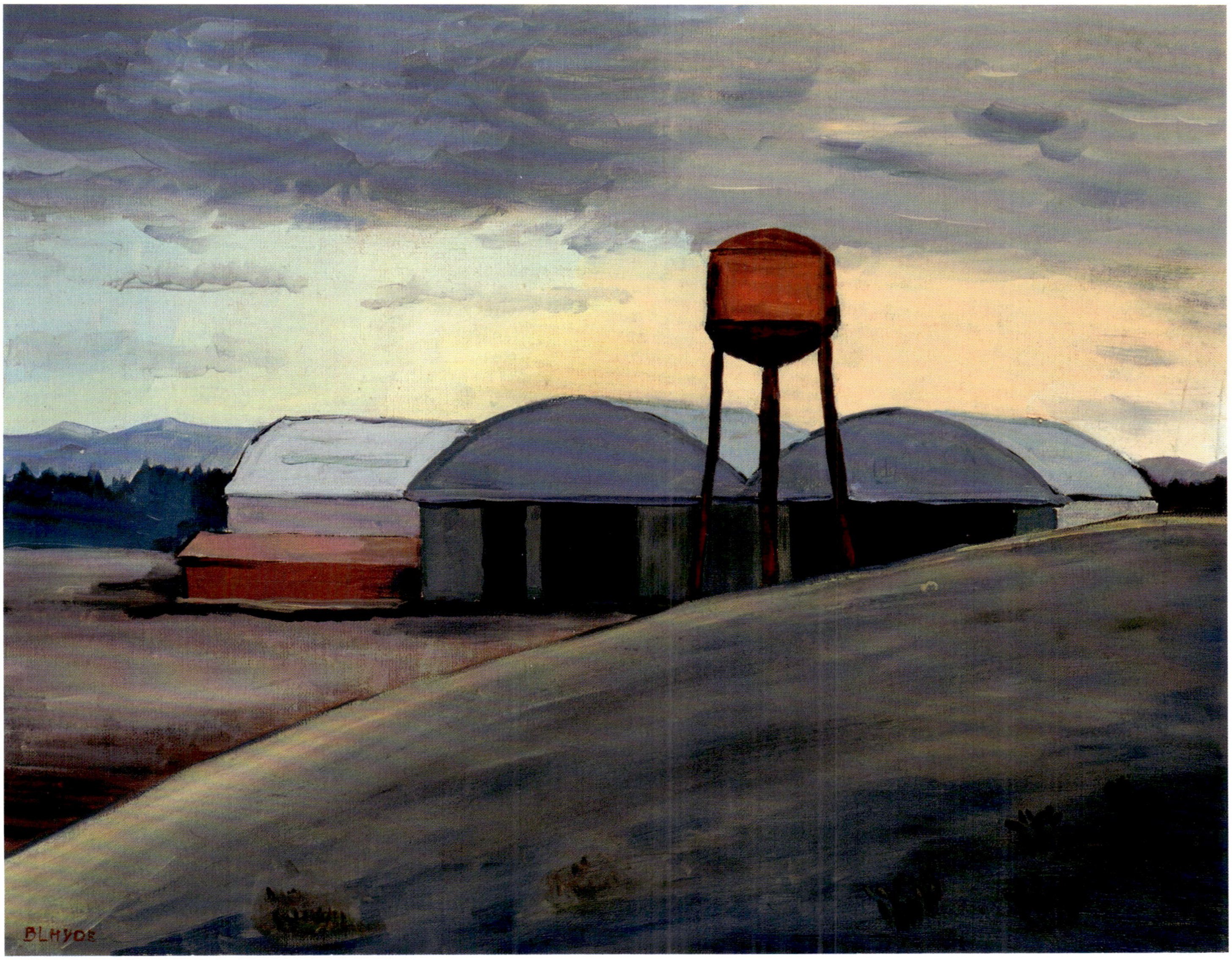

Beulah Loomis Hyde (1886–1983)
Untitled, ca. 1940–45
Oil on canvas
16 × 20 in.
Collection of Pamela Hyde Smith

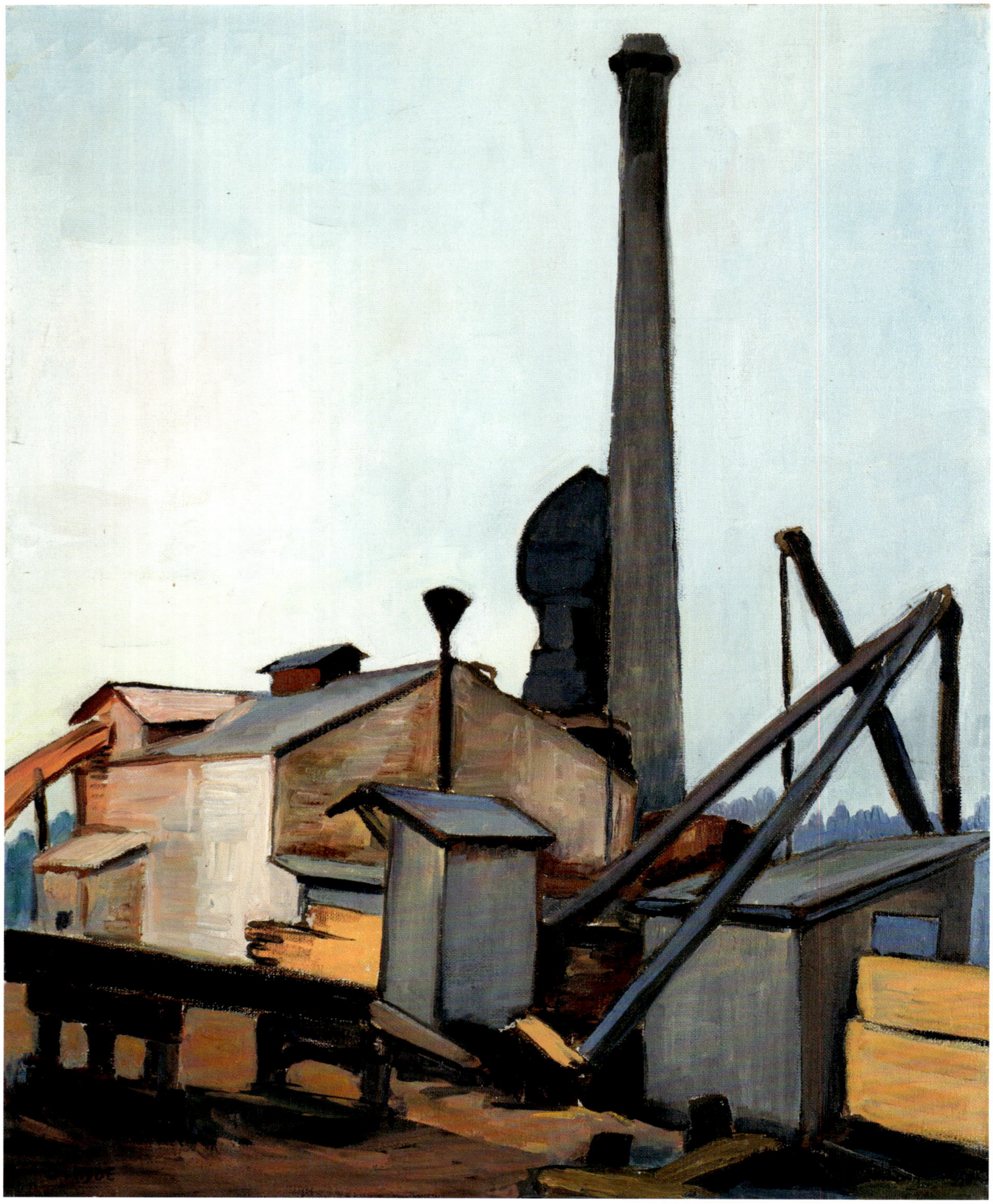

Beulah Loomis Hyde (1886–1983)
Untitled, ca. 1940–45
Oil on canvas
20 × 16 in.
Collection of Pamela Hyde Smith

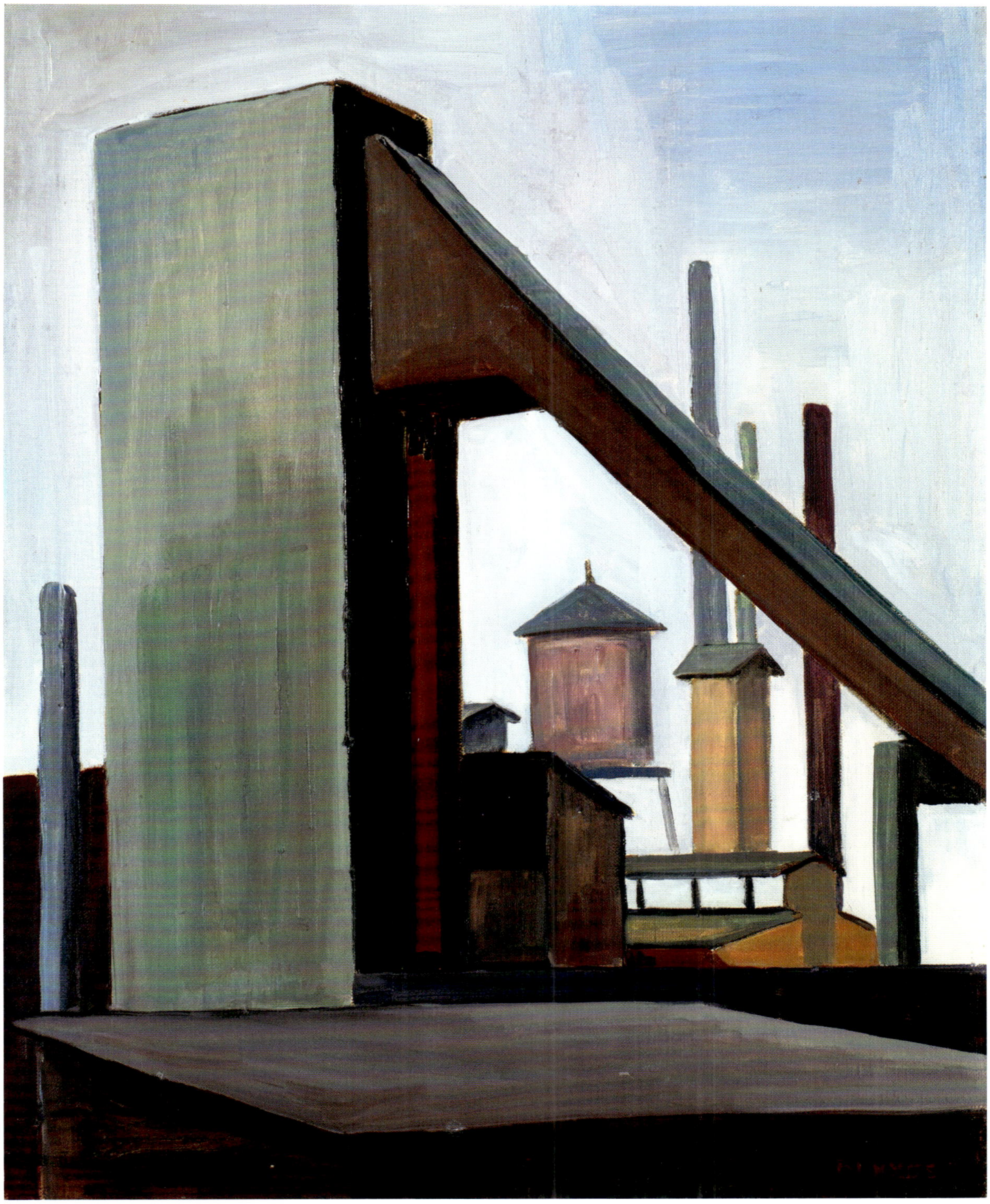

Beulah Loomis Hyde (1886–1983)
Untitled, ca. 1940–45
Oil on canvas
20 × 16 in.
Collection of Pamela Hyde Smith

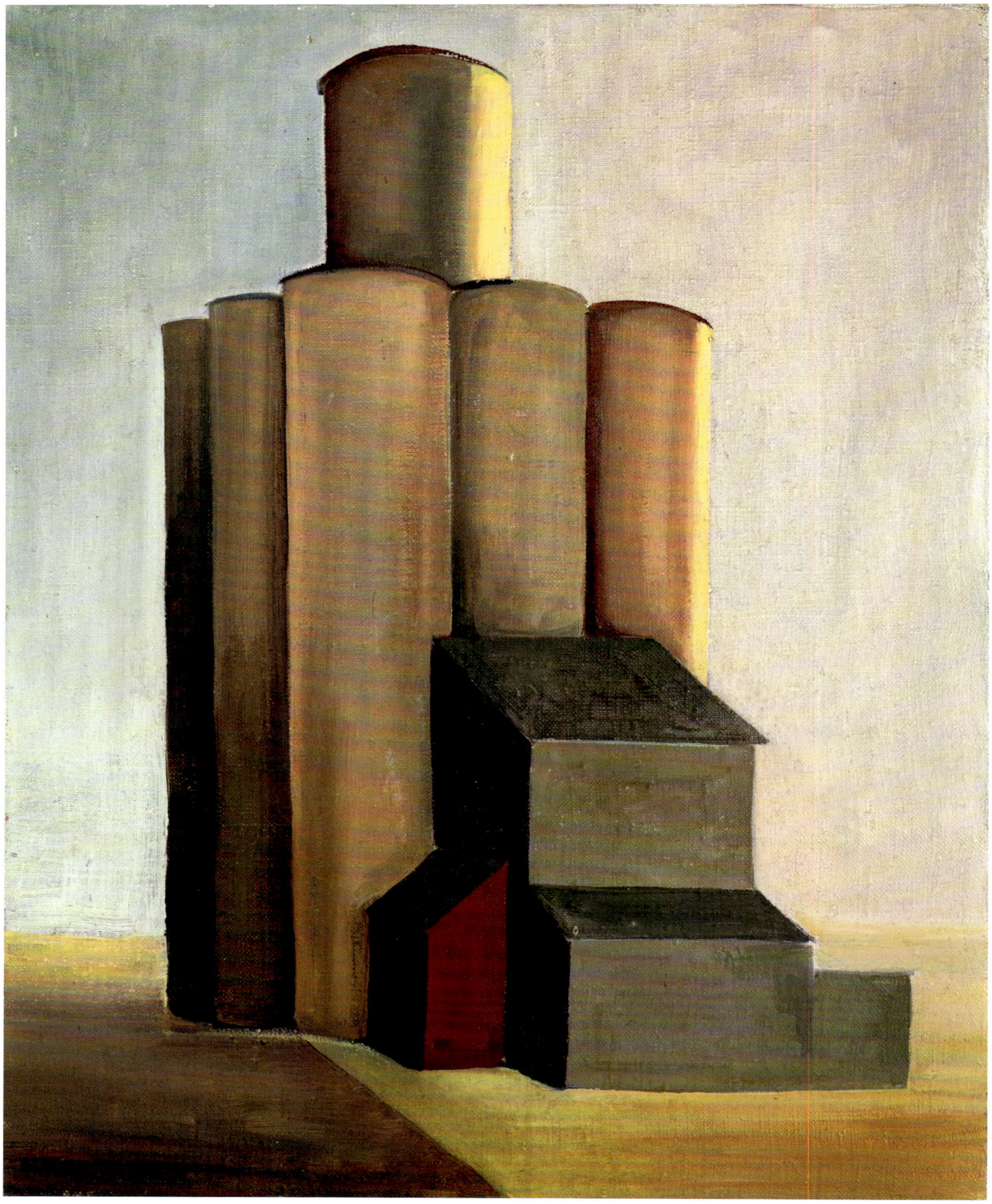

Beulah Loomis Hyde (1886–1983)
Untitled, ca. 1940–45
Oil on canvas
20¼ × 16¼ in.
Collection of Pamela Hyde Smith

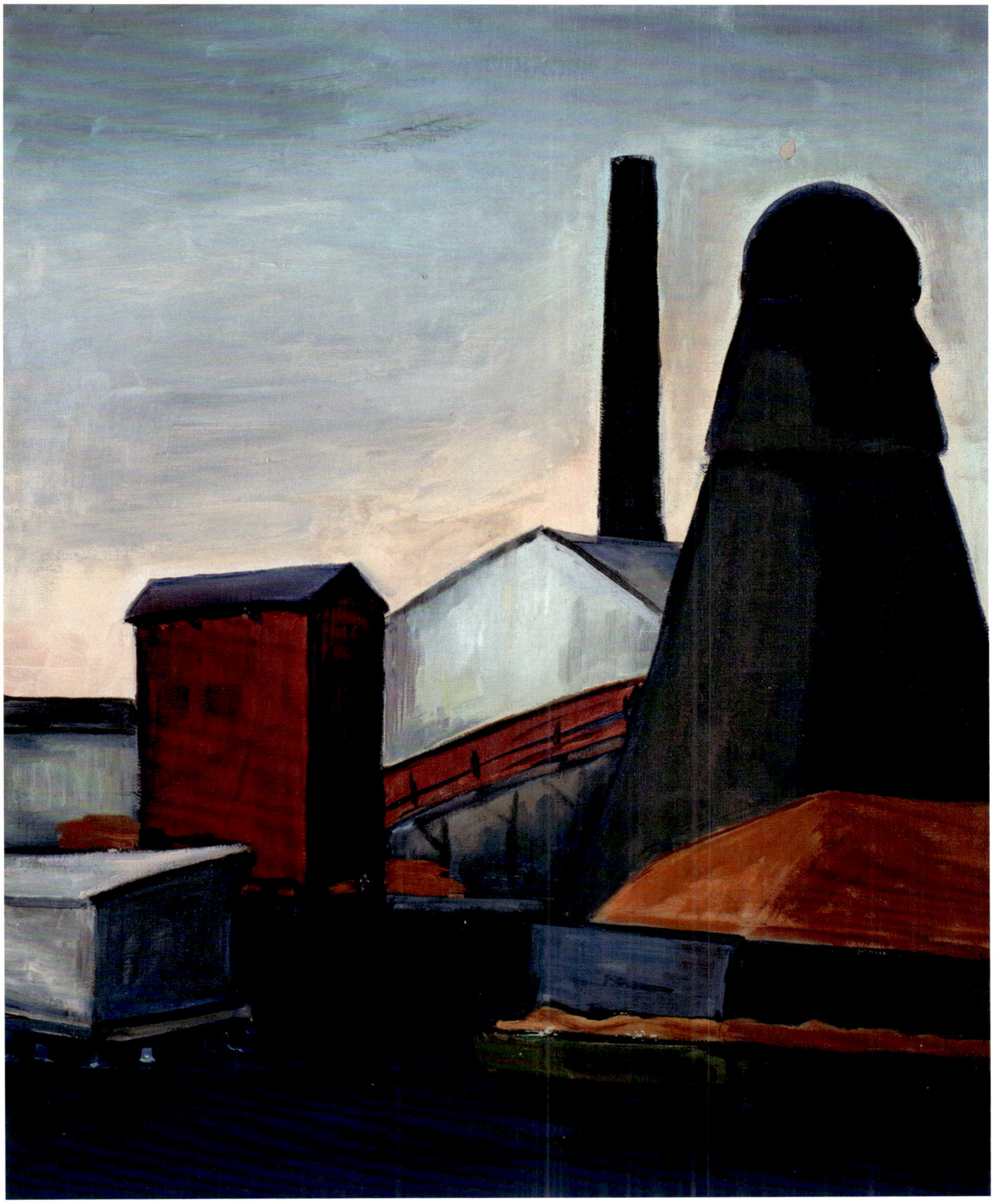

Beulah Loomis Hyde (1886–1983)
Untitled, ca. 1940–45
Oil on canvas
20 × 16 in.
Collection of Pamela Hyde Smith

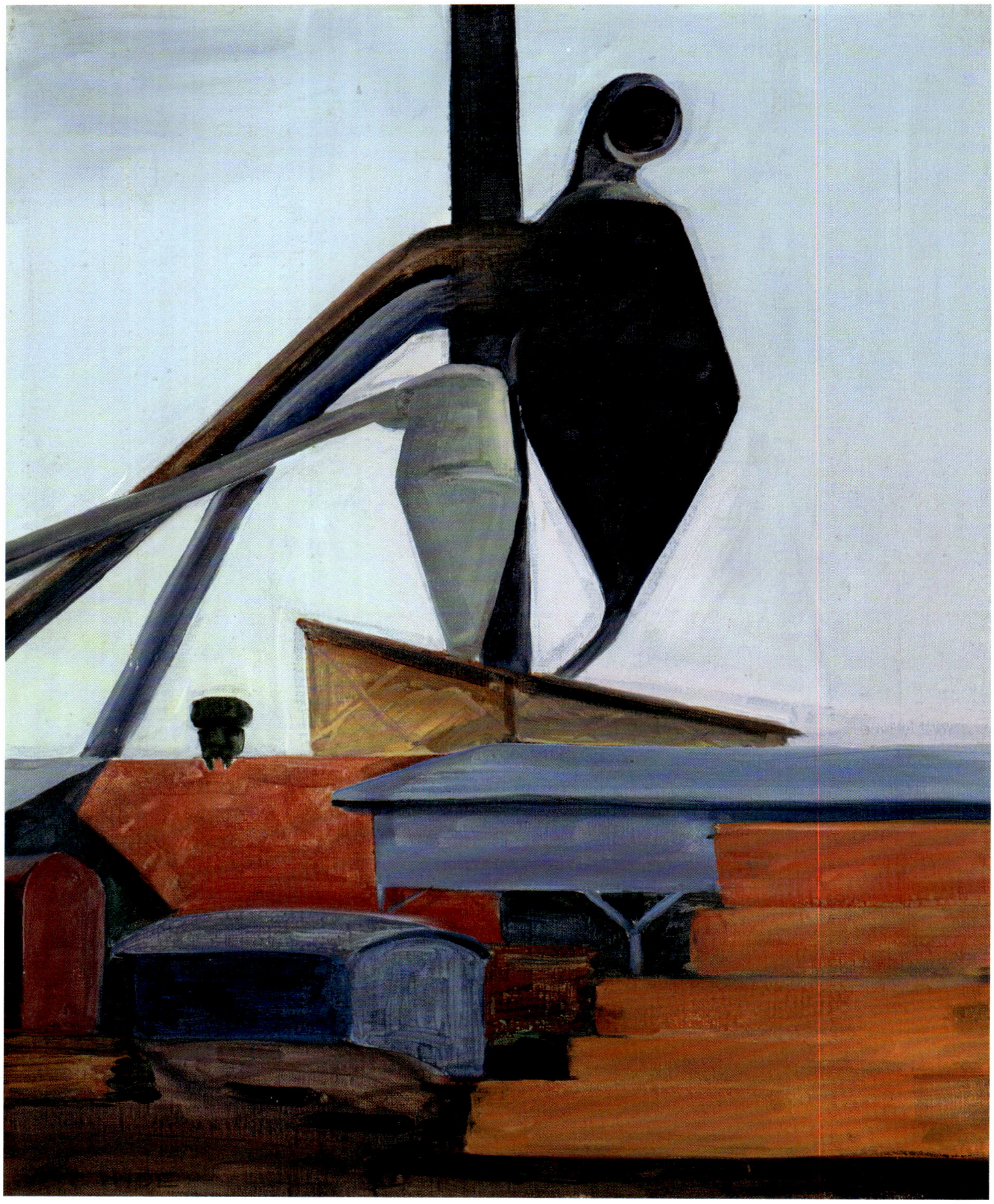

Beulah Loomis Hyde (1886–1983)
Untitled, ca. 1940–45
Oil on canvas
20 × 16 in.
Collection of Pamela Hyde Smith

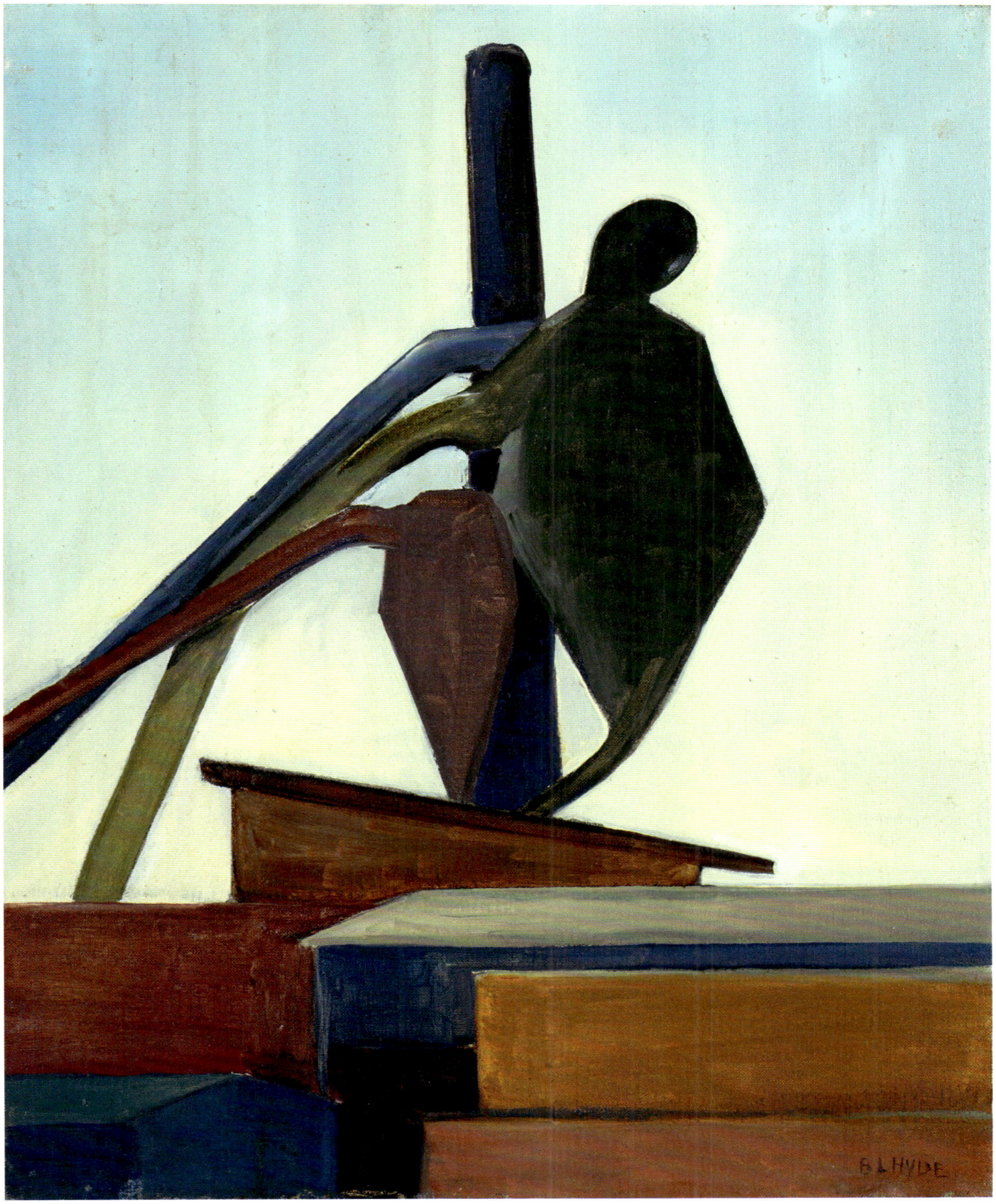

Beulah Loomis Hyde (1886–1983)
Untitled, ca. 1940–45
Oil on canvas
20 × 16 in.
Collection of Pamela Hyde Smith

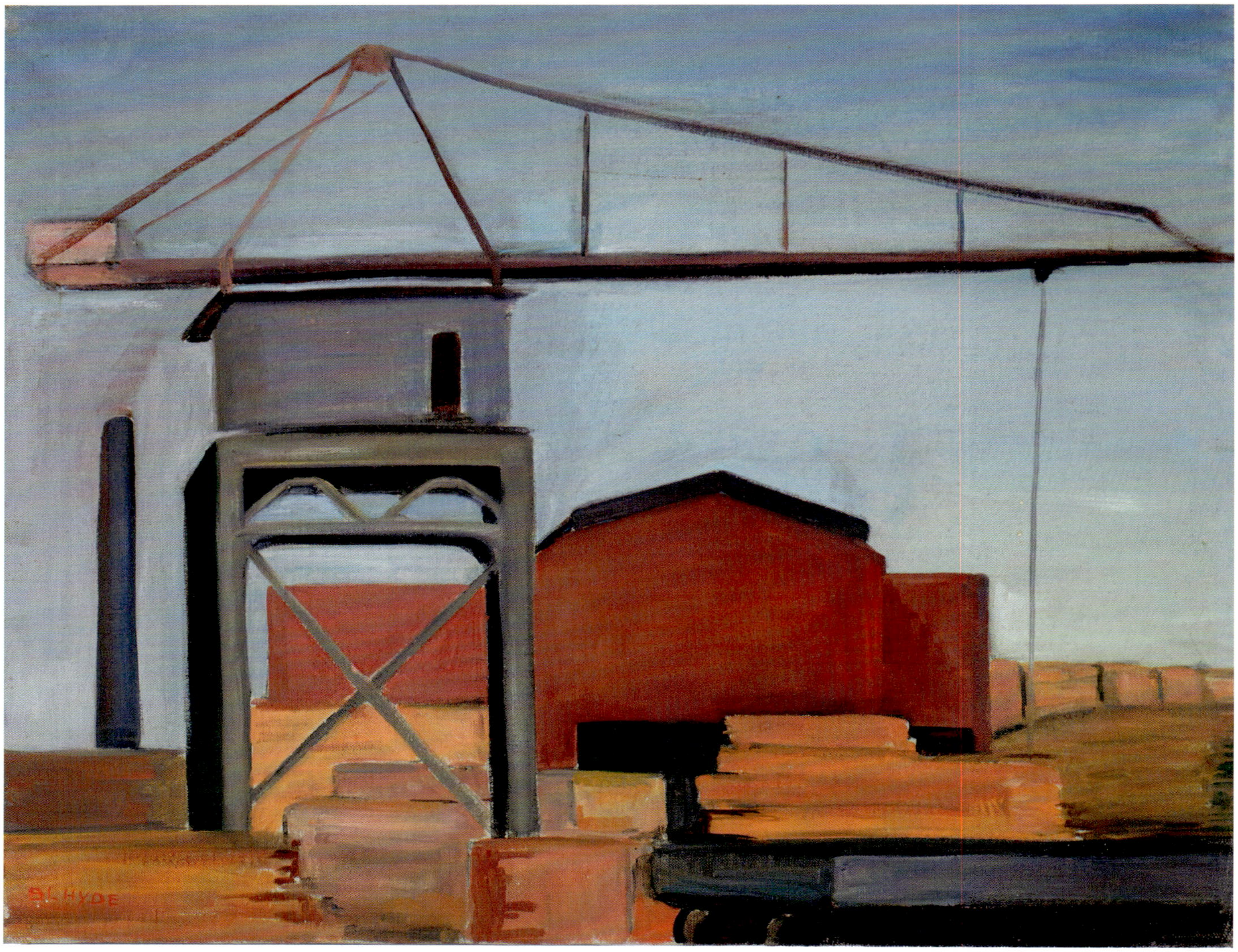

Beulah Loomis Hyde (1886–1983)
Untitled (Cheney Lumber Co., Tacoma), ca. 1940–45
Oil on canvas
16 × 20 in.
Collection of Allison Hyde and Jake Nellis

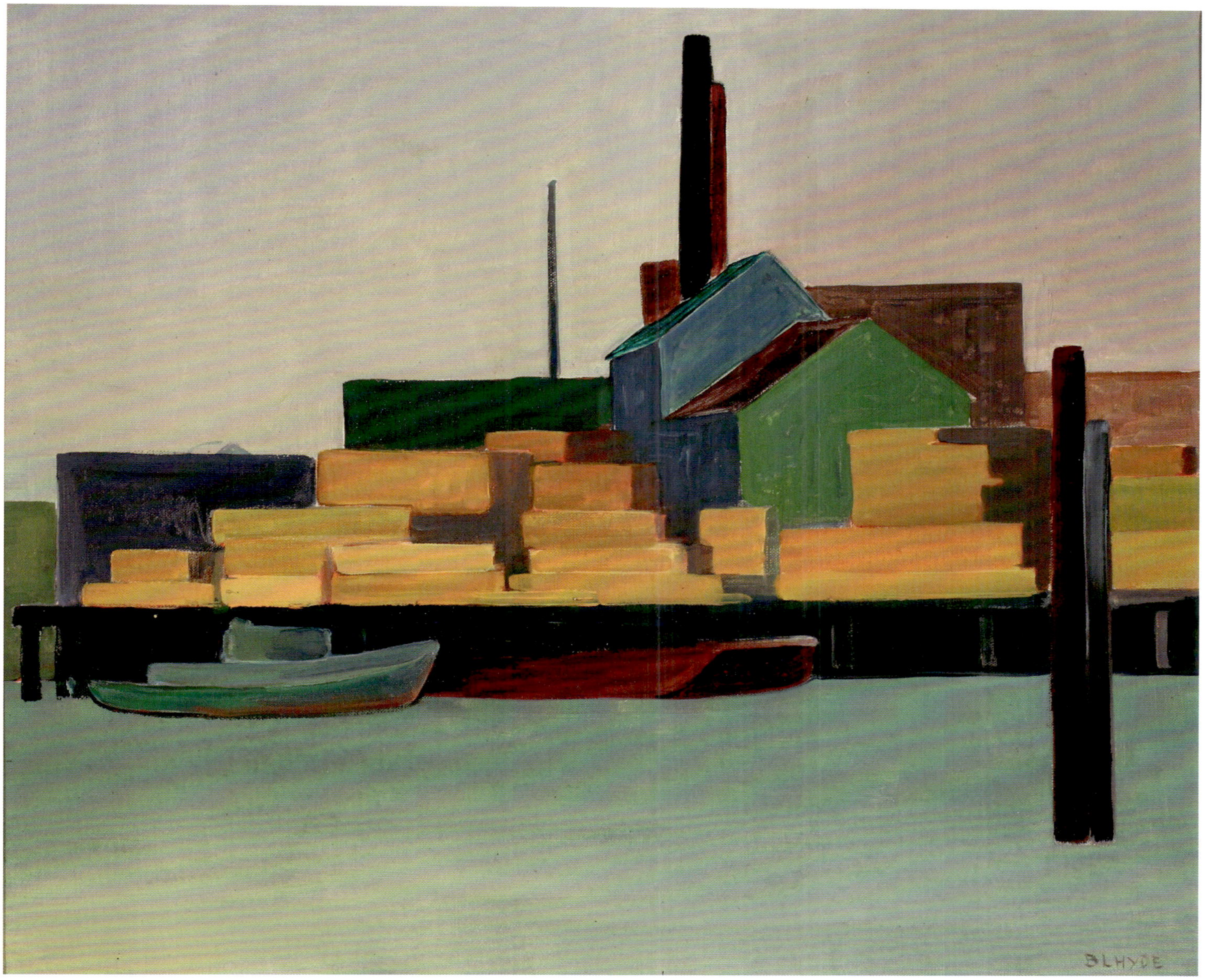

Beulah Loomis Hyde (1886–1983)
Untitled, ca. 1945–50
Oil on canvas
Sight: 19⅝ × 23½ in. (49.8 × 59.7 cm)
Tacoma Art Museum, Gift of William B. Hyde, 1999.8

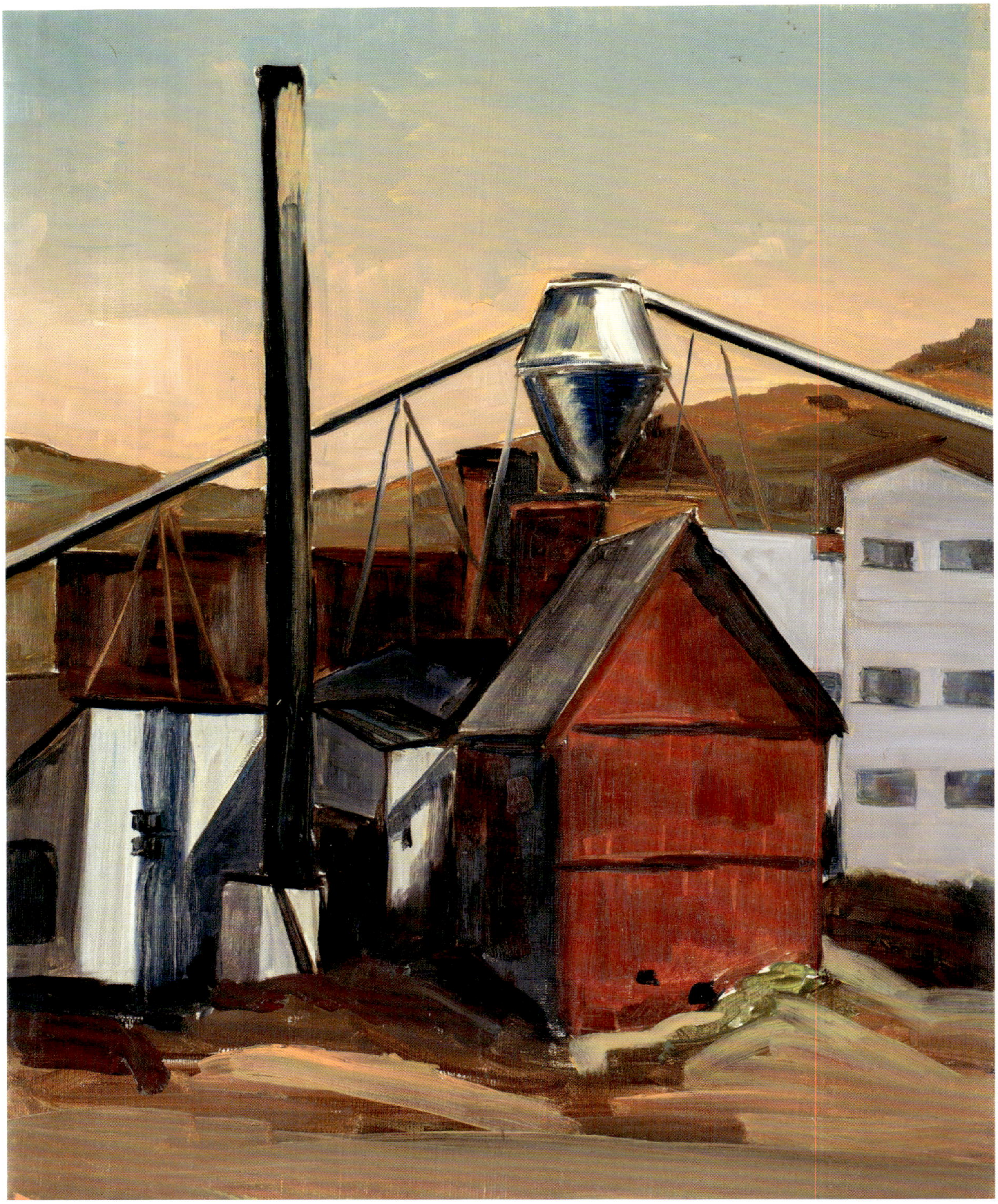

Beulah Loomis Hyde (1886–1983)
Untitled, ca. 1940–45
Oil on canvas
20 × 16 in.
Collection of Pamela Hyde Smith

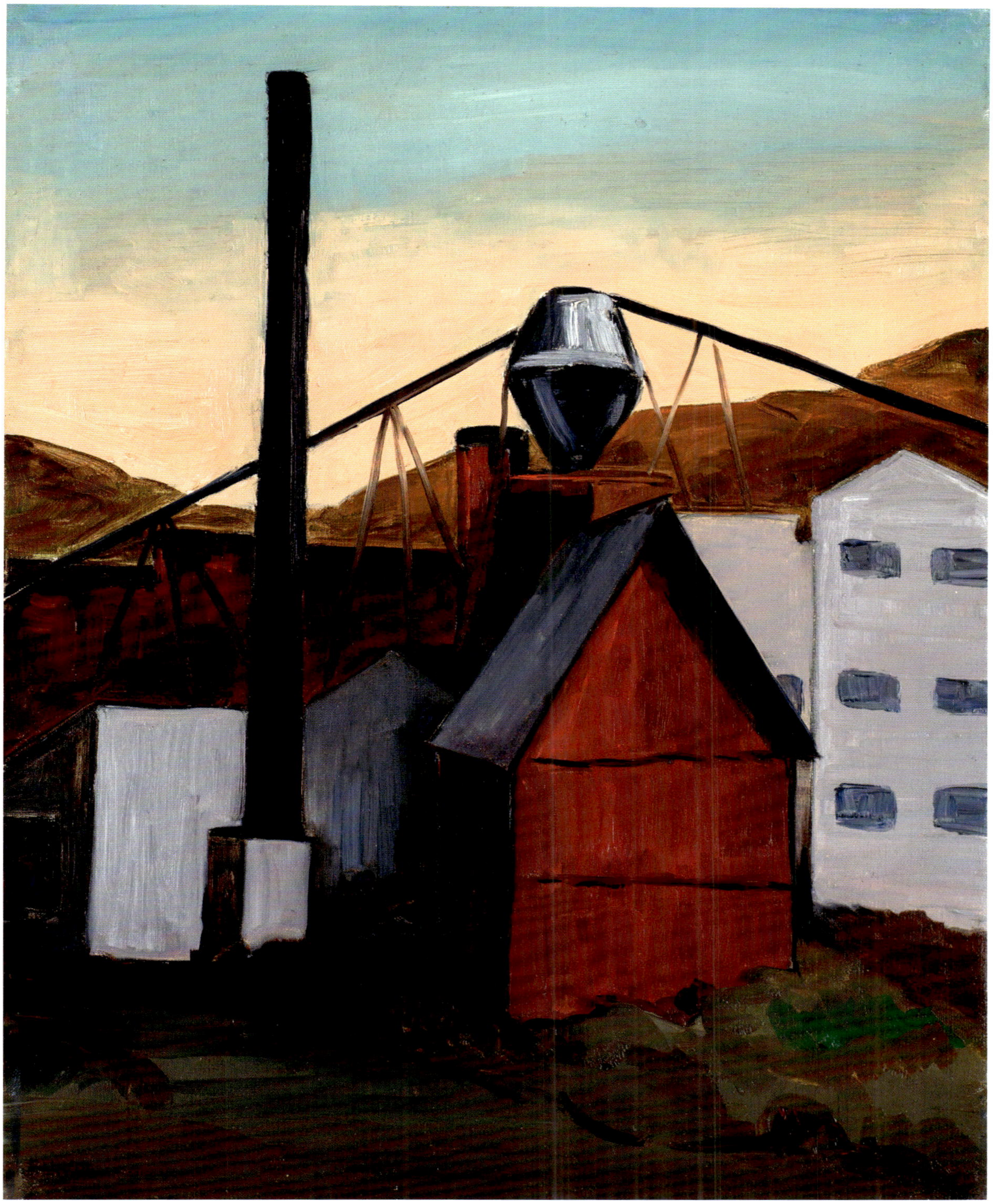

Beulah Loomis Hyde (1886–1983)
Untitled, ca. 1940–45
Oil on canvas
20 × 16 in.
Collection of Pamela Hyde Smith

Hyde used the exact same location to depict the subjects with two variant horizontal light sources such as sunrise and sunset. This allowed her to alter the atmospheric mood of the forms and emphasize different aspects of the underlying geometry of the structures.

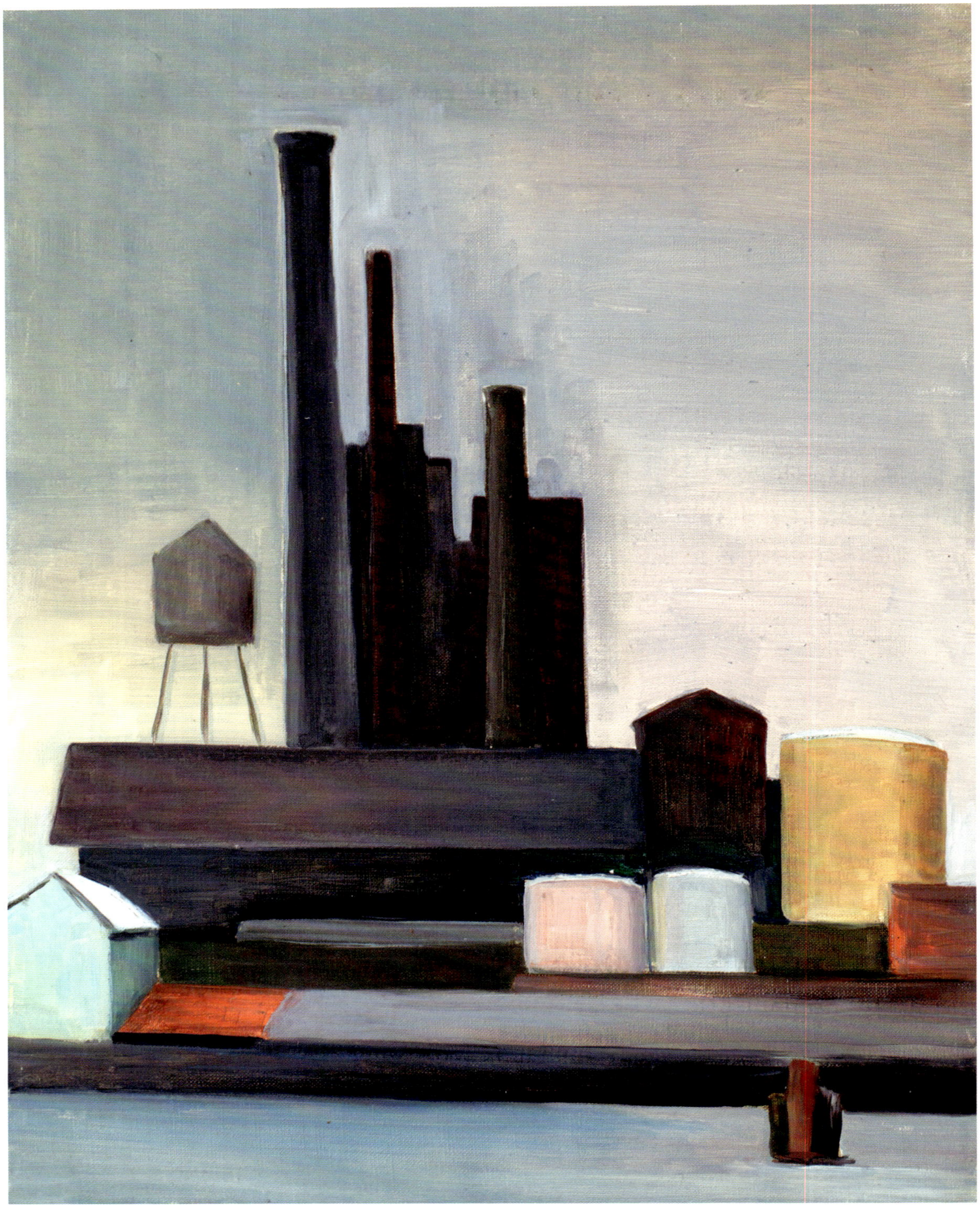

Beulah Loomis Hyde (1886–1983)
Untitled, ca. 1940–45
Oil on canvas
20 × 16 in.
Collection of Pamela Hyde Smith

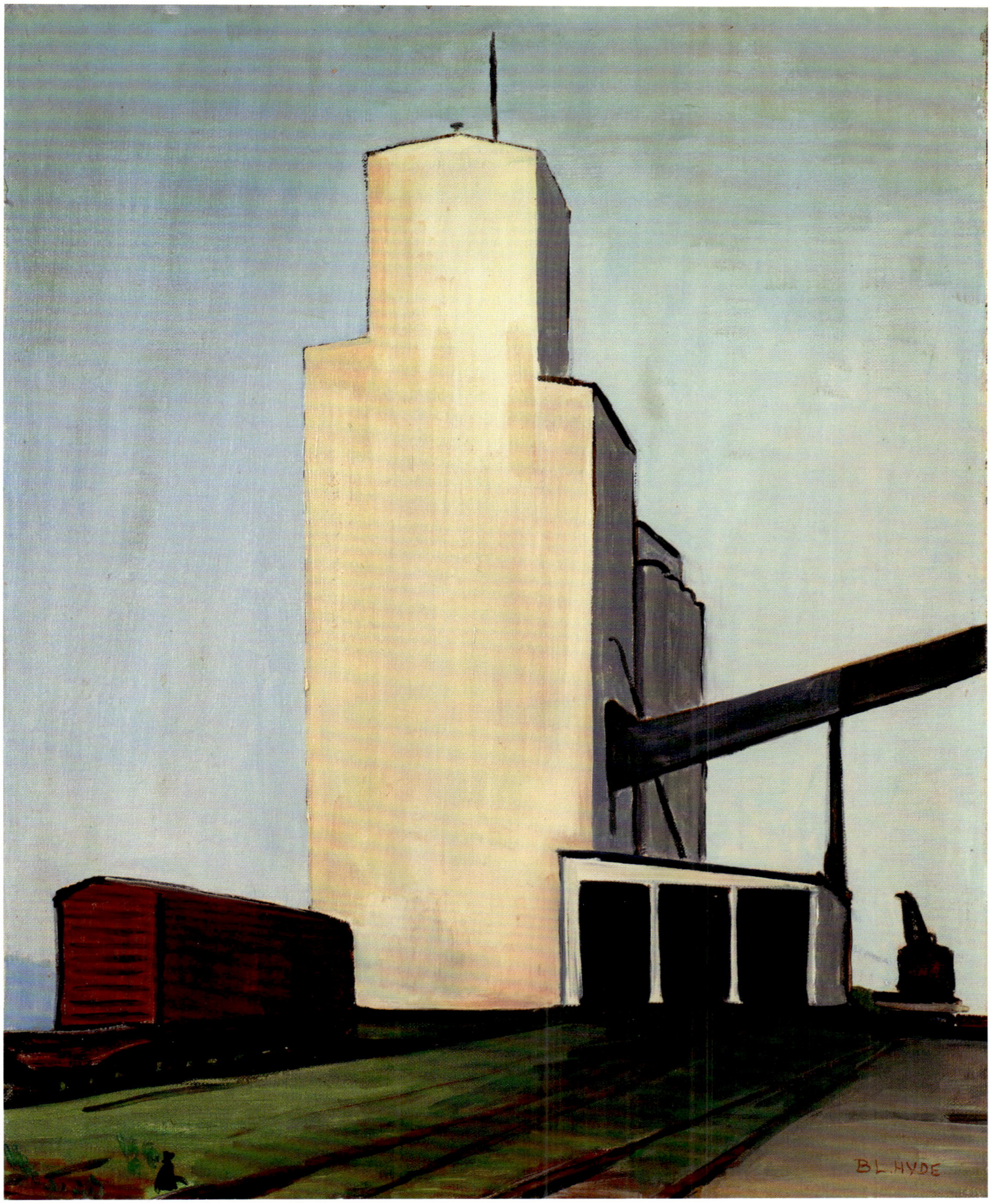

Beulah Loomis Hyde (1886–1983)
Port of Tacoma, ca. 1940–45
Oil on canvas
20 × 16 in.
Collection of Catherine S. Ebert

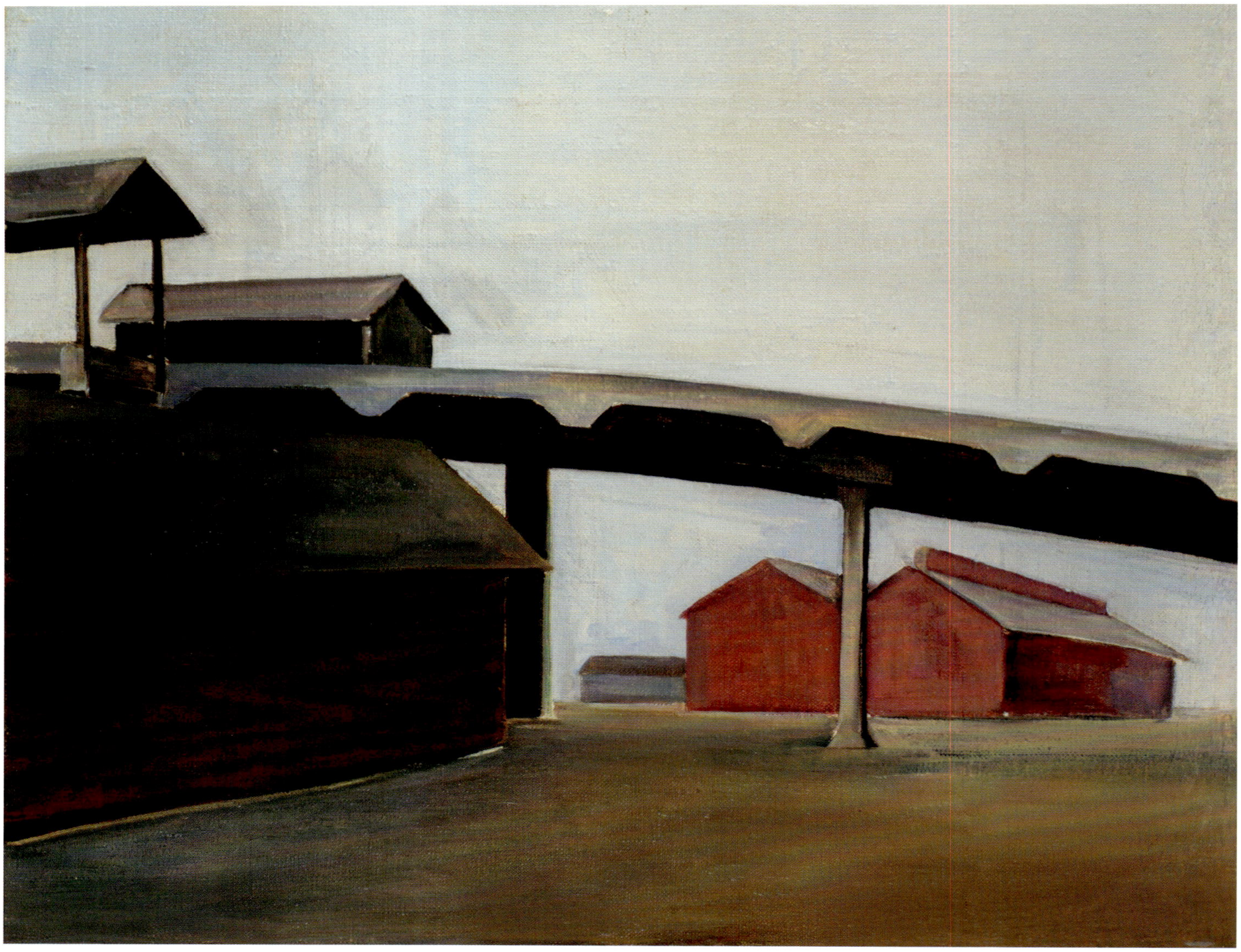

Beulah Loomis Hyde (1886–1983)
Bridge, ca. 1940–45
Oil on canvas
16¼ × 20¼ in.
Collection of Pamela Hyde Smith

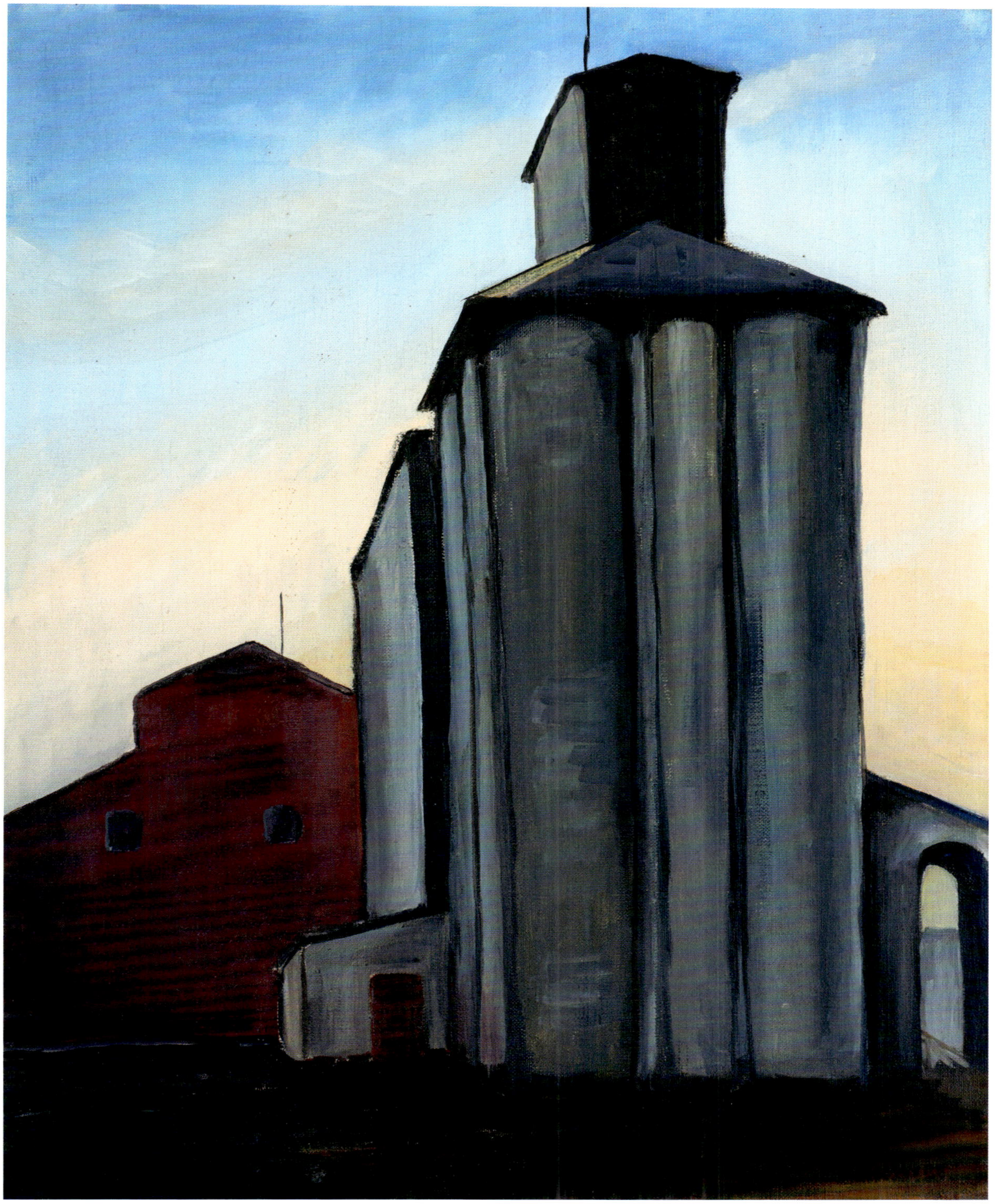

Beulah Loomis Hyde (1886–1983)
Untitled, ca. 1940–45
Oil on canvas
20 × 16 in.
Collection of Pamela Hyde Smith

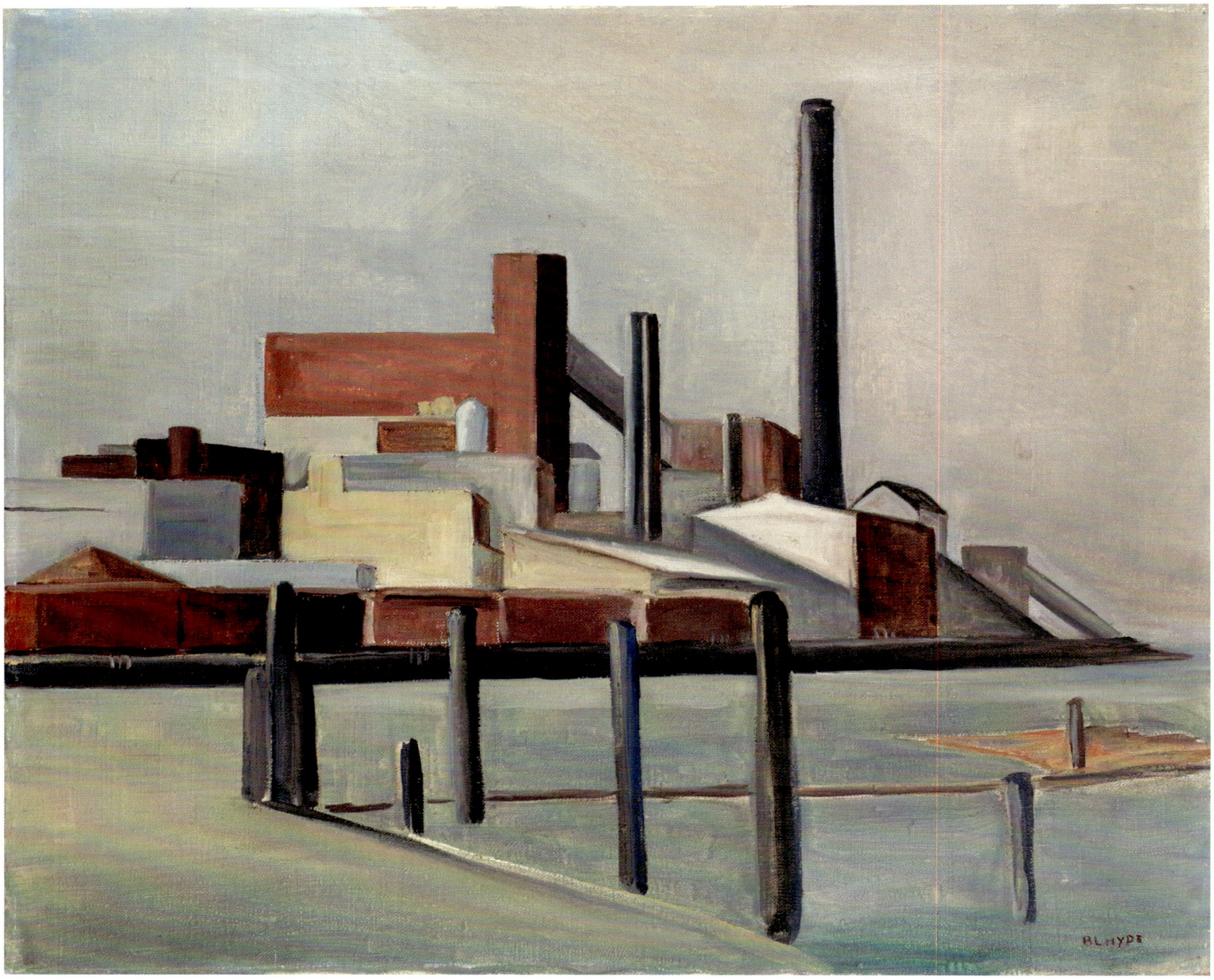

Beulah Loomis Hyde (1886–1983)
Waterfront, ca. 1940–45
Oil on canvas
20 × 24 in.
Collection of Allison Hyde and Jake Nellis

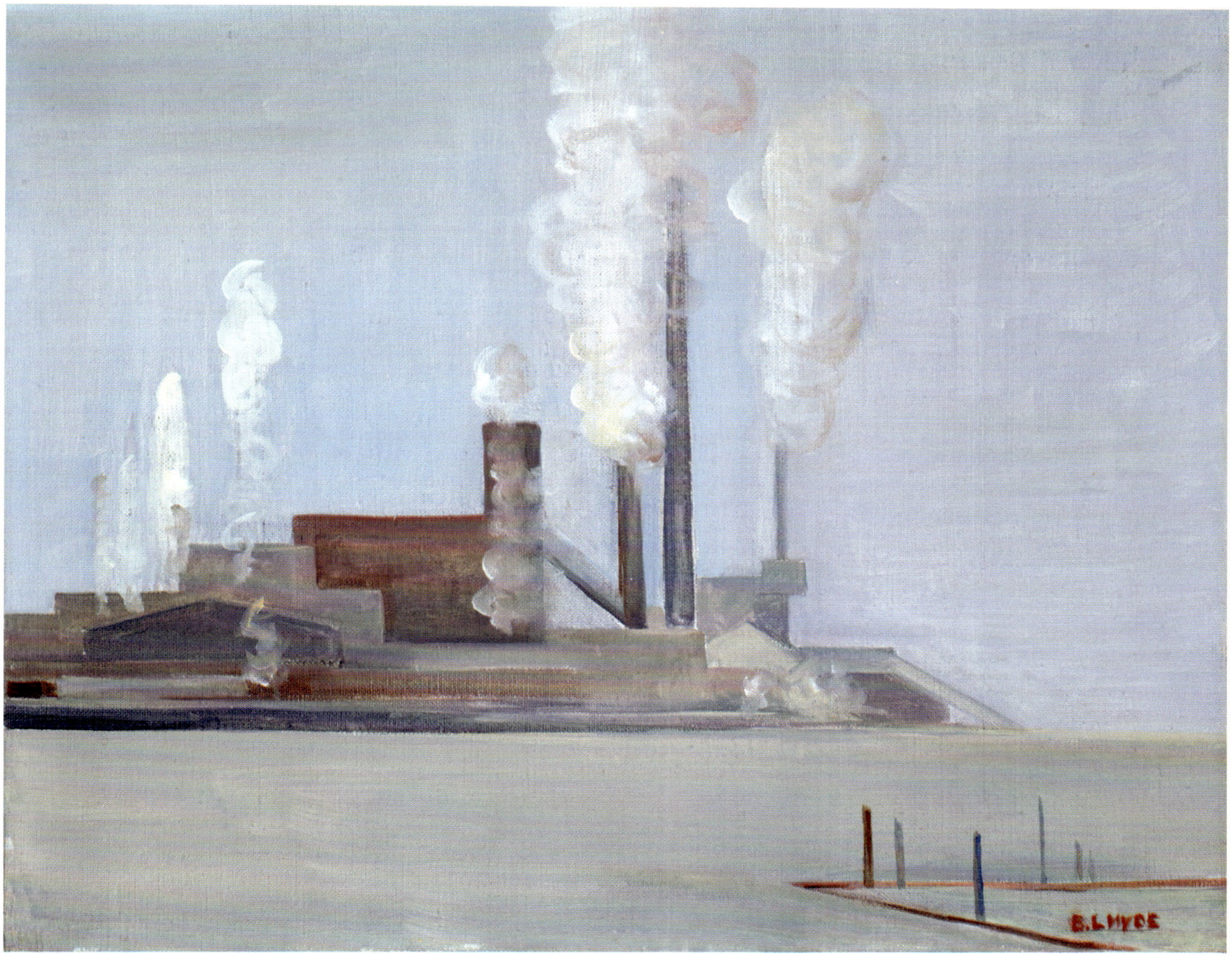

Beulah Loomis Hyde (1886–1983)
Untitled, ca. 1945–50
Oil on canvas
16⅛ × 20 in.
Cascadia Art Museum, Gift of Gretchen and Don Campbell,
Tacoma, WA, CAM 2023.19.1.a,b

Beulah Loomis Hyde (1886–1983)
Untitled, ca. 1949–50
Oil on canvas
24 × 18 in.
Collection of Catherine S. Ebert

One of her most abstracted images, Hyde used Tacoma's Washington Cooperative Farmers Association's grain elevator as the source for the painting. Located on the Hylebos Waterway, the structure was completed in 1949.

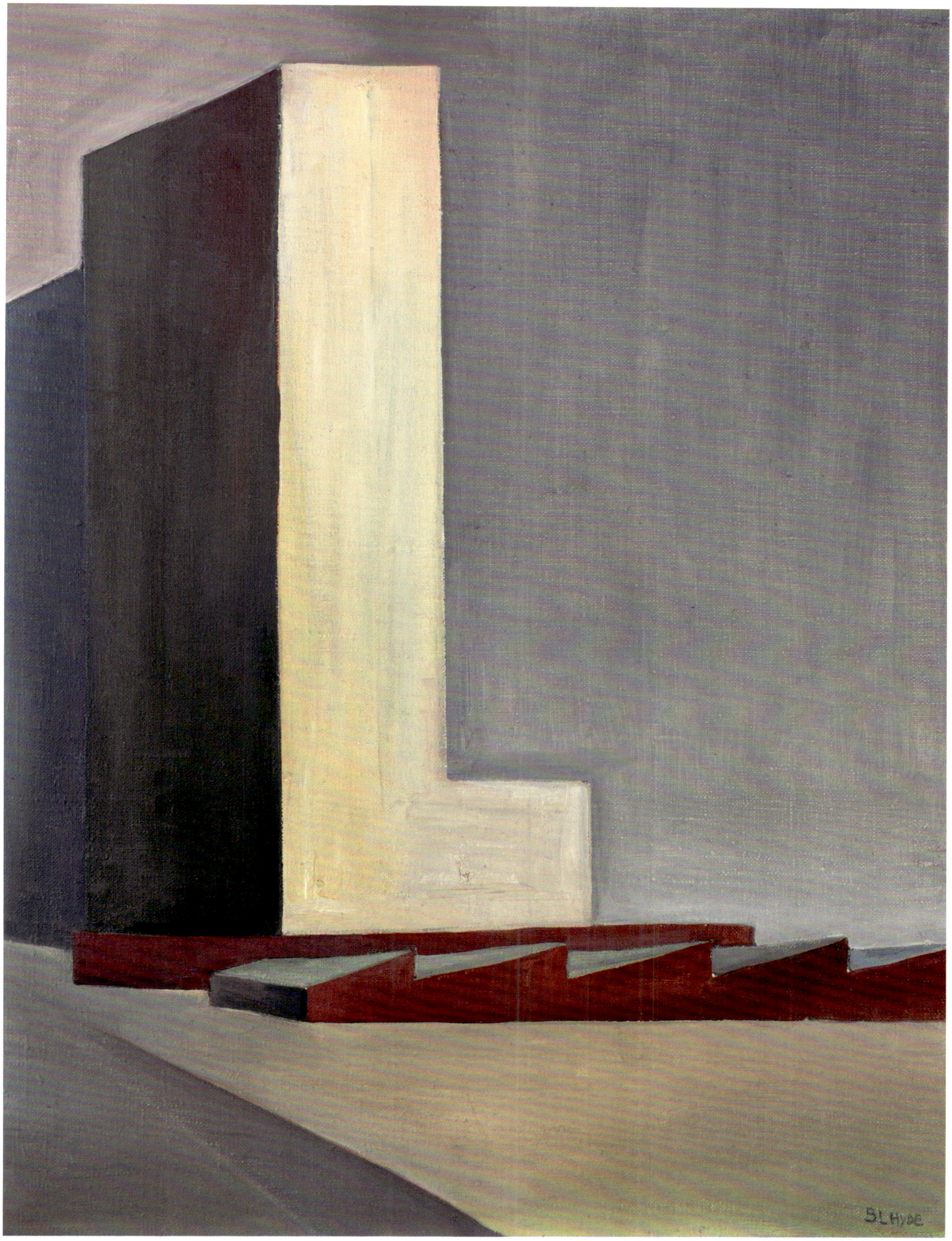
BLHYDE

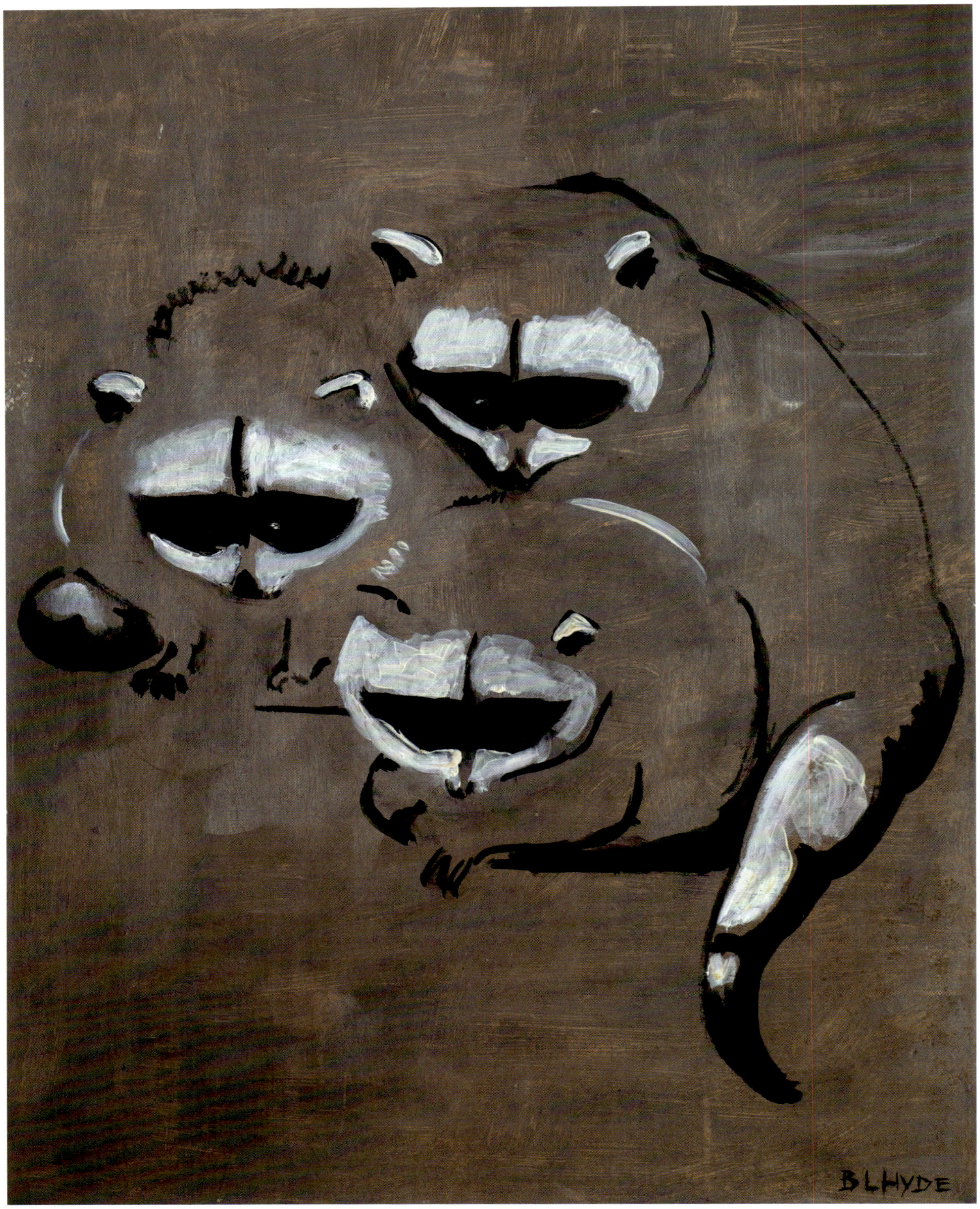

Beulah Loomis Hyde (1886–1983)
Raccoons, ca. 1945–50
Oil on paper mounted to Masonite
20 × 16 in.
Collection of Douglas Hyde Land

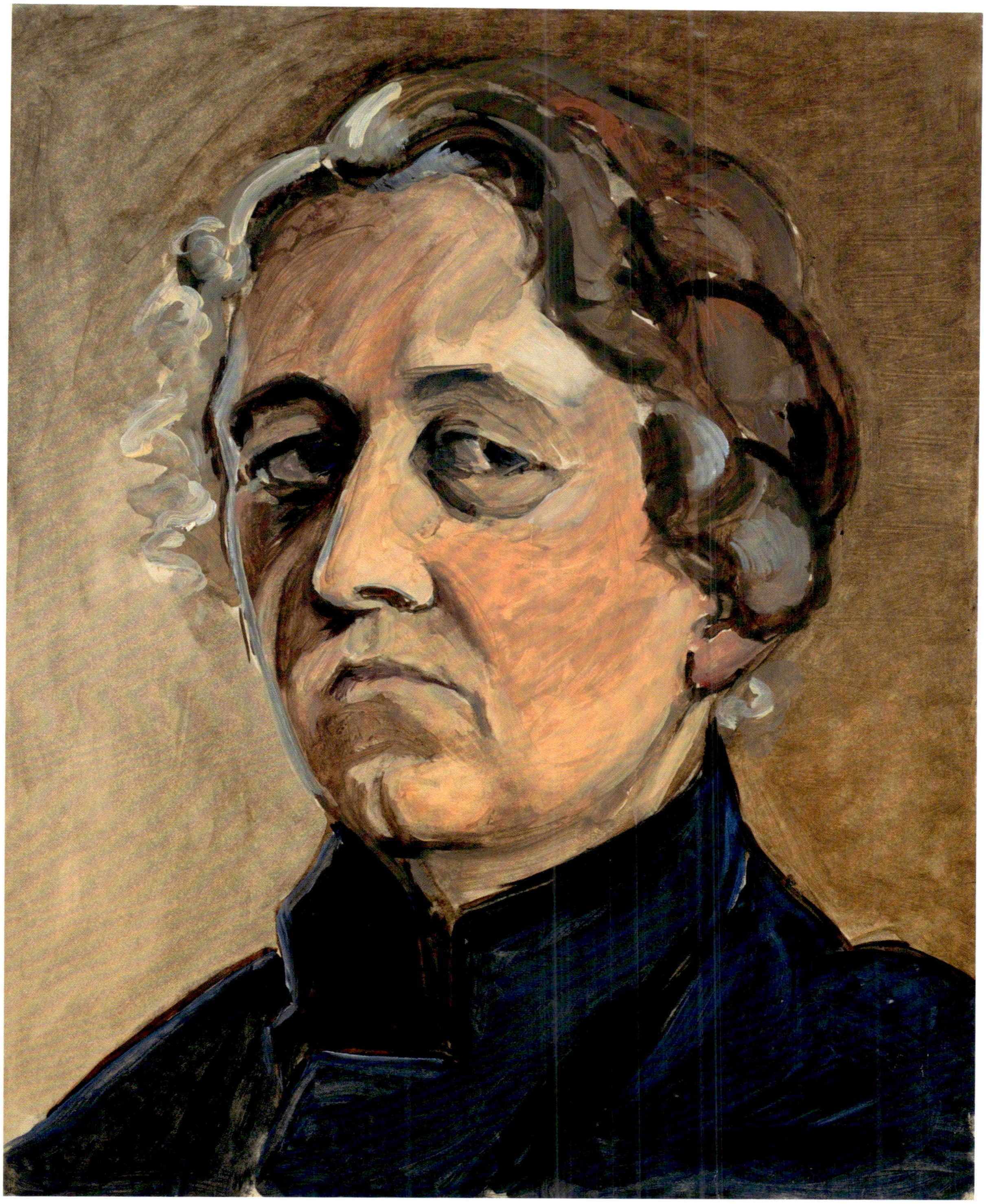

Beulah Loomis Hyde (1886–1983)
Self-portrait, ca. 1945–50
Oil on paper
20 × 15 in.
Collection of Pamela Hyde Smith

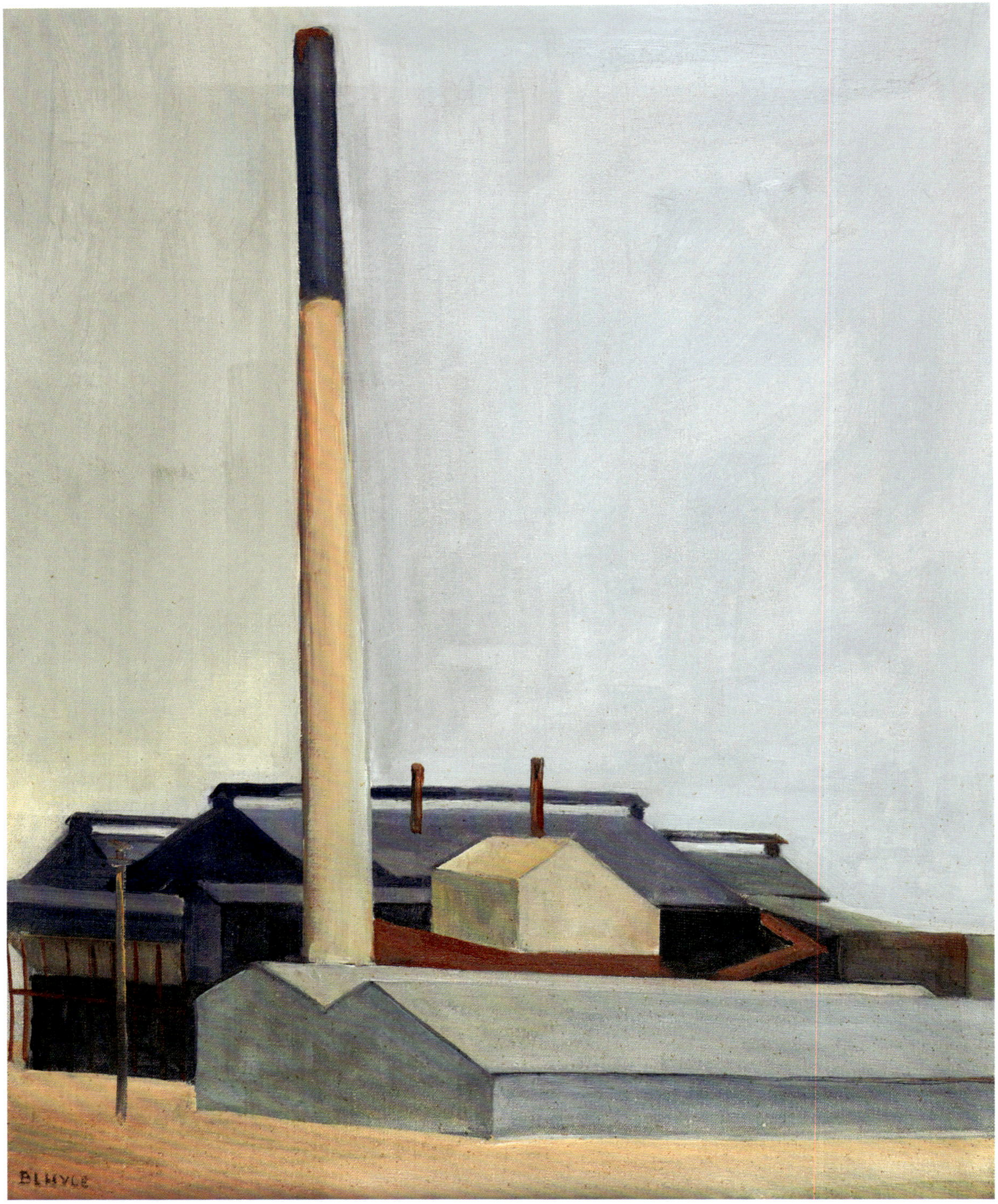

Beulah Loomis Hyde (1886–1983)
Smelter, ca. 1945–50
Oil on canvas
18 × 14 in.
Collection of Chris Hyde Lee

This painting depicts the Asarco copper smelter in the Tacoma suburb of Ruston. At the time, the smokestack was the largest in the world.

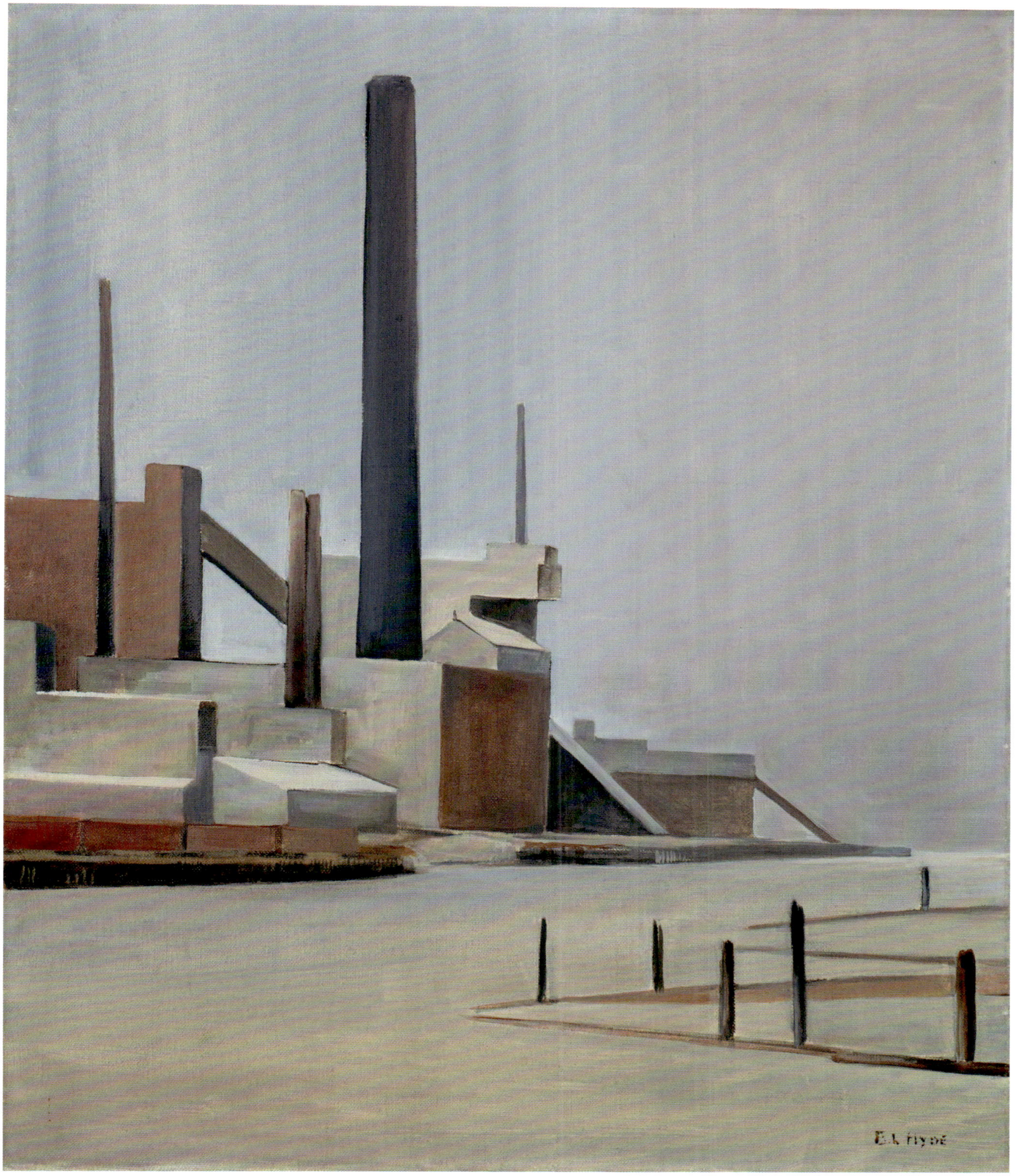

Beulah Loomis Hyde (1886–1983)
Waterfront, ca. 1945–50
Oil on canvas
24 × 20 in.
Collection of Charles Henry Hyde III

Beulah Loomis Hyde (1886–1983)
Untitled, ca. 1945–50
Oil on canvas
20 × 24 in.
Collection of Douglas Hyde Land

This painting matches a newspaper description of a Hyde painting titled *Hylebos Waterway*.

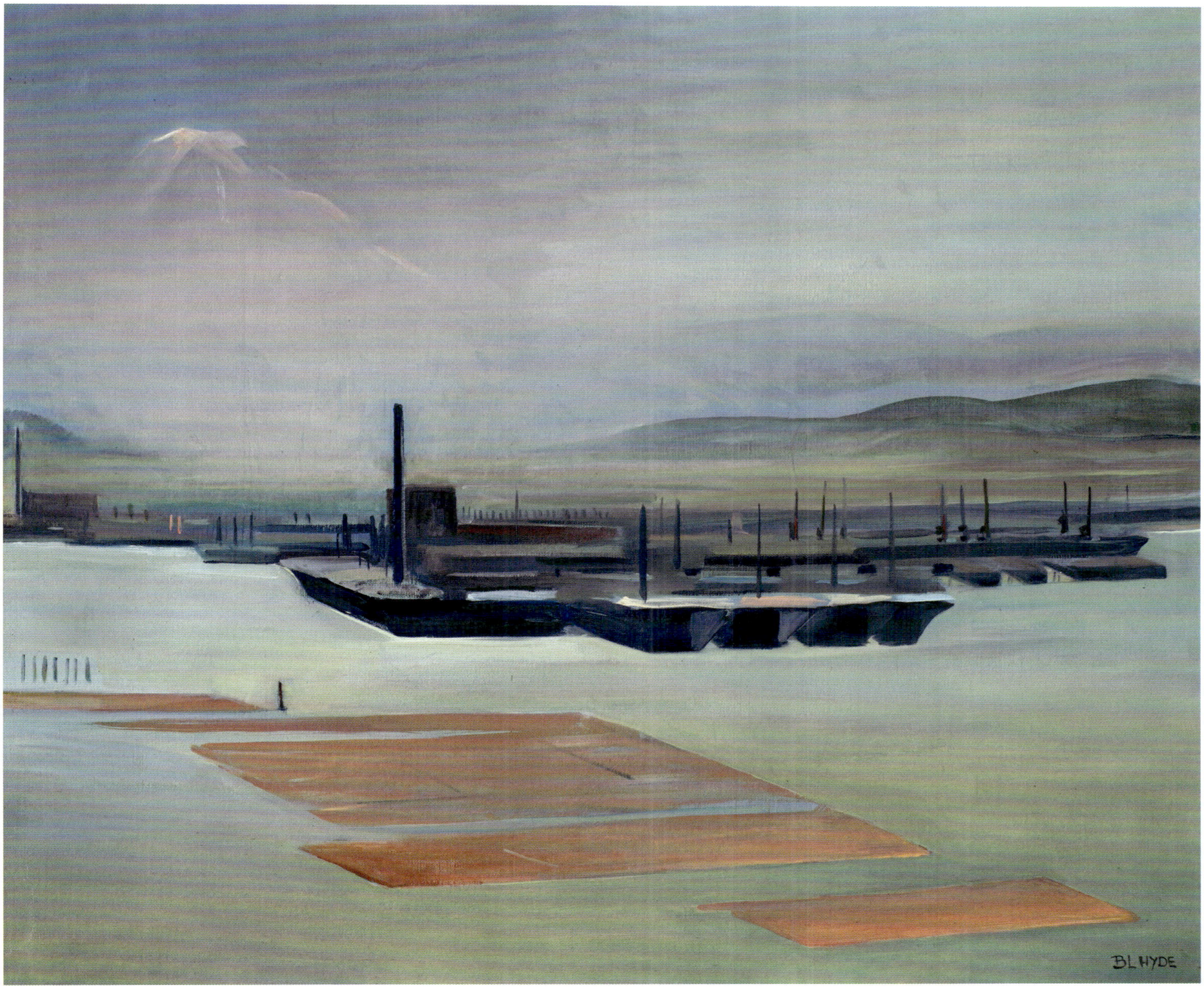
BL HYDE

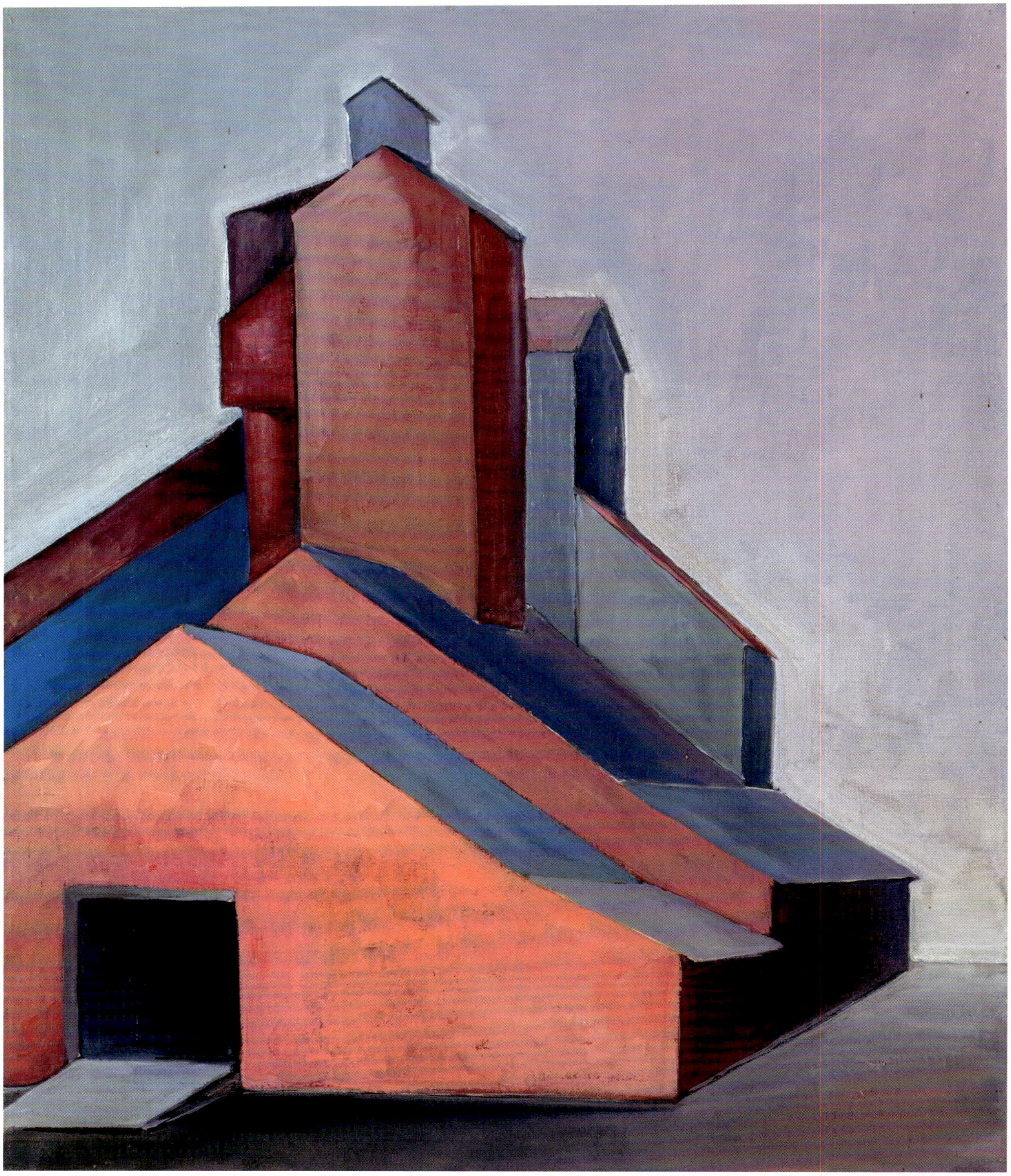

Beulah Loomis Hyde (1886–1983)
Untitled, ca. 1945–50
Oil on canvas
24¼ × 20¼ in.
Collection of Pamela Hyde Smith

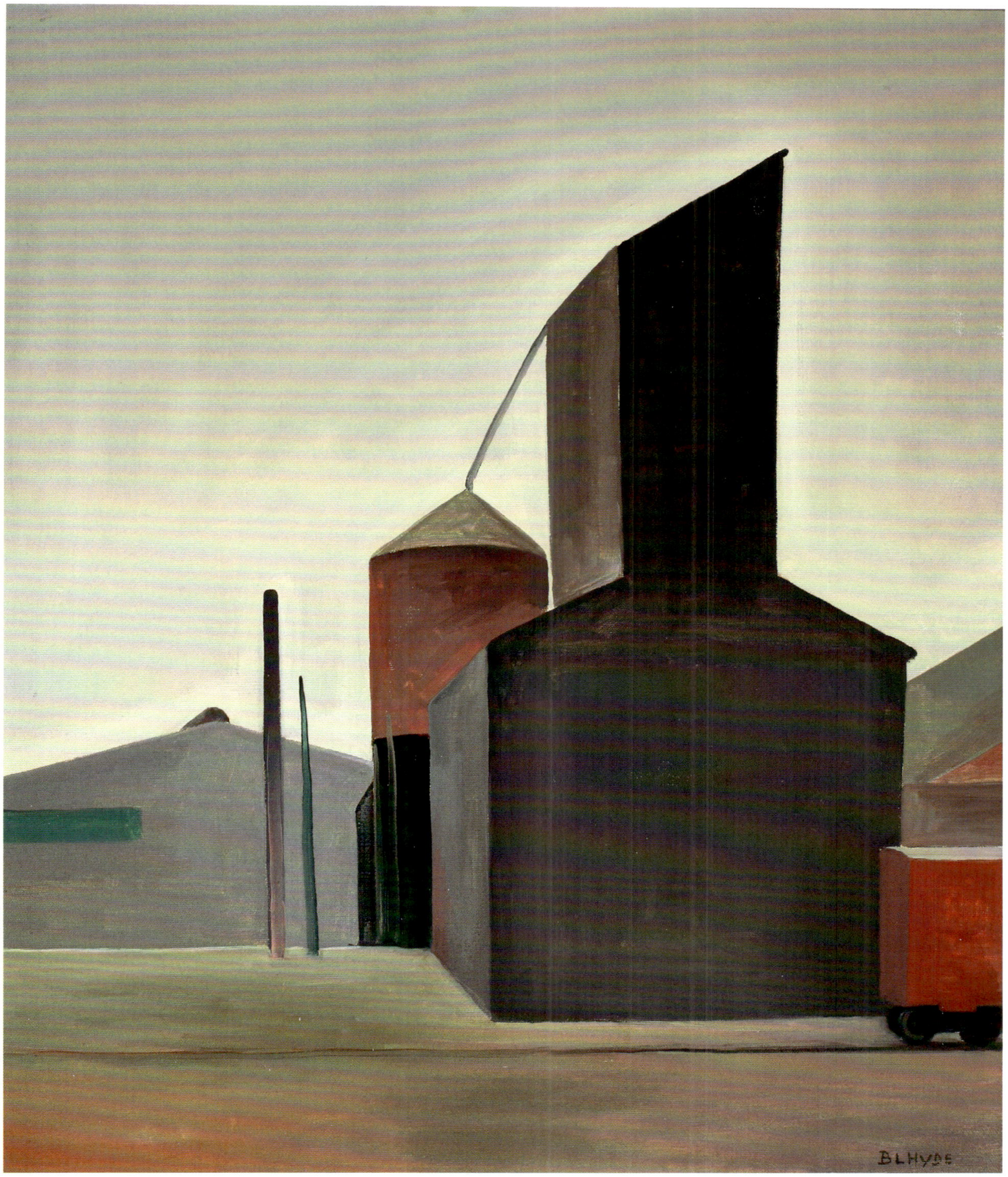

Beulah Loomis Hyde (1886–1983)
Old Mill, ca. 1945–50
Oil on canvas
24¼ × 20¼ in. (61.6 × 51.4 cm)
Tacoma Art Museum, Gift of the Aloha Club, 1971.11

Beulah Loomis Hyde (1886–1983)
Untitled, ca. 1945–50
Oil on canvas
20 × 16 in.
Collection of Pamela Hyde Smith

In this unusual composition, Hyde used the filter shapes as still-life components juxtaposed against the industrial background. The subtle tonal values and compacted, close relationship of the forms call to mind the still-life paintings of Le Corbusier and Giorgio Morandi.

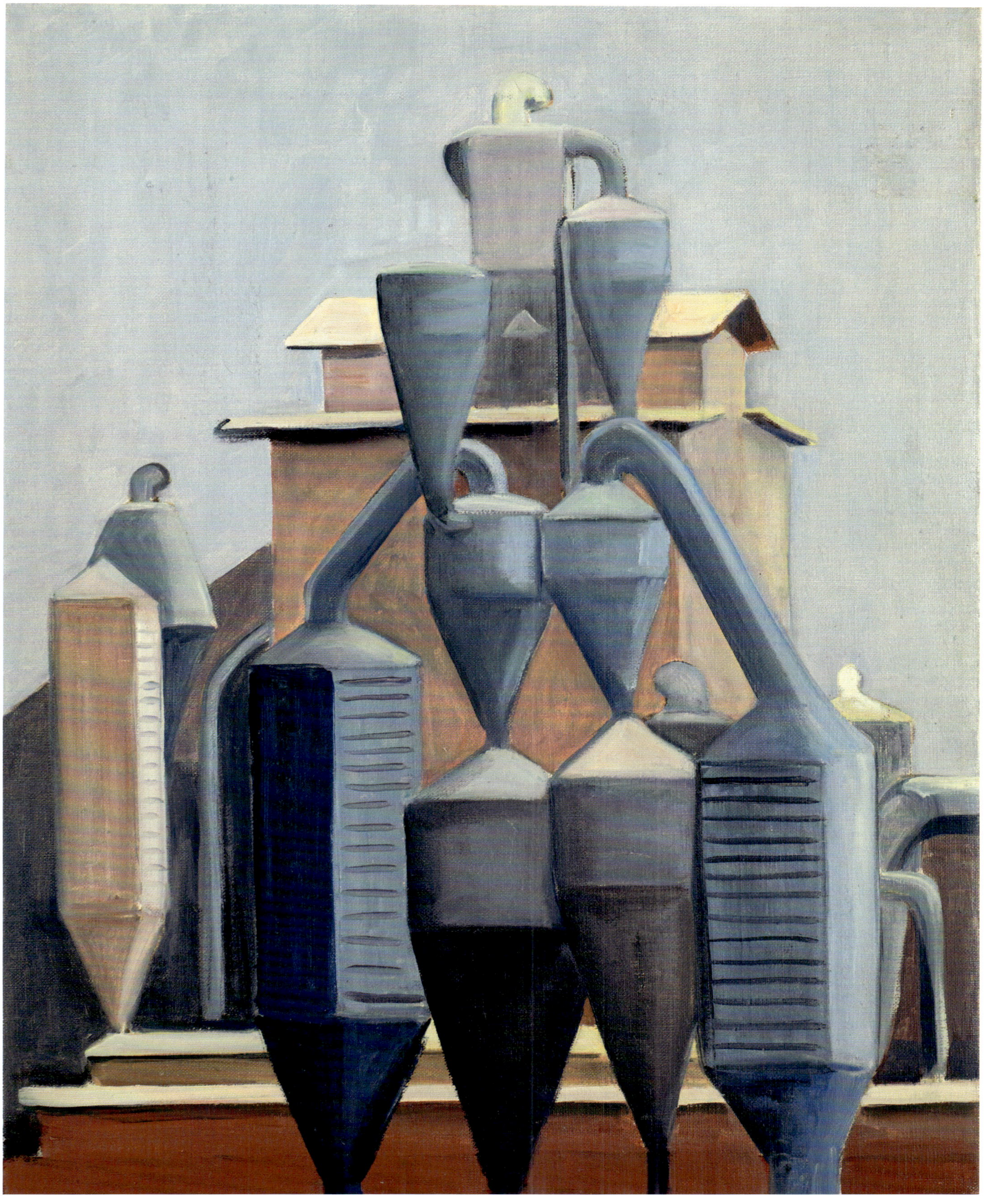

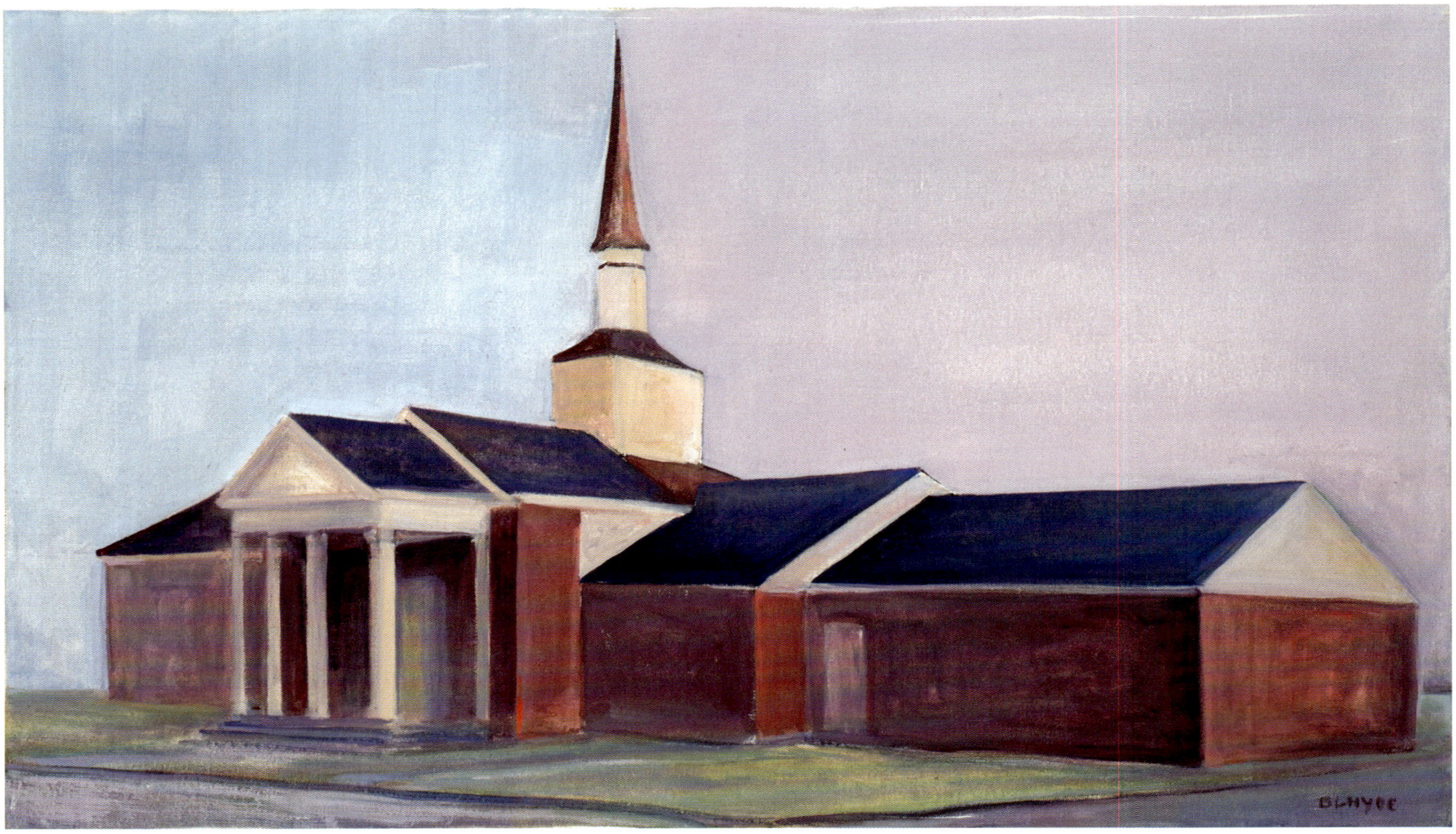

Beulah Loomis Hyde (1886–1983)
Church, ca. 1945–50
Oil on canvas
14¼ × 24¼ in.
Collection of Pamela Hyde Smith

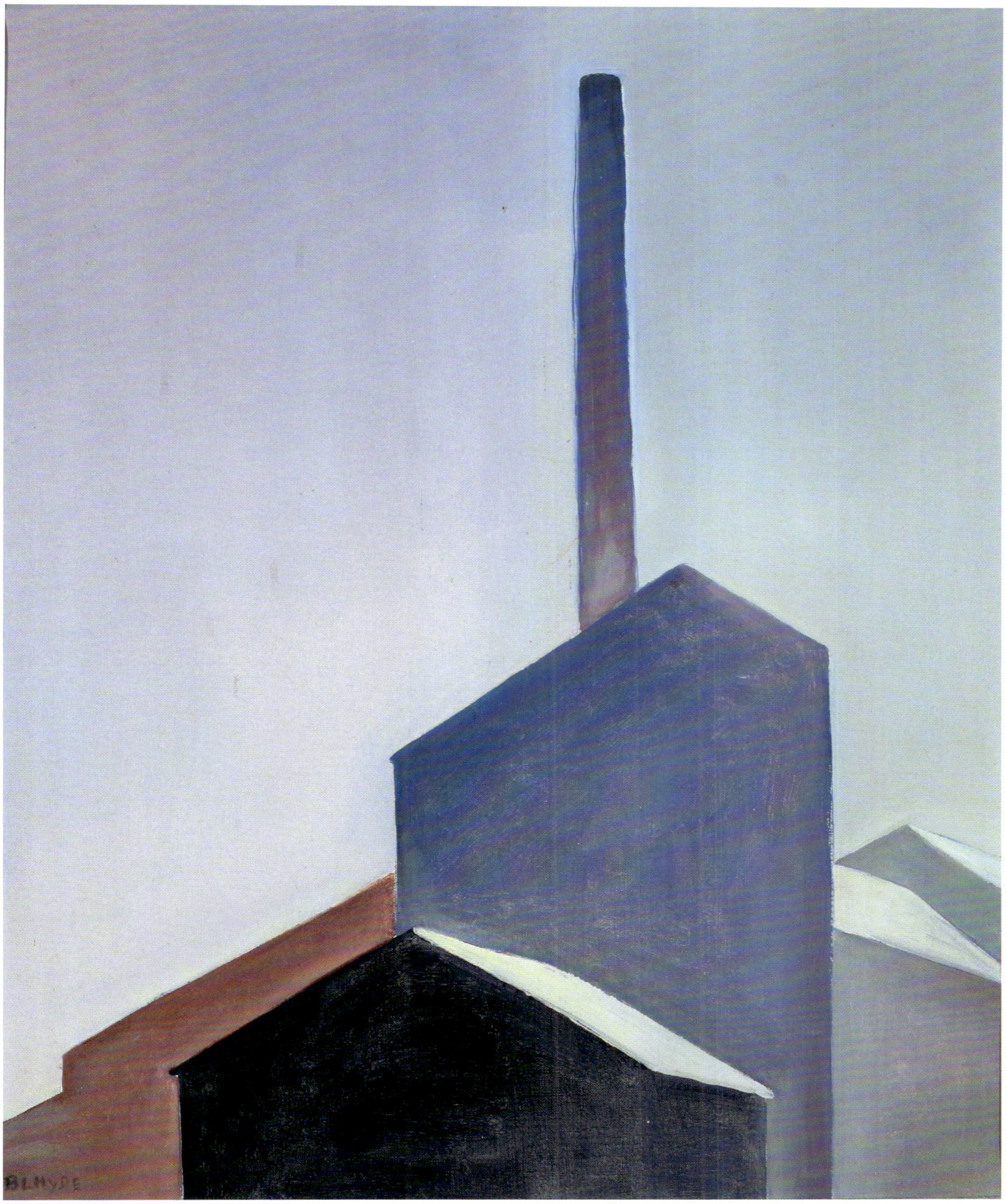

Beulah Loomis Hyde (1886–1983)
Factory, ca. 1945–55
Oil on canvas
24 × 20 in. (61 × 50.8 cm)
Tacoma Art Museum, Gift of Mr. and Mrs. J. P. Weyerhaeuser, Sr., 1963.4

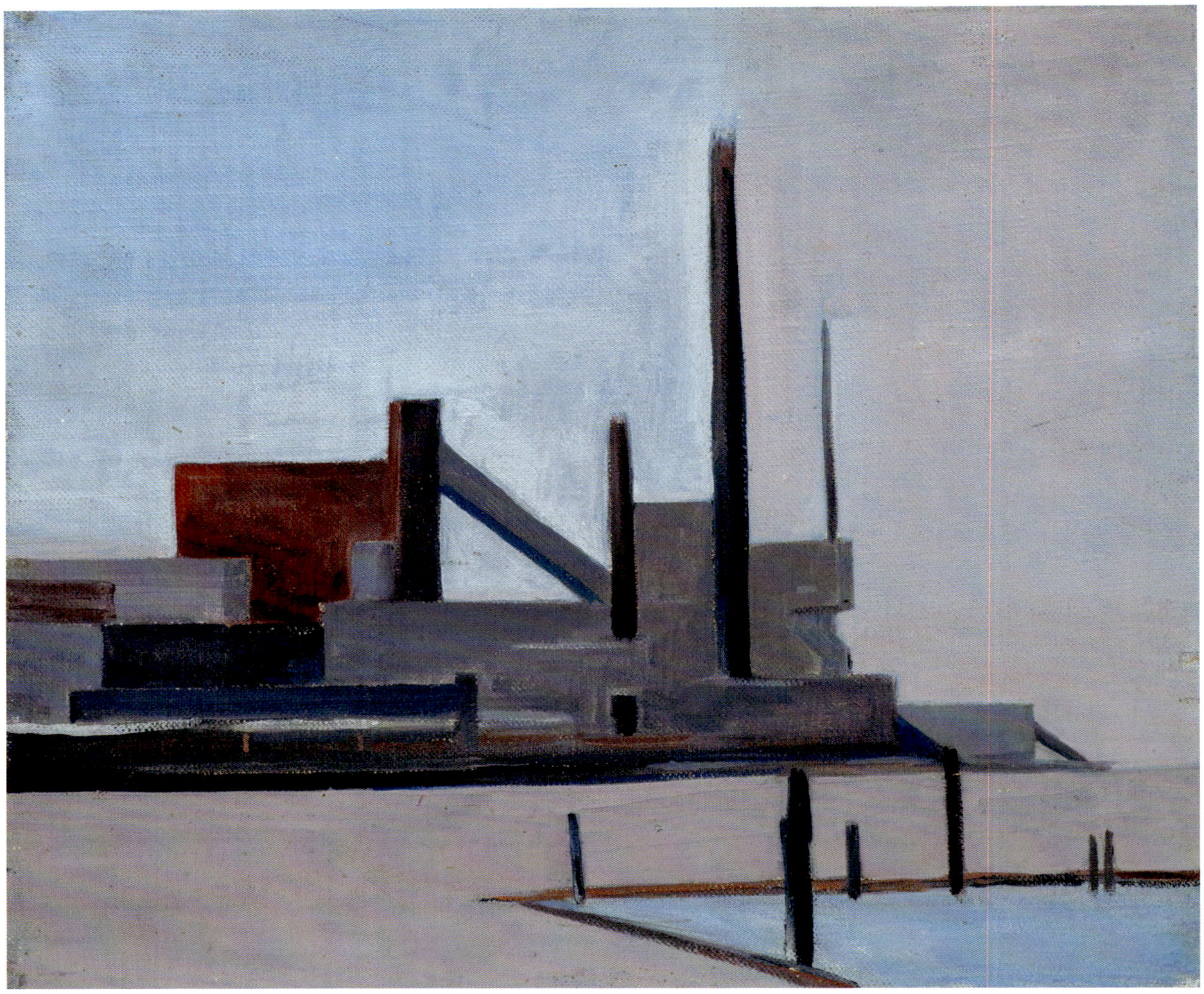

Beulah Loomis Hyde (1886–1983)
Untitled, ca. 1945–50
Oil on canvas
14 × 12⅜ in.
Collection of Allison Hyde and Jake Nellis

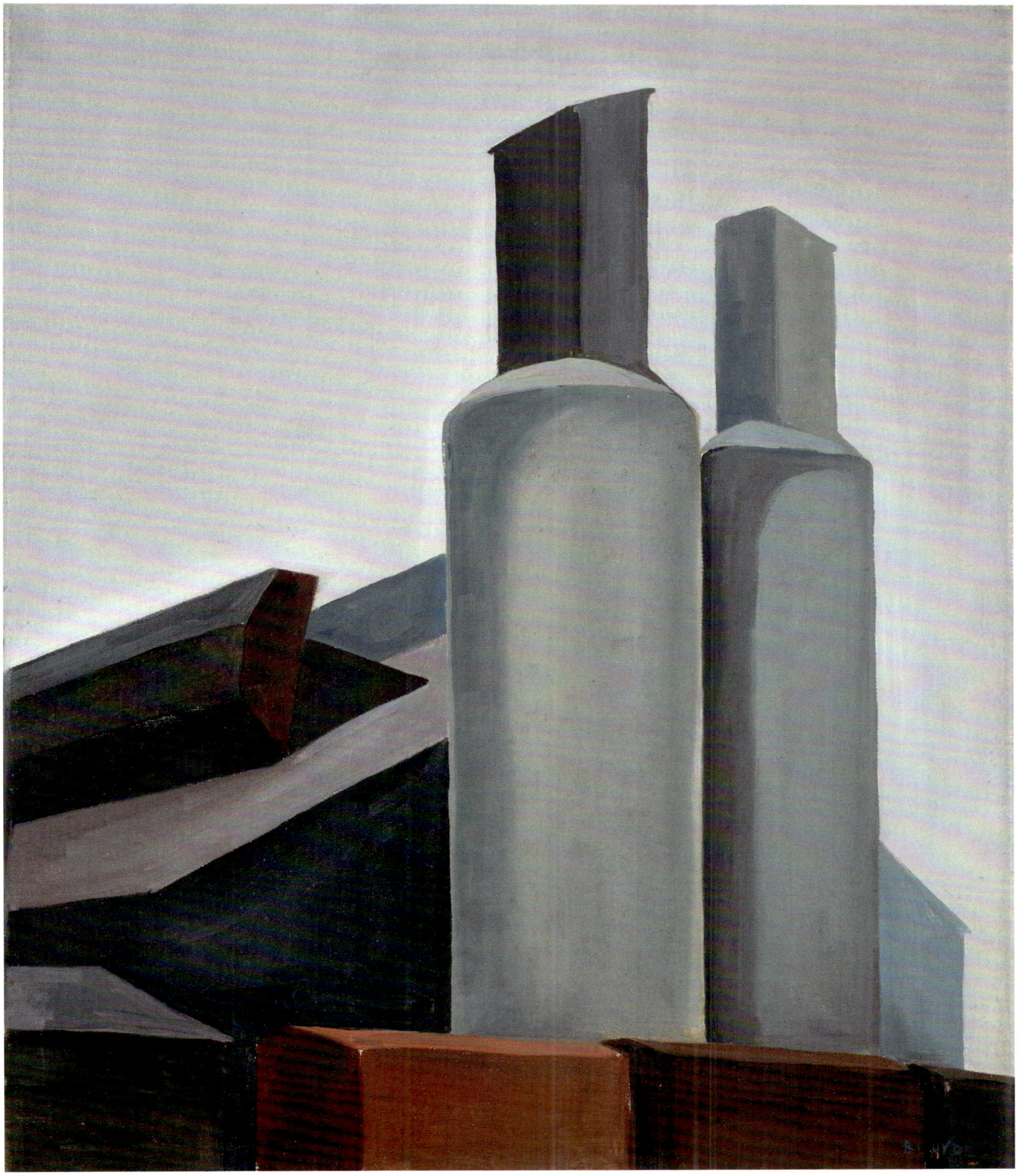

Beulah Loomis Hyde (1886–1983)
Aluminum Plant, ca. 1950–55
Oil on canvas
24 × 20 in.
Collection of Charles Henry Hyde III

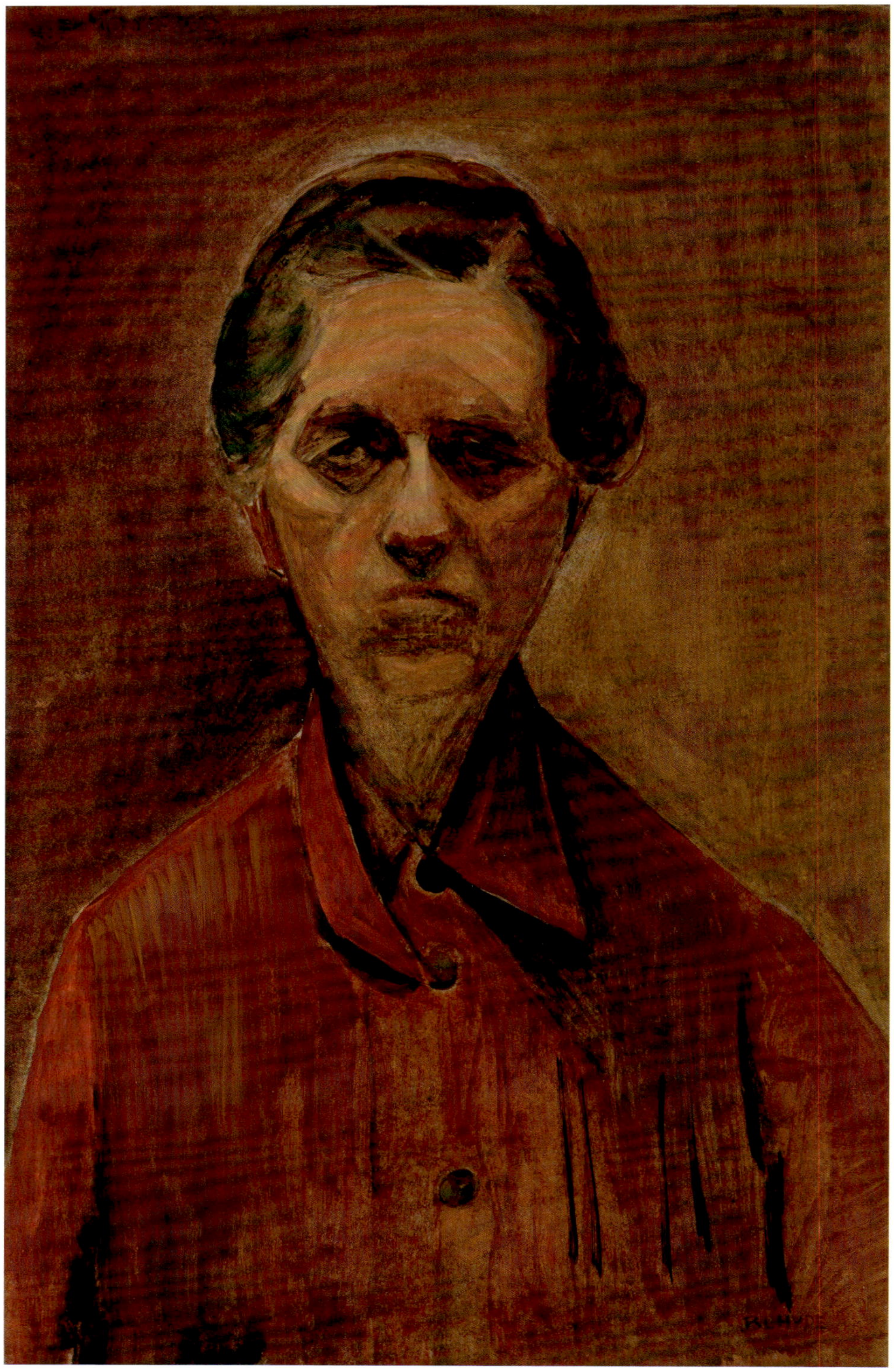

Beulah Loomis Hyde (1886–1983)
Self-Portrait, ca. 1950–55
Oil on paper mounted to canvas board
20 × 12¾ in.
Collection of Pamela Hyde Smith

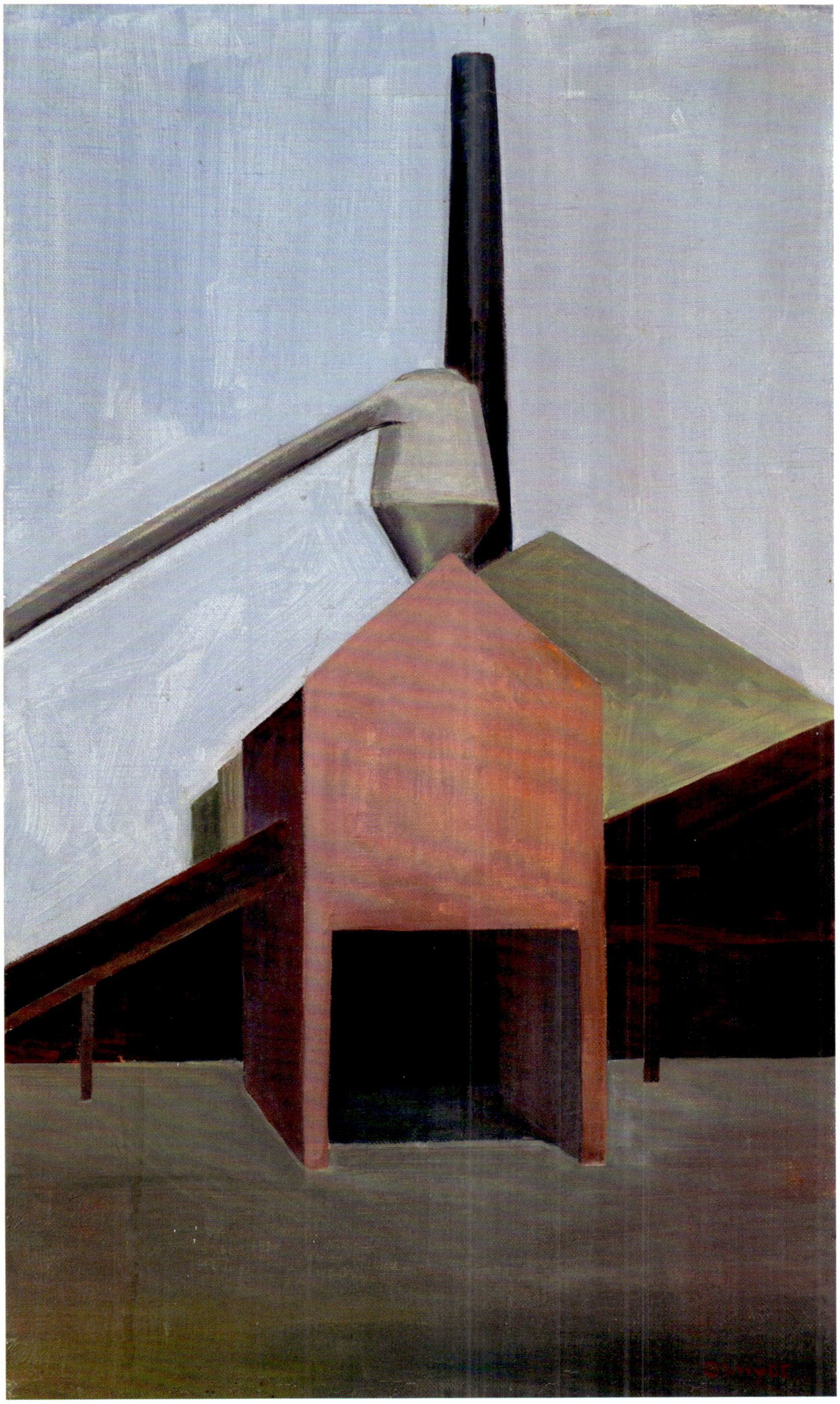

Beulah Loomis Hyde (1886–1983)
Untitled, ca. 1950–55
Oil on canvas
24 × 14 in.
Collection of Nicola M. Hyde

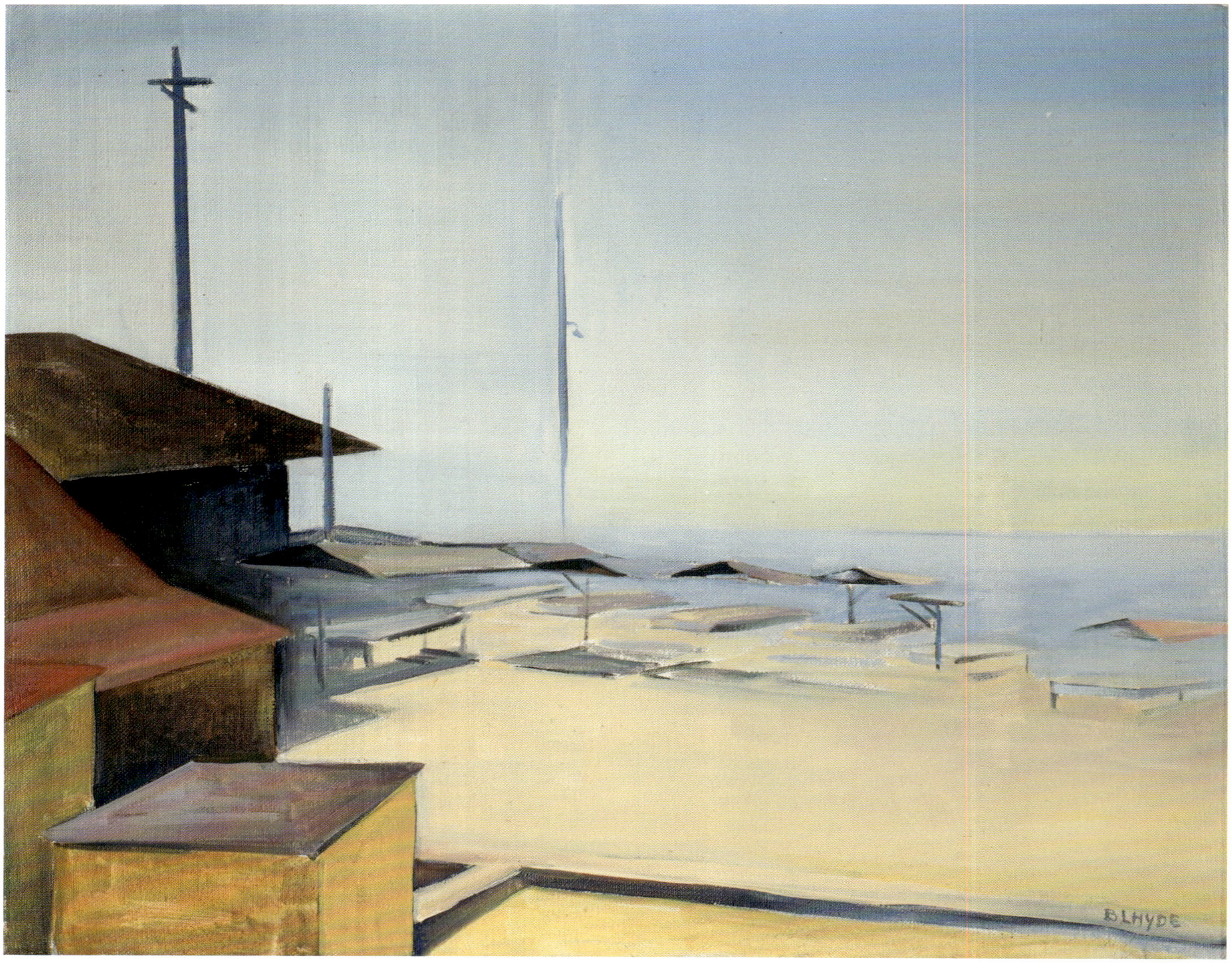

Beulah Loomis Hyde (1886–1983)
Beach houses, ca. 1950–52
Oil on canvas
Support: 16 × 20 in. (40.6 × 50.8 cm)
Frame: 26 × 30 in. (66 × 76.2 cm)
Tacoma Art Museum, Gift of Don and Gretchen Campbell, 2022.11.1

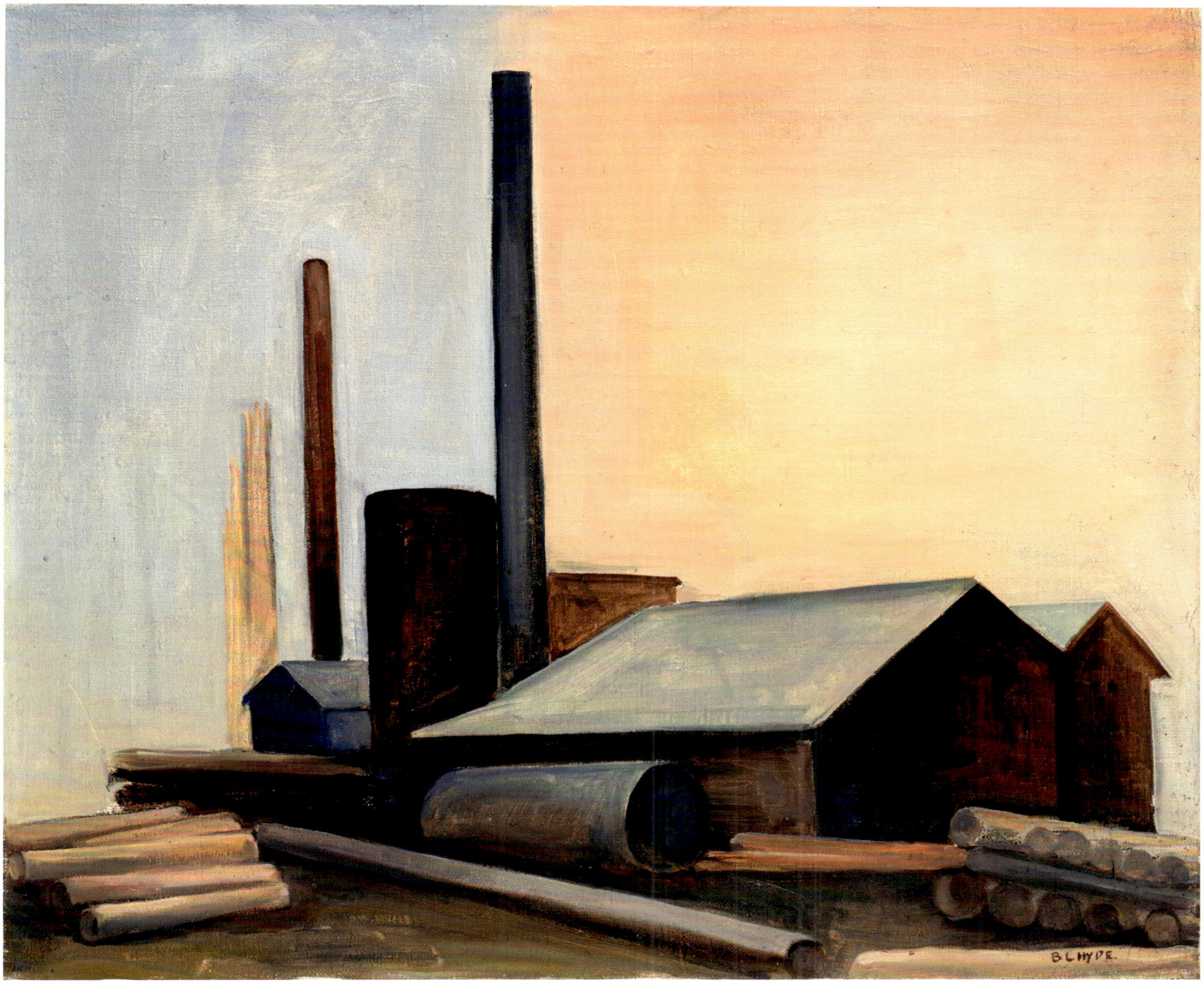

Beulah Loomis Hyde (1886–1983)
Pole Mill, ca. 1950–53
Oil on canvas
20 × 24 in.
Cascadia Art Museum, Gift of Gretchen and Don Campbell,
Tacoma, WA, CAM 2023.19.2.a,b

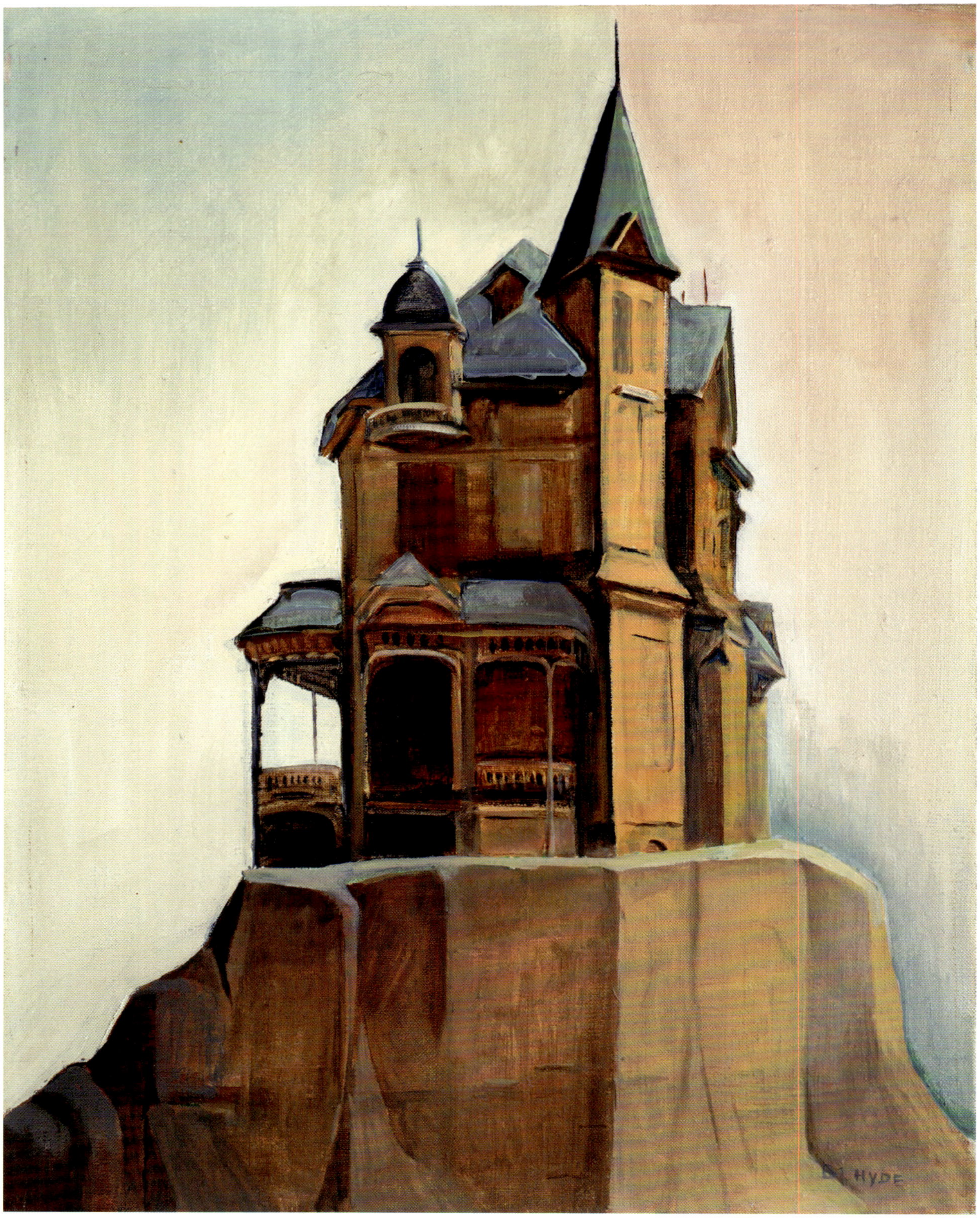

Beulah Loomis Hyde (1886–1983)
Last Landmark, ca. 1950–55
Oil on canvas
23 × 18 in.
Collection of Pamela Hyde Smith

This painting depicts a lone house standing on a hill during the Denny regrade in Seattle that flattened the landscape.

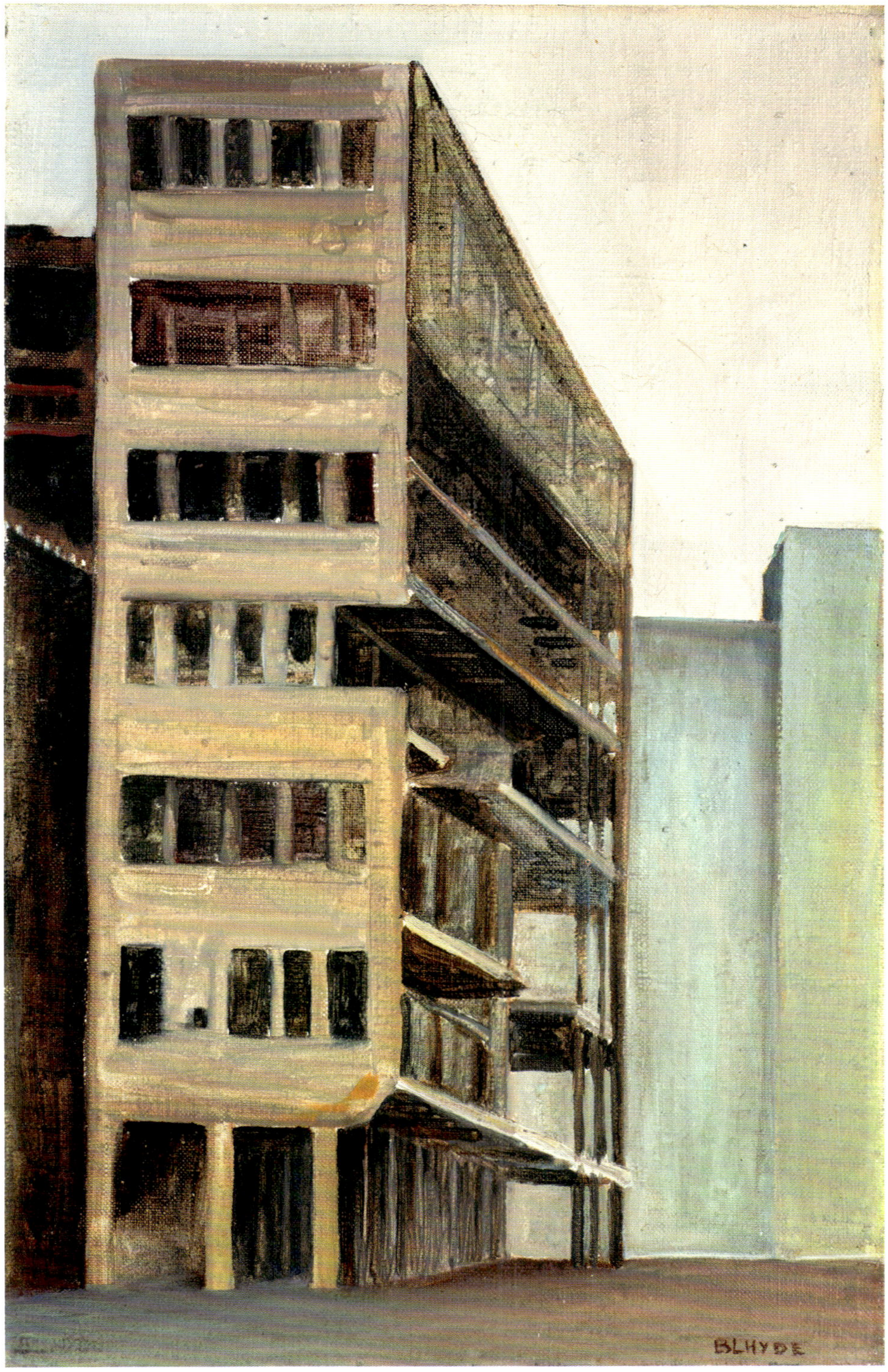

Beulah Loomis Hyde (1886–1983)
Untitled, ca. 1950–55
Oil on canvas
20 × 12¾ in.
Collection of Pamela Hyde Smith

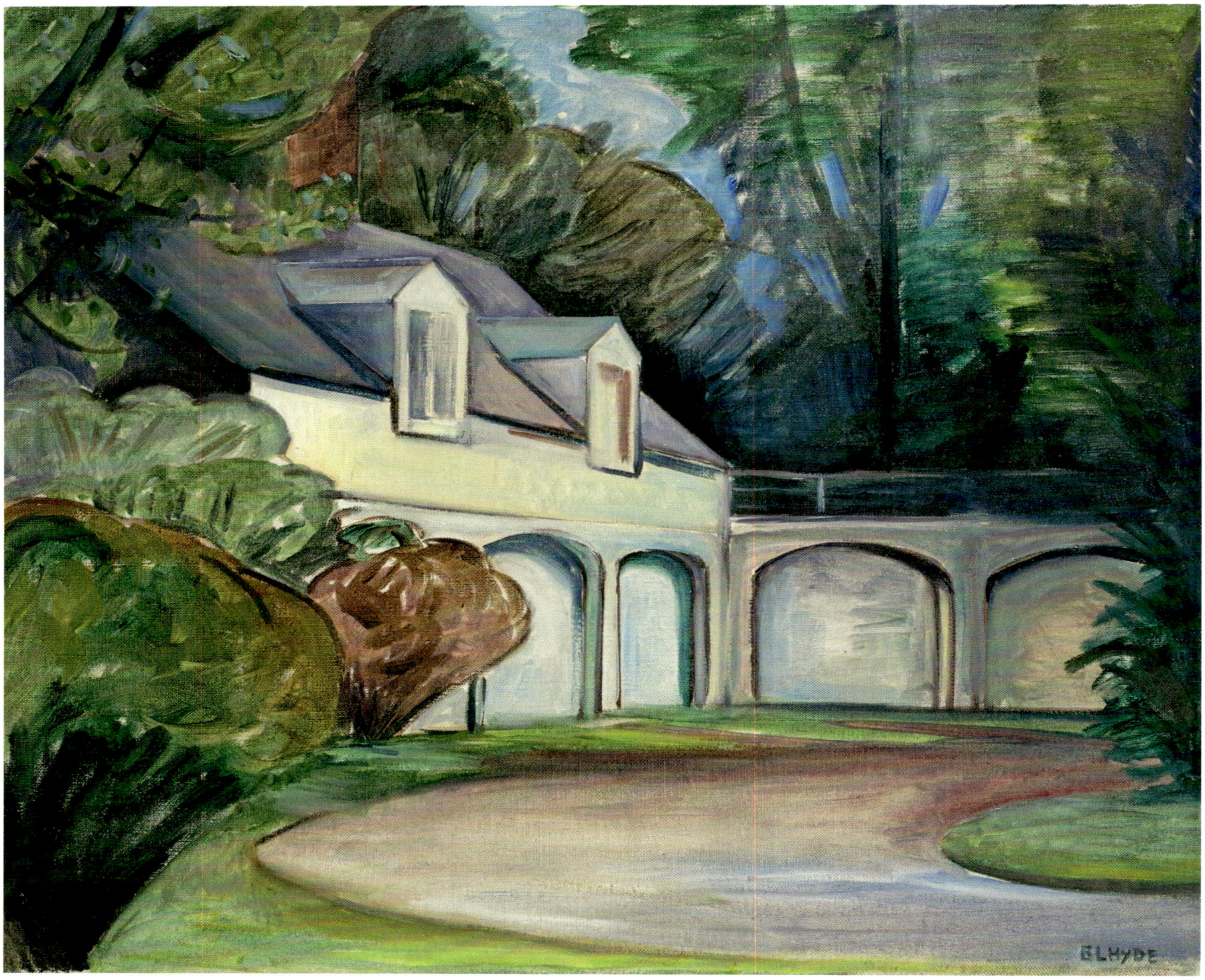

Beulah Loomis Hyde (1886–1983)
Garage, ca. 1950–55
Oil on canvas
20¼ × 24¼ in.
Collection of Charles Henry Hyde III

This painting depicts the artist's home studio in Lakewood, WA.

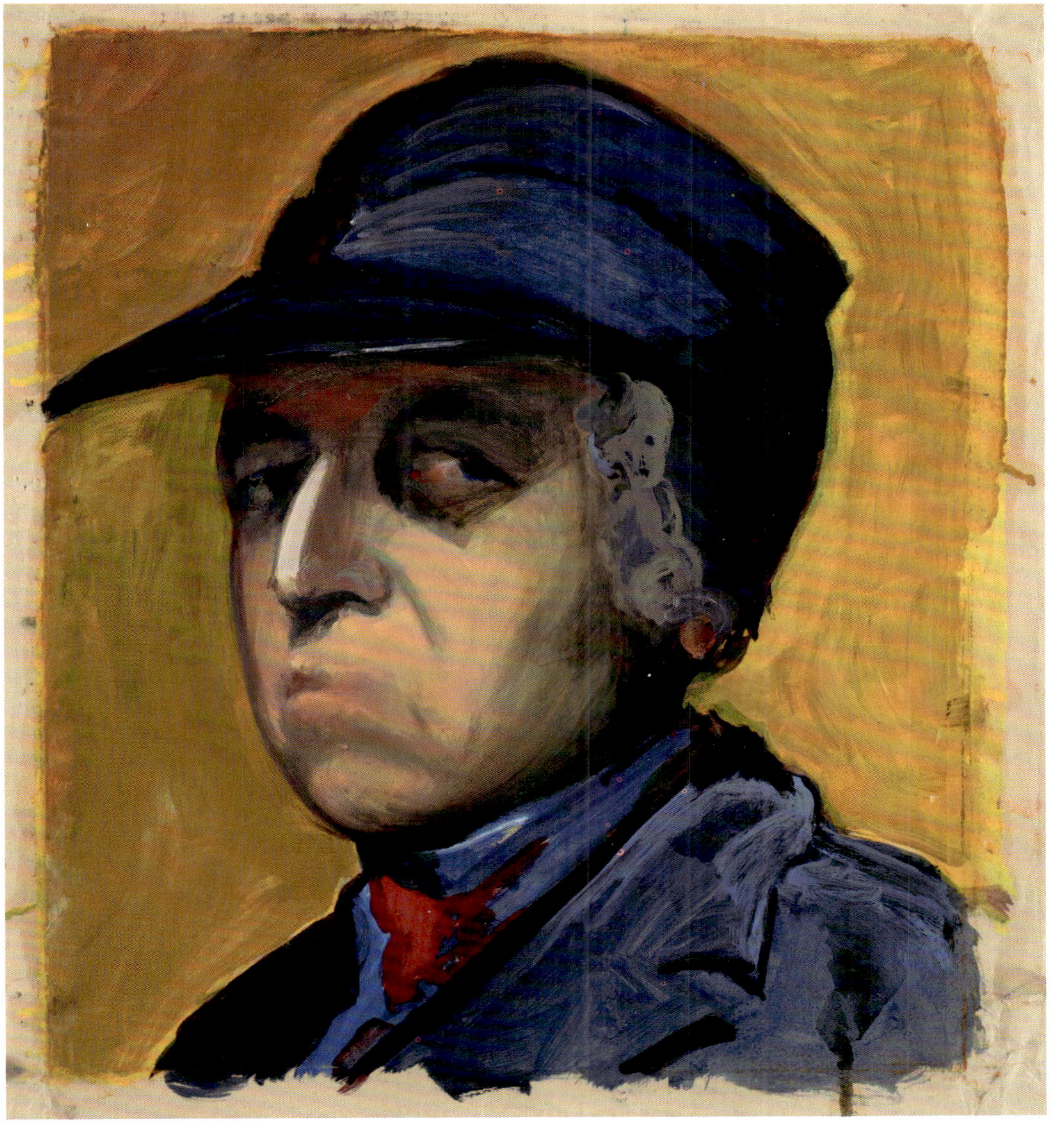

Beulah Loomis Hyde (1886–1983)
Self-portrait, ca. 1955–60
Oil on paper
18 × 15 in.
Collection of Pamela Hyde Smith

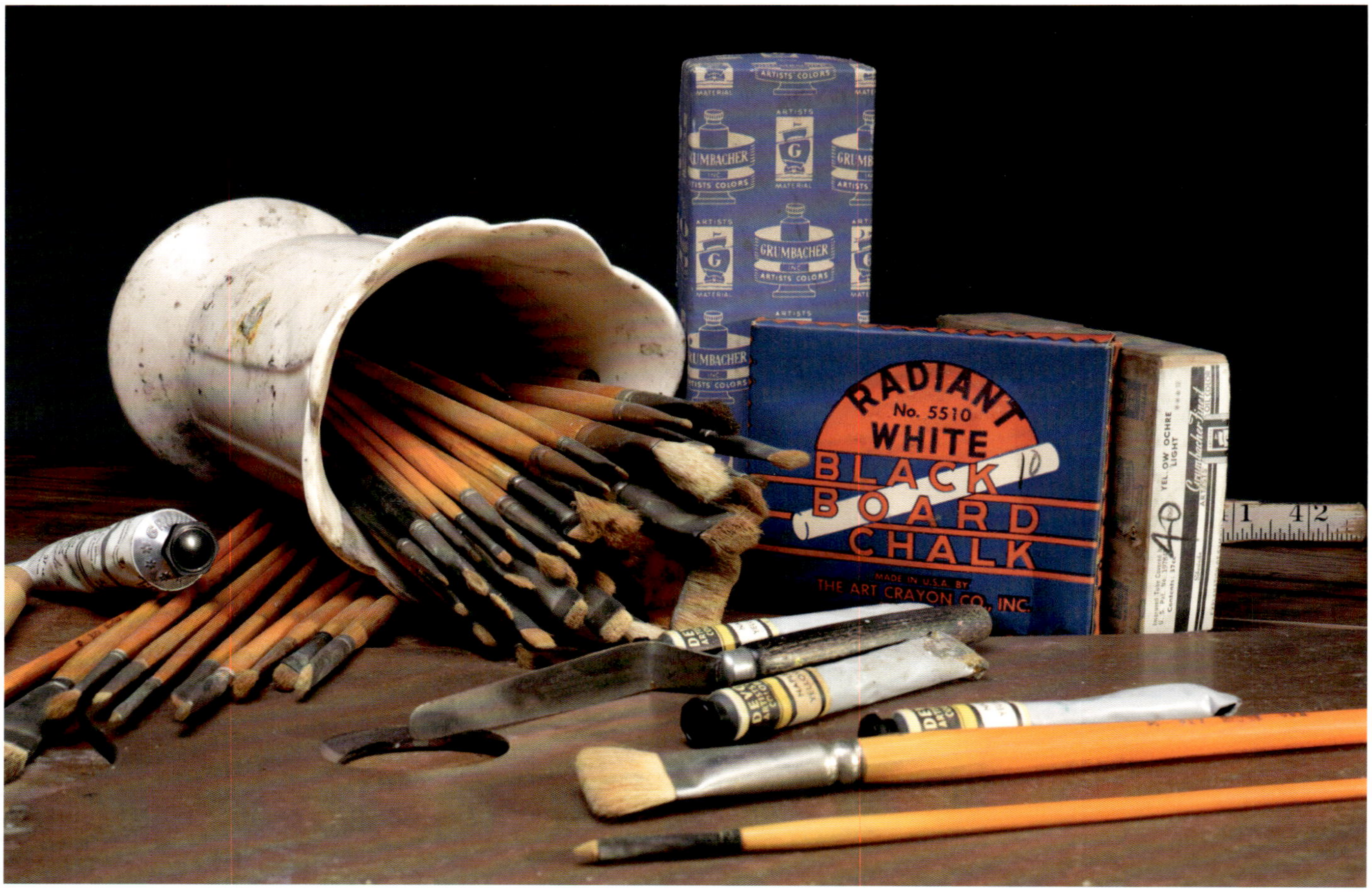

Beulah Hyde's painting supplies
Arranged and photographed by Bret Corrington
Artist Eye Portfolio Studio
Seattle, WA

ACKNOWLEDGMENTS

I am indebted to the following for assistance in making this publication possible:

First and foremost, I wish to thank the family of Beulah Loomis Hyde for such incredible support and for assisting me on numerous occasions in a warm and thoughtful manner. Pamela Hyde Smith, Douglas Hyde Land, Ben Land, Chris Hyde Lee, Charles Henry Hyde III, Allison Hyde and Jake Nellis, Catherine Ebert, and Marian Smith and Daniel Montalbano. They have made "Nonnie" come to life for me and have been diligent in the preservation of her artistic reputation. Besides Hyde's art, her family is an extraordinary part of her legacy.

Margaret Bullock, for championing the art of B. L. Hyde in her former position at the Tacoma Art Museum and for being such a wonderful person and thoughtful friend.

Special thanks to the amazing Spencer Bowman, Northwest Room librarian, Tacoma Public Library, for ongoing support and assistance.

Thank you to my friends at Tacoma Art Museum, Jessica Wilks, director of curatorial, and Ellen Ito, artist and curator.

Thank you to Marty Happy Behnke for sharing her University of Washington thesis on B. L. Hyde with me and Chris Hyde Lee for scanning and sending it to me.

Thank you to conservator Patty West for her expert rescuing of several paintings.

Photographer Bret Corrington, Artist Eye Portfolio Studio, Seattle, WA

Heide Fernandez-Llamazares, arts professional and lender to the book and exhibition

Steffi Morrison, collections manager, Wing Luke Museum of the Asian Pacific American Experience

Rod Koon, Tacoma historian

Deborah Healy

John Strong

Artist William Elston

Estate of Frank Herbert, John Silbersack and Brian Herbert

New Milford Historical Society, New Milford, CT, Kathleen Kelly, president

Carolyn Cruthirds, coordinator of image licensing, Museum of Fine Arts, Boston

Hannah Hirano, assistant registrar, rights and reproductions, Seattle Art Museum

Brooke Shelman Wagner, museum collections curator, and Kayla Tackett, director of exhibitions and collections, Northwest Museum of Arts and Culture, Spokane, WA

Kelly Carpenter, imaging, visual resources, and digital assets manager, Buffalo AKG Art Museum, Buffalo, NY

Sabah Ismail, collections assistant, Crystal Bridges Museum of American Art, Bentonville, AR

Laura Edgar, archivist, Annie Wright Schools, Tacoma, WA

Roberta Wagener, senior specialist, Access Services, Spencer Art Reference Library, Nelson-Atkins Museum of Art, Kansas City, MO

Sara DeCaro, curator of special collections and university archivist, Axe Library, Pittsburg State University, Pittsburg, KS

Nanaka Kishi, gallery and events assistant, and Izzy Morley, programs assistant, Daiwa Anglo-Japanese Foundation, London, England

Slava White and Jason Kable, estate of George Zell Heuston

Jane Connelly, archivist and special collections librarian, University of Puget Sound, Tacoma, WA

Phil Kovacevich, for another brilliant design and so much joy in our continuing collaborations.

Jane M. Lichty, for her superb editing and patient guidance.

Nicole F. Mitchell, director, and the staff at the University of Washington Press

Since 2015, Cascadia Art Museum has become one of the most important museums in the Northwest. I am grateful to the board, staff, and volunteers for providing me an opportunity to reintroduce the work of neglected Northwest artists and for giving the art and artists a home.

Lindsey Echelbarger, founder and board president, and his wife, Carolyn, have made such important contributions to Northwest art and culture. I am happy to call them friends for over thirty years and have witnessed the depth and sincerity of their commitment to the arts.

Thanks to our board: Ruthanne Weaver, vice president; Phil Grad, treasurer; and members Gary Faigin, Tori Force, Hylton Hard, Gwen Johnson, Alan Lawrence, Julie Long, Marni Muir, Mark Pomerantz, Meg Rankin, Janette Turner, Silvia Waltner, Richard West, and Kasumi Yamashita.

I also wish to thank committee member and museum supporter John Impert.

To our tireless staff:

Sally Ralston, executive director

Nate Hegerberg, director of operations (thanks for the Hyde family interview transcriptions)

Jason Bain, registrar

Julie Olson Anna, director of education

Carol Gordon, marketing and development manager

Breana Blackburn, bookkeeper and office manager

Sydney Kaemmerlen, store manager

I would like to remember with love, three close friends who were so important to me and my career, Dr. Susan Casteras, Maureen Duryee, and Lucy Hart.

Finally, and as always, I thank my partner Dominic Zambito, the Prince of Proxi on the Rue de Beaune.

Cascadia Art Museum extends our deepest gratitude to the Hyde family. Your generous contributions have made the art exhibit and publication possible. Your support has not only enabled the curation of an inspiring and thought-provoking collection but also facilitated the production of this publication, ensuring that the artworks and the stories of B. L. Hyde will live on to inspire generations to come.

PAMELA HYDE SMITH

DOUGLAS HYDE LAND

CHRIS HYDE LEE

CHARLES H. HYDE III

DONORS TO THE PUBLICATION

PLATINUM

Sarah Burns & Dennis Gannon
Mark Pomerantz
Nancy Rothwell

SILVER

Paul Carlson & Shawn-Marie Hanson
Michael Cunningham
Lindsey & Carolyn Echelbarger

BRONZE

Gwen & Steve Johnson
Lawrence Kreisman
Mary & Frank Montgomery Charitable Fund
Ray & Cate Taylor

FRIEND

Thomas Bingman & Sean Lane
Donald Eklund & Sharon Archer
Michelle Errecart & Robert Horsley
Donald Hall
Randall & Jan Holbrook
Stephen Lacy
Merch & Alice Pease
Kent & Inger Saltonstall

PATRON

Brenda & Jeffrey Atkin
Jan Bush
Gerald & Elizabeth Finkel
Todd & Christi Flynn
Carl Johansen & Lynne Galloway
Maurine Jeude & Charles Castellow
Julie Long
Carol Sund

Structure and Form: The Art of B. L. Hyde is published in conjunction with an exhibition of the same name, organized by Cascadia Art Museum and on view from October 10, 2024 to February 2, 2025.

Front cover: Beulah Loomis Hyde (1886–1983). *Waterfront* (detail), ca. 1945–50, oil on canvas, 24 × 20 in. Collection of Charles Henry Hyde III.

Page 1: Thomas Handforth (1897–1948). Ex libris for Beulah Loomis Hyde, ca. 1928, etching, 3½ × 4 in. Collection of Charles Henry Hyde III.

Frontispiece: Beulah Loomis Hyde (1886–1983). Untitled (Chambers Bay railroad bridge, Steilacoom, WA) (detail), ca. 1935–40, oil on paper, 16 × 20¼ in. Collection of Allison Hyde and Jake Nellis.

Page 4: Beulah Loomis Hyde in her studio, 1954. Photography by Chapin Bowen (1900–1956). Northwest Room, Tacoma Public Library.

Page 6: Beulah Loomis Hyde (1886–1983). Untitled (detail), ca. 1940–45, oil on canvas, 16 × 20 in. Collection of Pamela Hyde Smith.

Page 8: Beulah Loomis Hyde (1886–1983). Untitled (detail), ca. 1940–45, oil on canvas, 20¼ × 16¼ in. Collection of Pamela Hyde Smith.

Page 10: Beulah Loomis Hyde (1886–1983). Untitled (detail), ca. 1945–50, oil on canvas. Cascadia Art Museum, Gift of Gretchen and Don Campbell, Tacoma, WA, CAM 2023.19.1.a,b.

Back cover: Beulah Loomis Hyde (1886–1983). Self-portrait, ca. 1945–50, oil on canvas, 20 × 15 in. Collection of Pamela Hyde Smith.

All family photographs provided by the estate of Beulah Loomis Hyde unless otherwise noted

ISBN: 978-0-9989112-6-7

Cascadia Art Museum
190 Sunset Avenue South
Edmonds, WA 98020
cascadiaartmuseum.org

Distributed by University of Washington Press
uwapress.uw.edu

Design: Phil Kovacevich
Editing: Jane M. Lichty

Printed in Canada by Friesens Book Division